scanner handbook

2nd edition

scanner handbook

2nd edition

david d. busch, susan krzywicki, and laurel burden

IDG Books Worldwide, Inc.
An International Data Group Company

Foster City, CA ■ Chicago, IL ■ Indianapolis, IN ■ New York, NY

Scanner Handbook, 2nd Edition

Published by
IDG Books Worldwide, Inc.
An International Data Group Company
919 E. Hillsdale Blvd., Suite 300
Foster City, CA 94404
www.idgbooks.com (IDG Books Worldwide Web site)

ISBN: 0-7645-3523-4

Printed in the United States of America

10 9 8 7 6 5 4 3 2 1

1O/QS/RR/QQ/FC

Distributed in the United States by IDG Books Worldwide, Inc.

Distributed by CDG Books Canada Inc. for Canada; by Transworld Publishers Limited in the United Kingdom; by IDG Norge Books for Norway; by IDG Sweden Books for Sweden; by IDG Books Australia Publishing Corporation Pty. Ltd. for Australia and New Zealand; by TransQuest Publishers Pte Ltd. for Singapore, Malaysia, Thailand, Indonesia, and Hong Kong; by Gotop Information Inc. for Taiwan; by ICG Muse, Inc. for Japan; by Intersoft for South Africa; by Eyrolles for France; by International Thomson Publishing for Germany, Austria, and Switzerland; by Distribuidora Cuspide for Argentina; by LR International for Brazil; by Galileo Libros for Chile; by Ediciones ZETA S.C.R. Ltda. for Peru; by WS Computer Publishing Corporation, Inc., for the Philippines; by Contemporanea de Ediciones for Venezuela; by Express Computer Distributors for the Caribbean and West Indies; by Micronesia Media Distributor, Inc. for Micronesia; by Chips Computadoras S.A. de C.V. for Mexico; by Editorial Norma de Panama S.A. for Panama; by American Bookshops for Finland.

For general information on IDG Books Worldwide's books in the U.S., please call our Consumer Customer Service department at 800-762-2974. For reseller information, including discounts and premium sales, please call our Reseller Customer Service department at 800-434-3422.

For information on where to purchase IDG Books Worldwide's books outside the U.S., please contact our International Sales department at 317-572-3993 or fax 317-572-4002.

For consumer information on foreign language translations, please contact our Customer Service department at 800-434-3422, fax 317-572-4002, or e-mail rights@idgbooks.com.

For information on licensing foreign or domestic rights, please phone +1-650-653-7098.

For sales inquiries and special prices for bulk quantities, please contact our Order Services department at 800-434-3422 or write to the address above.

For information on using IDG Books Worldwide's books in the classroom or for ordering examination copies, please contact our Educational Sales department at 800-434-2086 or fax 317-572-4005.

For press review copies, author interviews, or other publicity information, please contact our Public Relations department at 650-653-7000 or fax 650-653-7500.

For authorization to photocopy items for corporate, personal, or educational use, please contact Copyright Clearance Center, 222 Rosewood Drive, Danvers, MA 01923, or fax 978-750-4470.

Library of Congress Cataloging-in-Publication Data

Busch, David D.
    Hewlett Packard official scanner handbook / David D. Busch, Susan Krzywicki, and Laurel Burden.– 2nd ed.
        p. cm.
    Includes index.
    ISBN 0-7645-3523-4 (alk. paper)
    1. Computers–Optical equipment. 2. Optical scanners. I. Krzywicki, Susan, 1952- II. Burden, Laurel, 1946- III. Title.
TK7895.O6 B87   2000
006.6'2–dc21   00-046127

ABOUT IDG BOOKS WORLDWIDE

Welcome to the world of IDG Books Worldwide.

IDG Books Worldwide, Inc., is a subsidiary of International Data Group, the world's largest publisher of computer-related information and the leading global provider of information services on information technology. IDG was founded more than 30 years ago by Patrick J. McGovern and now employs more than 9,000 people worldwide. IDG publishes more than 290 computer publications in over 75 countries. More than 90 million people read one or more IDG publications each month.

Launched in 1990, IDG Books Worldwide is today the #1 publisher of best-selling computer books in the United States. We are proud to have received eight awards from the Computer Press Association in recognition of editorial excellence and three from Computer Currents' First Annual Readers' Choice Awards. Our best-selling *...For Dummies®* series has more than 50 million copies in print with translations in 31 languages. IDG Books Worldwide, through a joint venture with IDG's Hi-Tech Beijing, became the first U.S. publisher to publish a computer book in the People's Republic of China. In record time, IDG Books Worldwide has become the first choice for millions of readers around the world who want to learn how to better manage their businesses.

Our mission is simple: Every one of our books is designed to bring extra value and skill-building instructions to the reader. Our books are written by experts who understand and care about our readers. The knowledge base of our editorial staff comes from years of experience in publishing, education, and journalism — experience we use to produce books to carry us into the new millennium. In short, we care about books, so we attract the best people. We devote special attention to details such as audience, interior design, use of icons, and illustrations. And because we use an efficient process of authoring, editing, and desktop publishing our books electronically, we can spend more time ensuring superior content and less time on the technicalities of making books.

You can count on our commitment to deliver high-quality books at competitive prices on topics you want to read about. At IDG Books Worldwide, we continue in the IDG tradition of delivering quality for more than 30 years. You'll find no better book on a subject than one from IDG Books Worldwide.

IDG
BOOKS
WORLDWIDE

John Kilcullen
Chairman and CEO
IDG Books Worldwide, Inc.

*Eighth Annual
Computer Press
Awards ≥1992*

*Ninth Annual
Computer Press
Awards ≥1993*

*Tenth Annual
Computer Press
Awards ≥1994*

*Eleventh Annual
Computer Press
Awards ≥1995*

Credits

Acquisitions Editor
John Gravener

Project Editors
Colleen Dowling
Martin V. Minner

Technical Editors
Robert Gann, Hewlett-Packard
Susan Glinert Stevens

Copy Editor
Nancy Rapoport

Proof Editor
Patsy Owens

Project Coordinators
Danette Nurse
Marcos Vergara

Graphics and Production Specialists
Bob Bihlmayer
Jude Levinson
Michael Lewis
Victor Pérez-Varela
Ramses Ramirez

Quality Control Technician
Dina F Quan

Book Designer
Kurt Krames

Illustrators
John Greenough
Gabriele McCann

Proofreading and Indexing
York Production Services

Cover Image
©Hewlett-Packard Company

About the Author

Two-time Computer Press Association winner **David D. Busch** has been demystifying arcane computer and imaging technology for PC and Macintosh owners since the early 1980s. As a writer, photographer, and contributing editor for more than a dozen leading computer magazines, he has more than 65 books and 2,500 articles to his credit, including *Digital Photography for Dummies Quick Reference* (IDG Books Worldwide). The *Scanner Handbook, 2nd Edition* is his seventh book devoted to desktop scanners.

Susan Krzywicki's background includes fine arts and computers. She worked for IBM, and ComputerLand as an Apple Business Development Manager, and studied art at Mills College (B.A. Studio Art) and the Rhode Island School of Design. She is currently working for Computer Associates and has taught classes in using scanners and color printers for crafts projects, including printing on fabrics.

Laurel Burden has been in graphic design longer than she likes to contemplate, working with the National Football League Properties for many years, and as an independent designer. Currently, Laurel is with TBWA/Chiat/Day Advertising in Computer Graphics. Laurel has a degree in fine arts from Mills College and has studied art and design at the University of California, Los Angeles and Art Center School of Design.

For Cathy
— David D. Busch

For my Dad
— Susan Krzywicki

For my family and friends
— Laurel Burden

Foreword

Hewlett-Packard is in a unique position to endorse a book that helps you use scanning technology successfully. We were a pioneer in desktop scanners in 1987, and remain the market leader today. In the *Scanner Handbook, 2nd Edition*, you have a resource that will enable you to use any scanner more efficiently, more creatively, and more productively.

Scanning has come a long way in the last decade. With low-cost, high-quality, easy-to-use color scanners, scanning technology is now available to anyone with a computer. Today, scanning is being done not just by professional graphic artists, but by people of all ages, occupations, and skill levels. Scanned images are appearing on community association newsletters, in family genealogy scrapbooks, on small-business letterhead, and in brochures.

The fun part about this technology is that its use is limited only by your own imagination. Once you've scanned an image or text into your computer, there's a wealth of things you can do and a wide variety of documents you can create. That's what makes this book so special: It not only teaches you how to set up and use a scanner successfully, but it also gives you inspiration in the form of project ideas and step-by-step guidance on how to work with images and text.

With this dual focus, the book benefits from three wonderful authors. David D. Busch, author of six scanner books as well as dozens of books on other computer topics, is the ideal person to cover the technology side of things. Susan Krzywicki and Laurel Burden bring their creative experience to the project section with fun, interesting, and useful scanner projects for users ranging from children to small-business owners. Together they've struck the perfect balance of technology and fun.

If you're new to scanning or own a scanner and want to get more out of it, you'll find this book a treasure trove of information and advice.

Carolyn M. Ticknor
President, Imaging and Printing Systems
Hewlett-Packard Company

Preface

If scanners give a computer eyes, the *Scanner Handbook, 2nd Edition* adds perspective to this newfound vision. While "pixel grabbers" are easy to use, the more you know, the more you can do with them. Within a few minutes of opening this book, you'll be able to:

- Convert letters, memos, blurry faxes, and other documents into editable text using the optical character recognition (OCR) software furnished with virtually every scanner.

- Grab images for World Wide Web pages. A few easy steps can optimize scanned images for Internet publishing.

- Enhance snapshots using sensational tools such as Adobe PhotoDeluxe or Photoshop, with no need to become an imaging guru.

- Apply your scanner expertise to your choice of dozens of interesting projects.

If images are important to the work you do — whether it's building your own Web page, creating newsletters, or assembling a personal photo collection — a scanner should be on your desktop. Today, anyone who can afford a printer can justify buying a color scanner. Computer owners are discovering that to get the most from their computers, a digital image grabber is just as important as a printer and, in fact, *multifunction devices*, which incorporate both add-ons in one unit, are already on the market.

InfoTrends Research Group projects that by 2002, more than 30 percent of home consumer PCs are expected to have a flatbed scanner attached. The same organization has found that 42 percent of existing scanner owners use them purely for personal applications, compared with 37 percent for business and 21 percent for both personal and professional applications. So, scanners are hot!

If you're a scanner user who is hungry for new ideas and clever techniques, you've come to the right place. We've packed this book with easy-to-understand information about how scanners work, everything you need to know to choose the best scanner for your work, and tons of tips on getting the best scans and finished images.

In the second part of the book, we take you through dozens of ingenious projects that apply what you've learned to inventive designs for home or business.

Bridging the Image Technology Gap

As discussed in Chapter 2, "How Scanners Work," building a high-quality color scanner is not a simple undertaking. The road to the modern scanner involved leaping over dozens of technology gaps, from the creation of versatile image sensors to the electronics necessary to convert scanned images to a format your computer can handle. As a pioneer in desktop scanners — from the first 16-gray-level ScanJet introduced with a multi-thousand-dollar price tag in 1987 to the latest color models costing only a few hundred dollars — Hewlett-Packard is in a unique position. With the dramatic changes in the market of the last year, HP has a brand name that's synonymous with desktop scanning, and a strong product line that covers every need from sheet-fed OCR applications to high-color color scanning for sophisticated desktop publishing. If anyone knows scanners and how to use them, it's Hewlett-Packard.

This book is not designed to describe, compare, or contrast the multitude of hardware options on the market, nor to conduct an exhaustive exploration of the software designed for them. Instead, we provide you with a compendium of universally useful information about the main scanner categories and the tools you need to work with them. When you've finished with the first part of this book, you'll be able to choose a scanner wisely (if you already don't own one) and use your image capture device to get great scans. You'll understand a little of how scanners work and how to use them to capture line art, grab photos for presentations and desktop publications, obtain images for World Wide Web pages, convert fax and documents to editable text though optical character recognition, or send faxes of hardcopies using their computer-based fax modems.

In the second part, you'll discover ways to use your scanner that you probably haven't thought of, through a rich treasure trove of easy projects.

Who Should Read This Book

We designed this book to appeal to both beginners to the scanner world as well as old hands looking for new ideas and better ways of doing their work. If you're a typical (or potential) scanner owner, you fall into one of these groups:

- Scanner owners who have read the documentation that came with their hardware and software and who are ready for more in-depth information. Owners who need information developed by users like themselves, who have squeezed every bit of performance out of a scanner.

- Potential scanner buyers who know that it's smart to "try before you buy" but even better to "learn before you're burned."

- Corporate trainers faced with users who need to use scanners in their work, and who are looking for a manual that will help those who may not have graphics design in their job descriptions and need to be brought up to speed quickly.

- Power users who may not have expertise in scanners, who are looking for some tricks that will save time, who want to do something unusual, or who need an edge over colleagues and competitors. Users who want to learn about resolution, color depth, dynamic range, and other technical things in a nontechnical way.

- Anyone looking for interesting projects that let them get more from their scanner.

Helpful Icons

This book uses four types of icons as visual cues to annotate the contents of the text:

Warning

Warning icons tell you when to watch out or when to take particular care when performing a procedure.

Cross-Reference

Cross-Reference icons tell you that information relevant to the topic you're reading about is located elsewhere in this book.

Note

Note icons offer an aside or extra information about a topic.

Tip

Tip icons signal the kind of information that saves you time, money, and aggravation.

How to Use This Book

A well-organized book requires no step-by-step instructions on how to use it. The ground rules for the *Scanner Handbook, 2nd Edition* are simple. If you want to know how scanners work, or learn more about specific image-editing techniques, check out the front half of the book. You'll find what you need to know, plus some enticing background material, there. If you want to put your scanner to use with an engaging project, check out the second half of the book for ideas.

Part I: Using Scanners covers how scanners, particularly the Hewlett-Packard family of image grabbers, can change the way you work and play. This part tells you only what you need to know to use an HP scanner effectively. Also, find out exactly what hardware you need to use scanners, how to configure and calibrate your scanner, how to optimize scanning to get the best images, and what tools can streamline your work.

Part II: Scanner Projects discusses how you can put your new knowledge to work. Part II is full of ideas for projects at the office, projects for all seasons, and projects to enhance a business or personal Web site.

Acknowledgments

Thanks to Pat Pekary and Bob Gann at Hewlett-Packard, who worked closely with us to provide both the latest products to work with as well as all the inside dope on scanners and scanning. Bob especially went beyond the call of duty, interrupting both vacations and pressing business trips to offer sage advice and correct little (but significant) errors, as well as a few larger (and even more significant) goofs. We'd also like to thank the folks at IDG Books Worldwide, including John Gravener, acquisitions editor; Colleen Dowling and Martin V. Minner, project editors; Susan Glinert Stevens, technical editor; Nancy Rapoport, copy editor; and Patsy Owens, proof editor. And we can't forget Father Caselli, who in 1863 cobbled together the precursor to the scanners and fax devices that have invaded all our lives.

Contents at a Glance

Contents

Part II: Scanner Projects   189

Chapter 16: Projects for Kids 309

→ Using Scanners

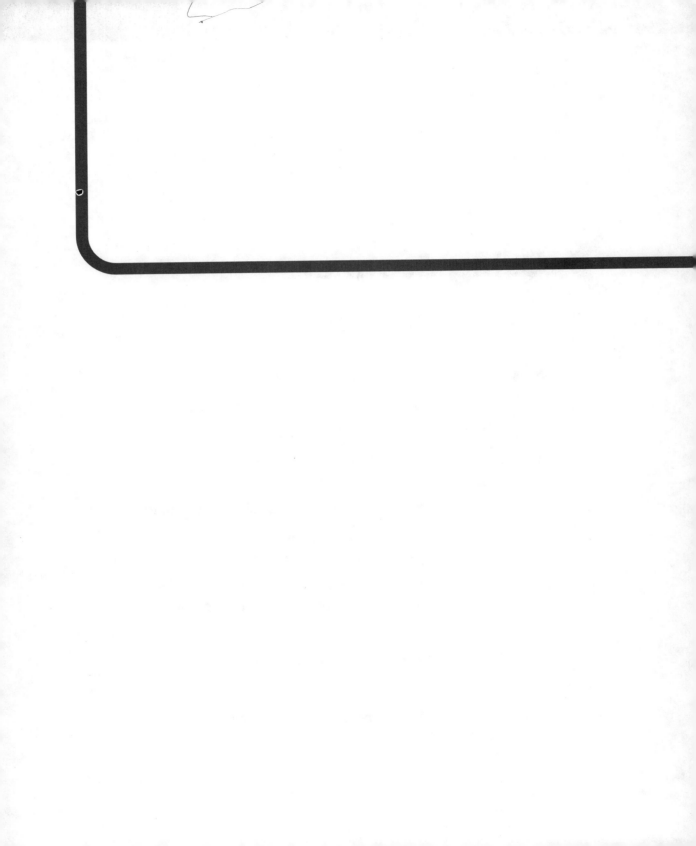

CHAPTER 1

Scanner Basics

IN THIS CHAPTER
- What can a scanner do?
- Types of scanners
- Current HP scanners
- How have scanners changed?
- Key scanner characteristics
- Hardware requirements

A scanner provides a computer with its eyes, bringing the gift of sight to computers, just as RAM serves as a computer's memory and the microprocessor behaves as its brain. The scanner's eyes provide the images that enable the computer to communicate ideas visually. Through paintings on cave walls, picture-symbols on highway signs, and word pictures such as black holes that stimulate images in the mind, humans instinctively rely on images to communicate. Although the personal computer excels at manipulating numbers and formatting text, a desktop system that lacks a scanner's eyes ignores the most powerful and efficient way to convey ideas. If you don't believe a picture is worth a thousand words, try to describe a scanned image using an 8-character DOS-style filename. Given the power and ease of incorporating images in your work and personal projects with a scanner, you won't have difficulty finding cool applications for an image capture device.

So What Can a Scanner Do?

Just look at what a scanner can do! Any reader of this book should find a half dozen uses for scanners from the following list:

- **Snag images for presentations.** Whether you're working on a computerized slide show of your family vacation or a presentation for work, a scanner is the perfect tool for turning still photos into digital images that can be merged with text or recorded narrations (using sound capabilities from your PC or Mac) in professional-looking presentations.

- **Scan directly to an Internet page with HP Scan-to-Web capability.** With new Web sites such as HP Cartogra.com, Myfamily.com, and xing.com you can create online albums for your family and friends to share images. You don't have to be an expert to use images on the Web. Scan-to-Web will even "register you" with the Web site if you haven't already signed up. This new capability really does scan files directly to the Web, unlike some alternative methods that just create an HTML Web page that you have to upload yourself.

- **Convert images for your own Web pages.** The next step up from scanning directly to the Web is grabbing pictures for use on your own Web page. A personal Web page can include images of your family. A page put together for work can incorporate product photos or other images. A few tasteful images can turn any boring text-only Web page from a distraction into an attraction. In addition, you can distribute your images widely. A scanner lets you combine the quality, flexibility, and low cost of traditional cameras and photofinishing with Internet distribution. Figure 1.1 shows a typical Web page with scanned art.

■ **Capture line art for publications.** You have a piece of line art — a one-color image such as a logo, decorative alphabet character, cartoon, or chart. You're on a short deadline and need to make some changes to the logo. Scanning and some touch-ups in an image editing program can provide you with the art you need in a few seconds. Although converting images to line art once required special programs, many scanners can do this for you automatically.

Cross-Reference

You'll find more information on line art and other kinds of original artwork in Chapter 2, "How Scanners Work."

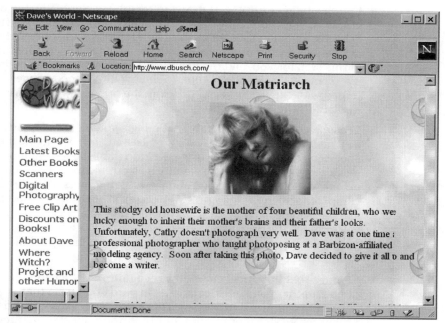

Figure 1.1 A Web page can be spiced up with scanned art.

■ **Capture photographs for placement in a publication.** If the final destination for your images is a desktop publication (whether it's a company or personal newsletter, a self-published book of poems, or your holiday greetings), pictures captured by a scanner can enhance any document. If your publication will be printed on a conventional printing press, you can even handle adding the dot patterns called *halftones* to the images to aid in reproduction.

Tip

Even information sheets that will be photocopied look better with an image scanned and manipulated, rather than just subjected to straight photocopying.

■ **Capture low resolution images for screen display or positioning in publications.** At times, super high quality isn't needed because the image won't be used as-is in the publication. Perhaps a high-quality scan using a professional device called a *drum scanner* is necessary. Even so, you can grab a version of the image using your scanner, for use as for position only (FPO) artwork. It's easier to visualize layout and finished appearance when you have a rough version of the actual image instead of a gray or black box on the screen or in your proof printouts.

■ **Capture images for use as drawing templates.** Sophisticated drawing programs such as CorelDRAW and Adobe Illustrator are available for Macs and PCs. A scanned image can be used as a template for tracing high-quality art. Some drawing programs even have an autotrace feature that takes care of this step for you, and the newest HP scanners have the built-in capability to convert images to outlines. When your scanned image has been traced, you can use it "as is" or refine the drawing with the various tools available in the drawing program.

■ **Create a computerized database.** Perhaps you are developing a computerized multiple listing database for a real estate firm. While the finished listings and scans could be printed using desktop publishing techniques, it may make sense to keep the publication in electronic form. Potential home buyers could look up information and view photographs of the house on the computer screen (or the firm's Web page). In such cases, superb images aren't essential, so quickie scans are just fine. In any case, the home buyers will examine the properties in person. They will just view the scanned image for an idea of a given house's appearance. Other image-rich databases could include personal hobby collections or online family trees.

■ **Capture text in optical character recognition (OCR) applications.** You'll often find that you have documents in hard copy form that you'd like to edit using your word processor. These documents may include letters, brochures, newspaper articles, or other printed material. Once you're certain you have the legal right to use these documents, how can you translate them into editable form without retyping from scratch? HP scanners integrate OCR right into the scanning application — you don't need to use extra packages. Converting a scan of text to an editable document is as simple as dragging the text into your word processing package where it is inserted as text. Of course, HP scanners work fine with more sophisticated OCR packages and document management programs (and may include them as part of their software bundles).

■ **Grab images of three-dimensional objects.** You have a product package or even a small product to include in a presentation, but no photograph.

Some scanners, including most flatbeds, can capture images of any object placed on the scanning bed. That makes it simple to capture images of three-dimensional objects. Place the object on your scanner's bed, and scan to produce a view suitable for your application. Figure 1.2 shows a background created by scanning an array of pennies directly on the glass of a scanner.

■ **Translate images into a format for facsimile transmission.** Fax modems receive or send faxes from your computer but don't include a provision for capture. That's where your scanner comes in handy. At home, a fax modem, scanner, and printer give you a complete two-way faxing system. At work, a scanner and a fax modem enable you to bypass long lines at the departmental fax machine. Personal fax capability lets you keep confidential documents safe from unauthorized eyes. Newer HP scanners will identify your fax software and provide a link to a button on the scanner that allows faxing with a single press.

Figure 1.2 Three-dimensional objects that are relatively flat can be scanned easily.

■ **Add photos to your e-mail.** Grabbing scanned images to incorporate in e-mail is fast and easy. What better way to get your message across electronically than with an eye-catching image?

Cross-Reference

Read more about adding scanned images to e-mail in Chapter 13, "Projects for the Office."

■ **Create original art.** Any scannable photograph or drawing can be further manipulated by the computer to produce a beautiful work of art. Figure 1.3 shows an image created by photographer/digital artist Peter J. Sucy. While the original photo is a powerful study in the strictures of inanimate bondage, a new layer of texture makes the image even more interesting after processing by Sucy.

■ **Make copies.** One of the most used scanner applications is to make copies at home or the office. With a low-cost color scanner and color printer, you can make vivid color copies.

■ **Capture documents into a document management system.** These software tools track letters, memos, faxes, and other documents and let you edit files or archive them. Such systems include optical character recognition to translate the documents into editable text and search ability so that you can find the information easily.

■ **Capture complex document formatting.** With recent HP scanners you can automatically capture a document with photos, text, drawings all in one step, in a new file that contains all the elements in their correct format and position.

■ **Send a document by e-mail.** With e-mail applications on most scanners and the e-mail scanning capability built into HP scanners, you can easily capture a document and send it to friends, family or business associates.

Tip

If you're interested in digital fine art, you can find more examples at Sucy's home page at http://www.home.eznet.net/~pjsucy.

Figure 1.3 Digital art created with photography and a scanner. (Image courtesy of P. J. Sucy)

Types of Scanners

We won't look at the mechanics of how scanners operate in this chapter. However, you should know that all scanners use a light source, some means of moving the sensor (or a mirror that reflects light to the sensor) over the surface of the artwork (or vice versa), and circuitry to convert the captured information to digital form. Different kinds of scanners usually arrange the components in various ways.

 Cross-Reference

You can find more information on how each type of scanner works in Chapter 2, "How Scanners Work."

Drum Scanners

The most expensive scanners are drum scanners, the high-price, higher-resolution color separation scanners typically found in the graphic arts industry. With drum scanners, the artwork is wrapped around a drum and rotated at high speeds. A bright focused light is usually used to illuminate tiny sections of the original. These scanners can provide highly detailed image files that can be used for sophisticated layout and page composition, electronic retouching, and color separating. High-end scanners can also generate halftone dots electronically while exposing films used to make the printing plates.

Flatbed Scanners

For good reason, the most popular style of scanner today is the flatbed type. This configuration provides the best and most flexible combination of features for most users. A flatbed can scan a variety of different originals, including thick originals such as books. If your artwork is too large to fit on a flatbed, you can scan it in pieces. With a special attachment, flatbed scanners can grab images of transparencies or color slides, and an automatic document feeder makes it possible to scan whole stacks of originals unattended. This versatility is hard to match.

Flatbed scanners look and work something like a photocopier: You lift the cover, place the original to be scanned facedown on the glass, and press a physical button on the scanner or click a button in your software. Figure 1.4 shows a typical flatbed scanner. The key advantages of flatbed scanners are as follows:

- **They can be used with a wide range of non-transparent artwork.** Anything that is flat and can fit on the glass platen can be scanned. As with photocopiers that have hinged lids, you can place books, large originals, and thick copy facedown. Images up to 8½ by 14 inches can be accommodated by the typical flatbed scanner, although some compact models limit you to 11-inch-long documents. As previously mentioned, very large originals can be scanned in pieces, and then "stitched" together within your image editing software.

Figure 1.4 A typical flatbed scanner and slide adapter

■ **You can scan some three-dimensional objects.** Keys, watches, human hands, and similar subjects can be captured with a flatbed scanner more easily than with sheet-fed models, unless you have a very thin, flexible object. Don't count too much on this capability, however. Results will vary widely, depending on the scanner (the least expensive models do a very poor job of this) and the object being scanned because the depth of focus (the distance above the surface of the glass that is sharp) is limited, and determined in part by the quality of the scanner's sensor.

■ **Artwork is fairly easy to align on a flatbed.** Originals can be placed precisely on the flatbed scanner's scanning bed, using the built-in rulers and alignment guides. Sheet-fed models can "drag" the original through slightly skewed, giving you a slightly warped image.

■ **Flatbed scanners can handle multiple types of original artwork.** Hewlett-Packard makes an especially nice model that comes furnished with both a 35mm slide adapter and a 25-page automatic document feeder. It's available with both USB and SCSI interfaces. Several of the newest models now include (or have available as an option) a device called an active TSA (transparency adapter) that will scan from 35mm up to 5×5-inch transparencies. Some can even scan color negatives.

Sheet-Fed Scanners

Sheet-fed scanners, once very popular, are today available only for a few niche applications and should be mentioned in passing just for completeness. These scanners, which sucked up sheets of paper for scanning in much the same way as a fax machine (which itself includes a sheet-fed scanner), were valued because of their lower cost at that time, but today flatbed scanners are just as cost effective (and are more versatile). While there are very few standalone sheet-fed scanners still available, you may find some models as part of "all-in-one" scanner/fax/printing/copying devices, described next.

All-in-One Devices

Scanners aren't just for scanning anymore! All-in-one units — also sometimes called *multifunction devices,* combine scanning, printing, copying, and faxing capabilities. They were developed to meet the needs of office workers, students, and home users with tight budget and space constraints. One of these devices may be your best bet for a scanner if versatility is at the top of your wish list.

All-in-one devices in the low price range are built around a color inkjet printer, which can be attached to your computer and used like any other printer. Some more expensive models, intended for the business market, use a laser printer for output. The vendor adds to the printer a sheet-fed (or, more recently, a flatbed) scanner, which can capture an image of any photograph or document supplied to the device. This simple add-on opens the door to several useful functions.

For example, a multifunction device can serve as a convenient photocopier. If you need a few copies, just enter the number of copies desired into a keypad on the front of the unit, and feed the sheets through. Many models can enlarge (blow up a 3×5-inch notecard to full-page size) or reduce (squeeze a legal sheet onto an 8½×11-inch copy you can punch and put in a notebook). The scanner also enables you to capture graphics for your image editing or desktop publishing program, and you can use it as a fax machine if the fax modem is either built into the device or if the computer has a fax modem. Most also are furnished with OCR software; as a result, text documents you receive via fax or fed in using scanner mode are translated directly into editable text in your favorite word processing format.

 Tip

Multifunction devices often contain their own memory so you can use them as a copier or fax machine even when the computer is turned off. You can also receive faxes while printing or copying is underway — each job will take its turn.

Other Scanners

There are a few more types of specialized scanners that we'll mention only briefly. One useful type is the photo scanner, which is aimed at consumers who want to grab images of their snapshots but don't need full-fledged scanning capabilities. Photo scanners are not widely available. These scanners accept snapshot-sized photos and convert them into scanned images you can manipulate or immediately print out with a photo-quality inkjet printer. Figure 1.5 shows a photo scanner.

Slide scanners are scanners designed specifically to scan 35mm slides, usually for professional applications, particularly reproduction in catalogs, magazines, or books. You'll also encounter transparency scanners for grabbing images from 6 cm by 6 cm and larger negatives or transparencies. Unless you're a photo buff with a large collection of slides, you probably won't need this capability. If so, there are attachments for many flatbed scanners that allow you to capture images from transparency originals, with quality that rivals dedicated slide scanners. The HP 5300, 5370, and 6300 can scan up to 5×5-inch transparencies.

Figure 1.5 Photo scanners are great for making copies of snapshots.

If you look hard enough, you may also find handheld scanners, video scanners, and overhead scanners that look like a photographic enlarger. In this book, we'll concentrate chiefly on the most popular type: flatbed scanners.

Key Scanner Characteristics

Although this section tells how much resolution to look for or expect in your scanner, for example, it doesn't explain in detail how each of the key features found in a scanner operates. If you want to know more about how scanner resolution is figured and other details, check out Chapter 2, "How Scanners Work," or Chapter 4, "Resolution, Interpolation, and Sharp Images."

Scanner Type

Before considering the other features of the scanner, you must decide which type of scanner you want. You should decide if you need automatic document feeding (and how many pages you'll want to be able to load at once) or transparency options. Some flatbed scanners do not offer these features so you'll want to avoid such models if those capabilities are important to you.

Scanning Size

Scanners typically limit the size of the originals you can scan in one operation. Sheet-fed models may have no practical limit on the length of an original, but won't accept any document wider than about 8½ inches. Flatbed models are friendlier to larger originals but still can capture only an image no larger than the scanning bed itself, which may measure somewhere between 8½ inches by 11 inches and 8½ inches by 14 inches. Some of these scanners are sized in-between at, say, 8½ inches by 13 inches, so be sure to check out the exact scanning dimensions if a particular size document is important to you.

Scanner Resolution

Today, a resolution of at least 600 samples per inch (spi) is standard among all flatbed and sheet-fed models. It's more common to find 800 to 1200 spi scanners. Resolutions above that standard aren't very practical (they produce very large files) or necessary. The resolution of scanners is over-emphasized today because the resolution specs of a scanner don't necessarily reflect the quality of finished scans. We'll take a longer look at this topic later in the book so you can see exactly when resolution is — and isn't — relevant.

Cross-Reference

See Chapter 2, "How Scanners Work," and Chapter 4, "Resolution, Interpolation, and Sharp Images," for information on the best resolution for specific kinds of applications.

Tip

Most scanners can interpolate the information contained between scanner dots and go beyond the unit's simple optical resolution of the unit. This capability can be useful if you need a specific resolution to avoid patterns when printing dithered halftones, or to make a grayscale halftone of a small photographic image and print it at a larger size. You'll learn about dithering and halftones — a way of reproducing tonal scales using a pattern of dots — later in this book.

Physical Size

Don't dismiss the importance of checking the footprint (the amount of space occupied on your desktop) of your scanner. A scanner will do you little good in day-to-day work if you can't fit it close at hand on your desktop. Some flatbed scanners are only a little larger than the largest area they can scan. Other heftier models use up more desk space than your monitor and keyboard combined. Weigh the tradeoffs between these two ends of the scale: a small flatbed may be portable enough to carry between two computers (including your machines at home and work), but you'll have to take care to protect them from image quality-robbing vibration. A bigger, more solid flatbed can be almost immune to outside interference while providing a more generously sized scanning area.

Color Depth

Color depth is the number of different colors a scanner can capture. The short answer to the color depth question (how many colors should your scanner be capable of handling?) is that the larger the number of bits (different shades of color) a scanner can capture, the more detail it can theoretically capture from image areas, including bright highlights and inky shadows. A 24-bit full-color scanner capable of 16.8 million different colors should be your minimum requirement. Most scanners, even the least expensive models, claim 30-bit or 36-bit (billions of colors) performance. In practice, a 30-bit low-end scanner might not produce colors as good as a comparable 24-bit model. Indeed, some of these models aren't even true 30-bit scanners: They capture 24 bits of information and interpolate the other bits using calculations similar to those used to interpolate higher resolutions.

Cross-Reference

You'll find a discussion of exactly what color depth means, and how to choose the best color depth for your applications, in Chapter 2, "How Scanners Work."

If the number of colors actually captured is important to you, your best bet is to compare actual samples from the scanners you are considering. Use challenging artwork with lots of detail in both the highlights and shadows. Then compare the scans on your screen with the original. They will never match the original, but the differences between them can help you decide which scanner to buy.

Speed

The speed with which a scanner operates can be important if you make many scans or scans of large originals. If you're grabbing occasional images of 4×5-inch photos, the speed of a scanner may not be especially important to you — just about any scanner will capture such images in 10 to 15 seconds. If you're feeding dozens of 8½×11-inch documents or many 8×10-inch photos, you'll prefer a scanner that can nab those images in 15 seconds over one that takes a minute or more for the same task. You may find typical scanning speeds listed in the specs for a scanner you're considering, but the best test is to try some actual scans using a computer with approximately the same speed and memory complement as your own.

Software Bundle

Scanners are always furnished with software that allows you to perform scans and control the basic features of the scanner (see Figure 1.6), but in the case of HP scanners, the software goes beyond the basic scan capability to include things like:

- Raster to vector (image to outline) conversion to create outlines from scanned images
- OCR to convert faxes and scanned documents to editable text
- Scan Destinations, which inserts the scanned image directly into an application, such as your word processor, instead of going through the "middleman" of a file
- Drag-and-drop, which lets you drag text from your scanner preview window into a word processing program, where it will be converted to editable text automatically using OCR technology.

Figure 1.6 Scanning software is the interface that enables you to control your scanner.

The software provided with scanners today, combined with one-touch scanning and an easier interface, really changes the way scanning works. Often you don't need to use other applications, such as image editors, to achieve your task. Scanning is a just a step to most people today — not an application or end in itself.

The HP scanners discussed in this book use one of these software interfaces (not drivers like TWAIN — that's the old way of working with a scanner) — PrecisionScan LTX, PrecisionScan LT, PrecisionScan, and PrecisionScan Pro. These will be discussed further in Chapter 6.

Hardware Requirements

One of the reasons why scanners have become so popular in recent years is that the hardware requirements are no longer as demanding as they once were. Any AMD K6, K7, Athlon, or Pentium-class PC, most 486 PCs, and any Power Macintoshes have all the horsepower and capabilities required to drive a scanner. In 1991, when David's first scanner book was published, a decent system would have set you back at least $5,000, without the scanner. Today, a $999 system will do the job, and, in some cases, that price will include a bundled scanner. So, it's hard to go wrong. In terms of memory, graphics capabilities and CPU speed, any recent computer has all you need and more.

However, full-color images require a lot of disk space, so if you're serious about scanning you should load up on hard disk space (a 40GB to 70GB drive is not excessive, and doesn't cost that much today). While SCSI hard drives were *de rigueur* for lightning-fast performance in the past, modern ATA-66 IDE drives are plenty fast enough.

Even the largest hard disk will fill up eventually. As you scan a lot of images that you want to keep, you'll need some sort of removable storage system for keeping images offline. Because you don't need to access these images daily, a storage medium slower than a hard disk is okay. The main options you'll want to consider have 100MB to 5.2GB of storage.

These include Iomega Zip drives, available in 100 to 250MB capacity, which can link to your computer either as IDE, SCSI, parallel port, or universal serial bus (USB) models. Iomega also provides Jaz drives with 1 to 2GB of capacity. The CD-ROM Recordable/Rewritable (CD-RW) disc is currently our mass storage favorite for long-term retention of images. Images that are "finished" (meaning that we don't expect to work on them soon, or want to keep a copy of this particular version of the image) are copied from my hard disk onto recordable CDs. The cost is incredibly low — just a few dollars for each 650 to 700MB CD-R or CD-RW disc. In addition, I don't have to worry about finding a computer that can access these discs, as virtually everyone has a CD-ROM drive. Figure 1.7 shows a typical CD-RW recorder.

Figure 1.7 CD-RW writers are a great option for backing up images.

Rewritable CD-ROM discs (CD-RW) are well on the way to replacing the earlier CD-R, pending only the universal availability of CD-ROM drives that can read them. Indeed, there are no CD-R-only recorders on the market anymore. All recorders can write both CD-R and CD-RW discs. CD-RW discs cost only a little more than CD-R media, but they can be written to, and rewritten to, dozens or hundreds of times. There's no worry about a slight computer glitch ruining a disc (although with the low cost of CD-Rs, this is scarcely a problem anymore) and you can reuse the same disc as often as you like. The downside? The recorders are still slooooow, roughly half the speed of CD-R writers.

CD-RW discs can be played back most reliably on the relatively new Multiread CD-ROM drives, and the media costs many times more than CD-R discs. If you plan to keep lots of images permanently, or want to exchange discs with friends or associates, CD-R is more cost-effective.

Farther down the road, digital video discs (DVD) are sure to wipe all the other options off the map. The large number of DVD movies you see lining the shelves at your local electronics superstore demonstrate that this is a format poised to take off in a big way. DVD can store movies, music, and computer data, and are compatible with players you attach to your television as well as DVD drives found in the latest computers. The first DVD drives were able to read discs but not write to them — however, DVD writers are now becoming available. Even the earliest DVD discs can store about 4.8GB of information; planned double-sided and double-layered DVD discs will multiply that capacity at least several times.

Moving On

In this chapter we've provided an introduction to what scanners do, the types of scanners, key scanner characteristics, and hardware requirements. This material should help you make an informed choice when you select a scanner for your work. In Chapter 2, we'll move into the details of how scanners work. Knowing how your scanner operates can help you work more efficiently and get better scans.

How Scanners Work

Of the devices that can be attached to a computer, a scanner is one of the easiest to understand. In one sense, a scanner captures information in the same way you read a book — line-by-line, starting (usually) in the upper-left corner and proceeding down the page. If you're reading — or scanning — a book page, a light source of some sort illuminates the document and your eye — or the scanner's sensor — grabs an image based on the reflected light. A color transparency can also be viewed in much the same manner by vision or scanners, except that the viewing light passes through the artwork instead of reflecting off it. Once captured, viewed or scanned images are converted to a format that can be understood by the human brain or a computer, and stored in organic, silicon, or magnetic memory. In a nutshell, that's all you really need to understand to get started using scanners.

However, few of us are satisfied with the contents of nutshells when we begin working with a tool in earnest. You don't need to understand internal combustion or physics to drive a car, but it helps to know what happens when your vehicle runs out of fuel — or that a particular sports utility vehicle has a tendency to roll over in sharp turns. This chapter provides a quick overview of how scanners work, with information you'll find useful when it comes time to really push your scanner in the projects in Part II.

Evolution of Scanning

Although low-cost scanners are a relatively recent phenomenon, scanners themselves are nothing new. They even predate computers by almost 100 years! Scanning was first proposed in 1850 as a method of transmitting photographs over telegraph lines. In 1863, a Catholic priest named Caselli achieved the first facsimile transmission when an image was sent between Paris and LeHavre, France. As odd as it seems, the first fax was sent 13 years before the invention of the telephone.

Another picture-scanning system was developed in 1884 as a precursor to television. Work by a German physicist in the early part of the twentieth century led to wire photos, which have provided photos of fast-breaking news events to newspapers and magazines worldwide for nearly 75 years. The first devices closely related to modern scanners were developed in 1937 to produce color separations for graphic arts applications. Desktop scanners arrived on the scene at about the same time as desktop computers.

Early Desktop Scanners

Be careful of what you wish for — or joke about — because it might come true. In 1981, one author of this book, David Busch, proposed, but only in jest, a scanner built around a dot-matrix printer with a sensor replacing the printhead. Four years later, he found himself the proud owner of a device called Thunder Scan, which operated in exactly the way he'd joked about, using the Apple ImageWriter.

This first desktop scanner was slow (requiring many minutes to capture even a small image), captured only black-and-white (not grayscale or color) graphics, and was saddled with relatively low resolution. Although wildly popular for a few years, ThunderScan eventually vanished from the scene as more advanced scanners became available. Some vestiges of the concept can be found in a few low-end scanner attachments for inkjet printers (costing less than $100 for the scanner add-on). These attachments can transform the hardcopy device into a document grabber by swapping a few components. A typical ThunderScan image is shown in Figure 2.1.

Figure 2.1 The black-and-white images produced by ThunderScan have a distinctive look.

Flatbed and sheet-fed scanners similar to those we use today followed within a few years, but the best of these cost $5,000 or more, at a time when you could purchase a new pickup truck for the same amount of cash. Desktop scanning didn't take off until the late 1980s, when Hewlett-Packard introduced the original ScanJet, which could capture up to 16 different gray tones and cost only a few thousand dollars ($2,500 to be exact). Good-quality grayscale scanning requires more than 16 different levels, of course, so HP followed its initial scanner product with the ScanJet Plus, which could capture up to 256 different tones.

Desktop publishing and graphics professionals flocked to the new flatbeds, but other scanner configurations were popular for specialized uses. Sheet-fed scanners, which could gobble up dozens (or hundreds) of letters, forms, or invoices one after another became an essential tool for *optical character recognition* (OCR, a process for translating printed text into word processing files) as well as document management.

Sheet-fed models costing anywhere from a few hundred dollars to tens of thousands of dollars proliferated. Other scanner types of this time included copystand models that used digital camera-like capture systems, hand scanners, and dedicated slide scanners. Video cameras and true digital cameras are also types of scanners (except they grab an image all at once, rather than a line at a time), but we won't be covering them in this book.

The Latest Scanners

Although grayscale scanners dominated the early part of the 1990s, color scanners eventually knocked their black-and-white brethren out of the picture. The progression from $2,000 grayscale scanners to $300 (or less) 30-bit and 36-bit color models in a span of less than ten years is an interesting one.

First, vendors began piling on features while keeping the suggested retail prices about the same. Scanners that could capture 16.8-million-hue color images at resolutions of 300 samples per inch (spi) were superseded by units that grabbed billions of colors at 600 samples per inch or more. The first color Hewlett-Packard color scanner, the ScanJet IIc was a 400 spi, 24-bit scanner that was priced at about $2,000. The ScanJet IIc was not the first color scanner, but it was revolutionary in that it was the first scanner that could capture red, green, and blue images in a single pass (instead of three), and used an advanced technology developed by HP Labs called an HP Trichromatic Beam Splitter to provide speed, quality, and color at the price of slower, three-pass color scanners.

Scanning speeds were boosted until a whole page could be grabbed in about the time it took to pick up the next document for capture. Software bundles, including image editors and optical character recognition (OCR) programs, became standard.

Then, prices began to drop precipitously, from roughly $2,000 to $1,000. The ScanJet IIcx, an improved version of the pioneering ScanJet IIc, broke the $1,000 barrier and really stimulated the market at this new, low price point. The IIcx also had an optional transparency adapter, which made it very attractive for those who needed to scan slides. Today, we've seen prices dip well below $500. You can now purchase a color scanner for a few hundred dollars that outperforms many of the best desktop units of half a decade ago. (You can also buy a cheap scanner that does not meet your needs — you tend to get what you pay for.) Scanners are also incorporated into multifunction devices, like the HP OfficeJet series, that combine scanner, color printer, fax, and copier capabilities in one compact, affordable unit. Scanners are everywhere.

Digitizing Images

Modern desktop scanners capture images a full line at a time, in contrast to high-end drum scanners, which use ultrasensitive photomultiplier tubes that capture information by changing their field of view across the surface of a rapidly rotating drum. Instead of tubes, personal scanners rely on silicon chips called charge-coupled devices (CCDs) or complementary metal oxide semi-conductor (CMOS) sensors to capture images. These chips, produced using technology similar to microprocessor-fabrication technology, are efficient light gatherers and are capable of recording both faint and strong amounts of light.

How Digitizing Works

Scanners consist of several components. On flatbed scanners, a glass platen or copyboard (the surface that appears when you lift the cover) holds reflective art or transparencies. With dedicated transparency scanners, a mount or transport mechanism supports the slide. Sheet-fed scanners, including fax machines, simply move the original past the fixed sensor. Some kinds of scanners have automatic document feeders (ADFs) that can deliver a stack of originals to the scanner one at a time.

The resolution — the capability of the scanner to resolve fine detail in the image — is determined by three factors:

- The quality of the optics in the scanner

- How many individual sensors are packed into the horizontal array (horizontal resolution)

- The distance the array moves between lines (vertical resolution)

A scanner includes a lens that is used to focus the reflected light from the original onto the CCD. In fact, as resolution ratings of scanners increase, the quality of the optics is more and more important. Just because a scanner has a higher resolution (spi rating) does not mean it is better at resolving detail. That requires better optics that are well focused and clear of distortion. The difference might be compared to the difference between a high-quality 35mm camera and a "single use" or disposable camera. You can have exactly the same film (the same "sensor") in both, and the SLR (single-lens reflex) will create much sharper images. The key is the optics. High-quality glass will beat mass-produced, low-quality optics any day. Lots of "out of focus" pixels are not much use.

With the common increase in resolution from 600 to 1200 spi and beyond, the value of that specification is more and more tenuous. This is a big issue for scanner manufacturers who have been forced by market pressures to increase spi — sometimes to the detriment of real performance. Vendors are starting to push for new standards that can be used instead of resolution. In a few years, the resolution issue may be dead.

Cross-Reference

Chapter 4, "Resolution, Interpolation, and Sharp Images," contains more information on resolution.

The image is captured as each individual sensor reads the amount of light reflected or transmitted by a small area on the original artwork and transfers the information in the form of a continuously increasing voltage, proportionate to the number of photons of light that have struck the sensor during its exposure.

Figure 2.2 is a simplified diagram that illustrates how the process works. The position of the light source and sensor is represented in two locations as they pass under first a light spot in the image and then a dark spot (as explained in a later section, the scanner illumination and sensor aren't really positioned as shown). The same number of photons, represented by arrows, arrive at the artwork in either case, but more are reflected from the light area than from the dark area.

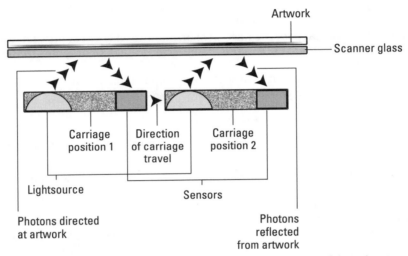

Figure 2.2 More photons are reflected from the lighter area of the subject, producing a lighter area on the final scan.

In many ways, scanner sensors are similar to the light-sensitive silver grains in the emulsion of photographic film. They can vary in sensitivity (like "fast" and "slow" films) and size (like "grainy" or "fine-grained" films) for the same reasons as in photographic film. Fast or large grain film is like a lower resolution scanner, and fine-grain, slow film is like a higher resolution scanner. The shorter the exposure or the lower the light level needed to produce an image on film or a scanner sensor, the faster both operate (allowing quicker scans, shorter exposure times, lower light levels, or a combination of all three). What is not obvious is that the higher "resolution" scanners with small pixels may actually require slower scans to produce higher quality, just as a fine grain or slower film needs more light.

As you might expect, the best ways to speed up a film or scanner include providing more light either by:

■ Upping the intensity of the illumination

■ Increasing the speed of the lens (a fairly expensive proposition)

■ Increasing the time, or exposure, of the sensor or film grain to the light source

The first option has an upper limit because of the cost of the lamp and the fact that the smaller pixels in new scanners cannot "hold" as much light — if you overexpose the pixels they overflow just like a bucket overflowing with water. This "overflow" runs into neighboring pixels and creates blooms or streaks in the image. In addition, lengthening the exposure slows down the process proportionately and also is limited because of the number of photons the CCD can capture. One of the problems encountered recently in new higher resolution scanners is that "noise," compared to the image information, increases, and images get "grainy."

Note

If you're a photo buff, you know that an exposure of f11 at ½₅₀ second is exactly the same as f8 at ½₀₀ second: doubling the amount of light reaching the film (by switching from f11 to f8) allows cutting the exposure time in half (from ½₅₀ second to ½₀₀ second). You also know that switching from a 100-speed film to a 200-speed film that's twice as sensitive allows cutting the amount of light or exposure time in half, too. Cameras and scanners are quite similar in this respect.

How a Scanner Grabs Images

Underneath the glass in most flatbed scanners you'll see a device called a carriage, which contains a light source and an optical system that gathers reflected or transmitted light and directs it to the sensor array.

Figure 2.3 shows a simplified rendition of the mechanical arrangement of an early flatbed scanner. There are many different ways to lay out a flatbed scanner's innards. Modern scanners don't stick to this easy-to-understand layout, but all include the same basic components: light source, optical system (lens), sensors, and a mechanism for scanning down the length of a page.

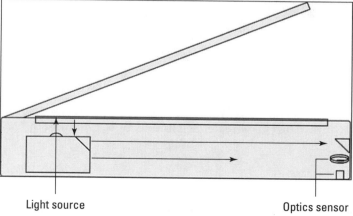

Light source   Optics sensor

Figure 2.3 Early scanners used a moving mirror carriage like this one.

Today, the same components are used, but with a fixed, single-piece carriage. The array is a line of CCDs or (in the future) CMOS (which should be available by late 2000) sensors that capture the image across the width, or short dimension, of the area being scanned. Scanners also contain memory to hold a portion of the scanned image as it is conveyed to the computer, and in higher-end scanners, some computer intelligence in the form of advanced image processing circuitry that can adjust brightness/contrast, scale images, and change the sample rate.

Scanners also include a component that converts the captured graphic from a continuous voltage to digital form before passing the information along to your computer using a process called analog/digital conversion.

Note

Analog/digital conversion is an important step in the capture of any image. The light reflected or transmitted by the artwork is received by the sensors as a continuous signal ranging from black to white, and an infinite number of increments in between. Computers can only work with such analog information after it has been converted into discrete chunks that can be represented by whole numbers. The A/D module converts the analog voltage to a number the computer can use.

For example, while a grayscale image may contain a full range of tones, the scanner may define each pixel of the final image in terms of digital values from 0 (black) to 255 (pure white). Figure 2.4 illustrates the difference between analog and digital information.

Figure 2.4 The image at the top shows a continuous grayscale, while in the bottom strip the tones are divided into discrete steps.

A continuous tone gray image (top) must be translated into individual digital steps by the scanner (bottom). The more "steps" available to represent the broad range of tones in an image, the more accurately an image reflects the original. We'll look at this idea in more detail in the section "Color Depth," later in this chapter.

Capturing Color

The sensor arrays in scanners are sensitive only to white light. To capture color, the scanner needs three separate images of an original, each representing the relative amounts of red, green, and blue for every pixel. In this respect, scanners sense and reproduce color images in the same way as your color monitor or television set: by combining various mixtures of the three primary colors of light. We're going to skip color theory for now because only a general knowledge of how colors are produced is necessary to understand how scanners capture color.

Because an unadorned sensor with no filters or other components added can interpret only white light, capturing color is accomplished either by filtering the white light reflected or transmitted by the original through red, green, and blue (R, G, and B) filters, or by using red, green, and blue light sources. The tricolor images can be captured in one of several ways.

Three-Pass Scanners

Some of the original desktop color scanners were three-pass scanners that made three complete passes of the original, each time using a different R, G, or B filter between the artwork and the optical system. Others used three separate red, green, or blue light sources consisting of fluorescent lamps, colored solid-state devices called light-emitting diodes (LEDs), cold-cathode tubes, or other types of illumination.

Theoretically, three-pass scanners should have been slower than those that required a single pass, but that wasn't always the case. Fast three-pass models were often speedier than less efficient models using another capture system.

These scanners required a high degree of accuracy in positioning the carriage for the three consecutive scans. The original had to remain rigidly in place to allow the three individual scans to be combined, or registered, without producing a rainbow effect called color fringing. The separate images were stored until the scans were completed and subsequently united. However, today the single-pass on-chip filter scanner has replaced the three-pass scanner — essentially, none exist.

One-Pass Scanners

Most one-pass scanners capture all three-colored images with a single trip past the original art. The scan can be done with a single CCD array, using three different exposures per line, each with a different red, green, or blue light source. In this kind of scanner you can often see the flashing lights as the scan progresses — of course, if you open the top to look at the lights during a scan, your image will not look so great!

Much more common today, the scanner includes a trilinear array — three duplicate sets of CCDs, each with a colored filter coated right on the chip during fabrication. The scanner's optics direct each of three white-light exposures per line to a separate set of CCDs. This on-chip filter technology is now used in virtually all desktop scanners and is used in all HP color scanners.

CIS or Contact Image Sensor Scanners

A type of scanner that is becoming somewhat more common at very low price points is the Contact Image Sensor or CIS scanner. CIS scanners are so-called because the original artwork is in contact with (or very close to) the sensor, unlike a CCD-based scanner, which has a folded optical path and lens between the sensor and the artwork (that's what is inside the optical carriage). If you unfolded the optical path (removed the mirrors) from a typical CCD-based scanner, you would find the distance between the CCD and the artwork ranges from several inches to a foot or more. In a CIS scanner, the distance between the sensor and the artwork is a few millimeters or less. Also, in a CIS scanner, the sensor is the same width as the page, whereas the CCD in a non-CIS scanner is only about 1.5 to 2 inches long.

In a CIS scanner, the color separation is achieved in the "3-colored light" mode like the older three-pass or one-pass scanners, but the lights are colored LEDs (light-emitting diodes): one red, one blue, one green. The LEDs flash in sequence as the CIS module moves down the page.

The primary advantage of a CIS scanner is the size of the carriage. The CIS scanning module, with LEDs and sensors included, is very small — maybe an inch on a side. This means the scanner can be smaller than a CCD scanner. Initially, CIS scanners were much cheaper than CCD scanners, but that advantage is nearly gone.

However, CIS scanners suffer from a number of limitations related to depth of focus and depth of illumination (the distance from the sensor at which a subject is represented sharply, and illuminated evenly). The LEDs are very dim and the focal range of the CIS sensor is short. This means that a CIS scanner, unlike a CCD scanner, cannot capture small 3D objects. Scanning a book, magazine, or a creased page may be a problem. CIS scanner modules are often used in color sheet-fed scanners.

Color Depth

Color depth (also called bit depth) is a way of representing how many different colors a scanner can capture. Because computers can't work with the continuous range of hues in your subject, the more colors and shades that can be differentiated, the more closely the tonal range of your scan approximates the original artwork.

Your computer assigns each individual shade and color a number based on its density and hue (for example, Red, 128; Blue, 63; Green, 0). The color depth refers to the number of bits used to store the information. We won't slog you down with binary arithmetic, but you probably know that your computer stores information in units called bytes, each of which contains 8 binary digits (or bits). A "2-bit" image could represent four tones with values 00, 01, 10, and 11. An 8-bit byte could represent any number from 00000000 to 11111111 (binary) or 0 to 255 (decimal). That's why an image saved with no more than 256 colors is often called an 8-bit image. Grayscale and some color images are 8-bit images. That's all the binary information we need for now. Just remember that a "byte" can store up to 256 variations of tone or color. Figure 2.5 shows the number of different tones that can be represented with 1 bit, 2 bits, and 4 bits.

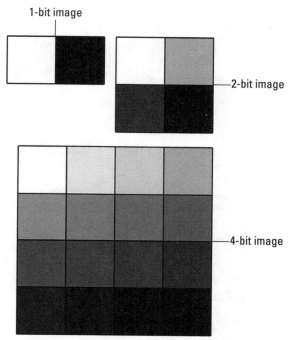

1-bit image

2-bit image

4-bit image

Figure 2.5 One bit can represent two shades; 2 bits, four shades; and 4 bits, 16 shades.

A color image is nothing more than three different grayscale images, each representing the amount of red, green, and blue in the original, as in our R128, B63, G0 example earlier. The three 8-bit red, green, and blue images are combined into one 24-bit file (which is why you hear full-color images referred to as 24-bit color). Where 8 bits can be used to represent 256 different colors, three sets of 8 bits can represent 256×256×256, or 16.8 million colors. As you can see, color scanners must be able to capture a minimum of 24 bits of information about each pixel.

There are other color depths in addition to 8-bit and 24-bit versions. Nearly all video cards today have enough memory to display 24-bit color, but older PC cards and some Macintoshes can show only 15- or 16-bit renditions of 24-bit files. These renditions result in 32,767 and 65, 535 colors on your screen, respectively. Keep in mind that the original color image can still be a 24-bit image even if it can't be portrayed as such on the screen; your video card converts it to "high color" (as opposed to "true color") to display it. Figure 2.6 shows an image presented at several different color depths. We're using black-and-white and grayscale images for our examples. The differences between the different types of images have been exaggerated slightly so they'll be visible on the printed page.

1-bit image

4-bit image

8-bit image

Figure 2.6 A grayscale image in 1-bit (black/white), 4-bit (16 tones), and 8-bit (256 tones) renditions

Many scanners now go beyond 24-bit color to capture 30, 36, or 48 bits of information per image. A 30-bit scanner, for example, grabs 10 bits per red, green, or blue color (30 bits total); a 36-bit scanner grabs 12 bits per color, and so forth. In fact, few applications can handle these ultra-color files, so scanners automatically convert them to 24-bit versions before they are stored on the computer or sent to the application. Even those few applications that allowed you to work with more than 24 bits limited what you could do to the image to the same kind of tonal transformation the scanner uses to create the 24-bit image from the 36-bit or higher scan. So, if you end up with a 24-bit image in the end, why grab 30- or 36-bit images in the first place?

Theoretically, 24-bit color should provide plenty of colors for most images because the human eye can't differentiate between anything approaching 16.8 million different shades. In practice, color scanners always lose a little information because of the inherent noise in any analog electronics system, much like the sound on your car stereo suffers when you roll down the windows. With the wind whistling past your ears, you may have to turn up the volume to compensate. Extra-color scanners work in a similar fashion.

Noise affects a scan only from the time of capture until it is converted to digital format. So, instead of 256 colors per channel, you may end up with only 128 different colors per channel. When a system is capable of reproducing 256 different colors but only 128 are available, it's likely that one of the available colors will have to be substituted for actual colors in an image. That scenario is especially likely to happen when scanning transparencies, which have a wider dynamic range — they detail all areas from deep shadows to lightest highlights — and may easily contain 256 or more colors in a particular color layer or channel. CCD scanners are notorious for coming up with bogus values in shadow areas because they lack sensitivity in dark regions.

The primary reason scanners capture extra data is to allow you to readjust the exposure of an image you scan. For instance, you may have a particularly dark photo — or a photograph in which the interesting subjects, the people standing in front of the bright snow, are badly exposed. With more bits in the scanner you can adjust the image to bring out the part of the image you want. Finally, to make a scan print or display well, you must apply something called gamma compensation. People often think gamma compensation is a correction for the scanner but, in fact, gamma compensation in the scanner precompensates the image for correct display or printing. Without gamma compensation, the scan will print or display too dark.

Cross-Reference

Chapter 10, "Optimizing Color," provides more information on gamma compensation.

So, many scanners now grab more bits per channel — 30-bit scanners can discern 1,024 colors per channel, nearly 11 billion colors overall, while 36-bit scanners grab 4,096 hues, which is 6.8 trillion colors. With so many extra colors, these scanners can afford to lose a little information to noise and still retain plenty of data to create an accurate 16.8 million color image. Even grayscale scans can benefit from the extended range of such units. Extra-color scanners often can sense 1,024 or more different gray tones and reduce the information to the best 256 shades for your final image. In practice, however, higher bit-depth scanners may not show a demonstrable improvement in quality because so many other factors can affect the image.

A Warning About Bit-Depth Specs . . .

A final word about bit-depth specifications. Scanners claiming more than 36 bits may or may not be actually capturing more bits of image. A recent trend in scanners is a form of "software enhanced" color depth. It is very unclear if these enhanced claims are really providing any benefit to the scanned image — so use care when comparing bit-depth specification. Unfortunately, there is no standard definition of what defines "bit depth" or "color depth" and many scanners with high bit-depth claims may not, in fact, deliver either that performance, or even a better image. In fact, since a good 24- or 36-bit scanner will provide all the quality most people need, it is probably better to pay more attention to other features and capabilities of the scanner than the bit depth. A well thought-out scanner is a solution comprising many features, one of the least of which is the bit depth specification.

Scanners and Resolution

Some discussion about what determines scanner resolution is appropriate here. As you learned in Chapter 1, "Scanner Basics," resolution isn't simply a matter of "more is better." This section explains how a scanner's resolution is determined.

Cross-Reference

Chapter 4, "Resolution, Interpolation, and Sharp Images," contains more information on resolution.

As we mentioned in a previous section "How Digitizing Works," true resolution, or optical resolution, is, in the broadest terms, the number of samples per horizontal and vertical inch that the scanner can discern. The width of the sensor strip in the scanner is one factor that determines the theoretical maximum number of samples per inch the device can capture. (The quality of the optical system actually limits the amount of resolution you can expect.) A scanner must have 5,100 individual sensors to capture a single strip 8½ inches wide at 600 samples per inch. That means the sensor bar is crowded, and every sensor must work to provide the scanner's top resolution. Designing a high-resolution sensor array is a complex task.

In practice, the actual width of the sensor strip itself is less than the widest band it can capture; that is, smaller than 8½ inches because a lens/mirror system is used to reflect and focus the light from the subject matter onto the array. While these more compact sensors are a challenge for CCD designers, their smaller size is actually an advantage when figuring vertical resolution. In this case, size does matter.

Obviously, the same linear sensor is used to scan each line of an image. The vertical resolution is determined by the distance the array is moved between lines. That is, if the carriage is moved ⅟₄₀₀ inch between lines, the scanner has a vertical resolution of 400 samples per inch. Some scanners capture the same line twice, slightly overlapping. That's why you'll see scanners with specifications listing 300×600 or 400×800 optical resolution. In practice, however, these specifications do not reflect a higher resolution (ability to see detail) in the vertical direction. Because of blurring introduced by the motion of the scanner, the actual resolution in this direction can be lower than the horizontal resolution.

In fact, the real limit to the "resolution" of a scanner — how small a detail it can resolve — is the lens, not the sensor resolution. Still, today's scanners can "see" things far smaller than your eye can see. This is useful if you want to enlarge something.

Interfacing with Your Computer

Once an image has been captured and converted to digital format, it must be passed along to your computer for storage, printing, editing, or other manipulations. The connection between your scanner and computer is called an interface, and it allows the two components to talk to each other. The scanner can communicate its status to the computer and transfer captured documents, while the computer can transmit commands to the scanner over this two-way link. Scanner interfaces take one of four different forms, not counting proprietary interfaces (which worked with only a particular vendor's scanners and have now completely vanished from the scene). The others are discussed in the following sections.

Serial Port Interface

The standard serial port — the same COM1 or COM2 connection you use for your modem and possibly your mouse — has largely fallen from favor, chiefly because serial connections transmit information a bit at a time, rather than in parallel like most other options that transfer a byte (or multiple bits) all at once. Serial ports are generally slow, limited to 115K bits per second at best, compared to the multi-megabit transfer rates of even the slowest SCSI interfaces.

Note

Another nail in the serial port coffin is that available ports in most Windows machines are very scarce. COM1 and COM2 are often dedicated to a modem and serial mouse. Other ports, numbered COM3, COM4, and higher, can be available, but they often must share a computer resource called an IRQ (interrupt) with the lower-numbered ports, and can't be used simultaneously.

Some multifunction devices use a serial connection for their scanner in tandem with a parallel interface (for the device's printer) to allow scanning and printing simultaneously. The newer universal serial bus (and eventually the even faster FireWire serial connection) described later in this section will replace the standard serial port and many other scanner interfaces in the future.

SCSI Interface

The small computer system interface (SCSI) connection started to gain favor in the scanner world when all Macs — starting with the Macintosh Plus — began to include this interface as a standard component. Today, SCSI has become a popular add-on for Windows machines as well because it is a fast system that allows multiple devices (up to six per SCSI bus) to communicate with the computer simultaneously. These devices can include removable cartridge drives such as Iomega Jaz and Zip drives, SyQuest SparQ units, recordable and rewritable CD-ROM drives (CD-R and CD-RW), DVD drives, and fast hard disks.

Many higher end current scanners use a standard SCSI host adapter, which you may use with any of these other components as well as the scanner. Those adapters furnished with scanners are likely to be low-end cards with few extra features.

Note

If you'd rather have a SCSI card with a ROM that allows booting from a SCSI device, or a faster interface compatible with Wide and Ultra-SCSI devices, you're free to buy one and use that instead. Scanners designed for a SCSI interface usually work well with all name-brand host cards.

Parallel Interface

Parallel scanner interfaces use the same connection as a printer on Windows-based machines. They're faster than standard serial ports, and the bidirectional parallel ports on most computers built in the last decade allow the scanner and computer to "talk" back and forth. Parallel port connections are used for some kinds of Zip drives, video capture devices, portable CD-ROM drives, and even parallel-to-SCSI adapters. While the parallel port isn't as fast as SCSI in all these applications, it's quick enough for many uses and doesn't require opening your computer to install a card. Many — but not all — parallel port devices have a so-called "pass-through" connector that enables you to use the device and your printer at the same time.

This kind of interface is very common, and can be found in multifunction devices, lower-cost scanners, and other peripherals. Unfortunately, the parallel interface was never designed as a general-purpose interface. Multiple devices may conflict or work only a portion of the time.

USB

The universal serial bus (USB) is included in all new Windows computers (anything with a Pentium II or compatible processor) and is directly supported by Windows 98. It invaded the Macintosh world in mid-1998 with the iMac, which uses a USB connector instead of the trio of serial, SCSI, and ADB (Apple Desktop Bus) ports found on previous Macs. USB devices include (take a deep breath) keyboards, mice, joysticks, scanners, video cameras, audio devices, modems, ISDN adapters, monitors (which use USB primarily to "talk" to the video card), as well as external low-speed drives from Iomega. Look for other applications, including telephone systems, in the future.

Like the standard serial port, USB conveys information in a continuous stream of bits, but up to 100 times faster at up to 10 megabits per second. As more devices are added, the bandwidth is shared. If two high-bandwidth devices are used on a USB interface, say a scanner and a disk drive, the performance is not as fast. In practice, for reasonable scans, USB works quite nicely for scanning because other factors often limit the speed (such as image processing or disk writing time).

While slower than SCSI, the rate is fast enough that a USB scanner, printer, and mouse should be able to communicate with a computer simultaneously without noticeable degradation of speed. Unlike standard serial ports, USB can support up to 127 devices on a single bus, similar to the way you can connect a string of devices with a SCSI interface.

However, SCSI is limited to 6 peripherals per bus, and each must be assigned a unique ID number and arrayed in a daisy chain with a device called a terminator at each end. USB requires no ID numbers and can be connected in multiple branches, using an intermediate gadget called a hub.

USB scanners are very common and much easier to connect than parallel or SCSI. If you have a newer computer that came with Windows 98 or Windows 2000 and USB, this is a very good option for you.

A faster version of USB, called USB 2.0 will become available in late 2000 and could provide a faster interface for the scanner and become a very strong competitor to SCSI or FireWire.

Types of Artwork

Scanners handle different kinds of originals — commonly called "artwork" — in different ways. The following section explains the differences between line art, grayscale images, previously halftoned art, and color.

Line Art

Line art is any piece of artwork that consists only of black-and-white areas, such as a pen-and-ink sketch, architectural plans, mechanical drawings, electrical schematics, and other artwork drawn only with lines and shapes. The key difference between line art and other kinds of images is that lines or areas of only one density are used to outline the art. The color of the line can be black, dark blue, or any other color. An example of line art is shown in Figure 2.7.

Because a single density is used to draw line art, scanners can capture such images as single-bit, binary images, although some allow no fewer than 16 different shades.

Line art can include patterns or fills, such as the cross-hatching and other effects used to differentiate between adjacent areas. Pattern fills, for example, are often used on bar charts. Because the regular patterns alternate black and white lines, our eyes blur the two to provide a grayish image. Line art may contain only lines of the same density, but still appear to have gray.

One important distinction with line art is the higher the scanning resolution, the sharper the image appears to be. That's because many more pixels are available to represent the edges of the lines, which may otherwise be represented by "jaggy" or "stairstepped" pixels. Higher scanner resolution is most important when scanning small originals, such as finely engraved postage stamps, stock certificates, or currency (where legal!).

Figure 2.7 Line art consists only of black and white (or, white and one other color).

You can see that a 1-inch square postage stamp scanned at 300 samples per inch would contain 90,000 (300×300) different bits of information. At 600 spi, you'd end up with four times as many bits — 360,000. This excess could make a significant difference in sharpness of diagonal lines, which reveal stairstepping most blatantly. However, in practice, most people may not be able to see the difference between 300 and 600 spi when the image is presented at normal size. In addition, if the end application is for a Web page, the higher resolution will be wasted.

So, even if you generally scan grayscale or color images, which often look their best at less than a scanner's top resolution, as you'll learn later in this chapter, you should know that line art generally looks and reproduces best when scanned at the highest available optical resolution.

Line art images don't put many demands on your scanner. The range of tones that must be captured — two — translates into a short dynamic range, which is a way of describing the distance separating the lightest tones and darkest tones with detail. With line art, this distance is virtually nothing: tones that are brighter than a particular value, or threshold, are represented as white. Those that are below this threshold are shown as black. The two areas where line art may demand much from the scanner are resolution (not spi, but the real capability of the scanner to capture fine detail in the original) and scaling — enlarging or reducing the image. Scanners that capture binary and then scale will often do a very poor job, introducing scaling defects that become obvious. A much better result will come from a scanner that enlarges based upon grayscale or color data — and then converts the enlarged image to binary.

Color Drawing — or Spot color

Color drawings are like black-and-white line art, except a drawing is made of solid colors — like crayons or markers. Also called spot color, color drawings are often used for ads, business cards, or letterhead. Some scanners have the capability to scan spot color and recognize the single colors — re-creating the drawing faithfully. This is useful if you want to scan a logo and preserve the color.

Converting Line Art to Scaleable Line Art

Some HP ScanJet scanners provide a method to convert a scan of line art from a raster "bitmap" to a vector drawing. A vector drawing is the kind of drawing you draw with a pencil. The nice thing about vector drawings is that you can enlarge or reduce them, or change colors of lines, after the scan. For instance, if you scan a very small logo as a vector drawing, you can then enlarge the logo dramatically in your word processor — and the image will not suffer from "jaggies" or loss of resolution like a raster bitmap would. While some third-party programs can do this, some HP ScanJets do this automatically, without requiring you to use another program.

Grayscale

Another kind of image is called grayscale, or, as they were labeled in the past, continuous tone, because these images appear to have a continuous scale of shades from pure white to black, with all the grays in between. A black-and-white photograph is a typical grayscale image. (Color images can also have continuous tones, with the added component of hue.) A typical grayscale image is shown in Figure 2.8.

Even though grayscale images may have smooth gradations through all the different shades of gray, it is convenient to think of such images in terms of individual steps or gray levels, as your computer does. Photographers do this all the time when they use one of the various systems of exposure. When we use photographs and other continuous tone images for desktop publishing, we'll need to think of gray levels, too.

Grayscale prints may have a long dynamic range, depending on how the picture was exposed and printed. If you've seen prints made by Ansel Adams or Edward Weston, you've doubtless marveled at how these images have subtle detail in the deepest shadows, while retaining detail in the brightest highlights. This range can be a challenge for scanners to reproduce, particularly those that grab monochrome images using 8 bits of information. A total of 256 tones is often not sufficient to represent the rich array of shades in a well-made black-and-white print. Add to that the need for gamma compensation for display or printing and the result may be pretty disappointing.

Figure 2.8 Grayscale images contain a full range of monochrome tones.

Cross-Reference

In Chapter 9, "Getting Better Scans," we look at some ways to improve your chances for a good scan.

Previously Halftoned Art

Halftoning is a technique that allows printing presses and laser printers to reproduce continuous tone images, even though they use solid-color inks and toner. Some kinds of printers, such as dye-sublimation models, are capable of varying the density of individual pixels, but most hardcopy devices rely at least partly on some kind of halftoning technology. Halftones convert the various gray and color values to black dots and magenta/yellow/cyan dots of various sizes. The eye merges these dots with the surrounding white area to produce the perception of a gray tone or color image. A halftoned image is shown in Figure 2.9.

While you'll want to learn more about converting images to halftones, you also need to consider them as original input for scanning. At times, you may discover that an image that has already been halftoned must be recaptured for a publication. Generally, you'll obtain poor results in capturing such images. Scanning halftones as if they were the continuous tone images they appear to be works only until you try to apply your own halftone effect to the image, which will happen as soon as you try to print the graphic. The extra set of dots usually results in an objectionable effect called moiré. Some scanners can automatically filter out these effects.

Figure 2.9 Halftoned images consist of a pattern of dots.

Color

When using the term color, we generally mean continuous tone color images, such as photographs or transparencies. Certainly, line art can be made and scanned in color (a kind of "spot" color), and grayscale images can be given a sepia, silver, or other tone for effect. Color halftones are a category unto themselves. In this book, however, color images are full-range color graphics, including photographs, paintings, and similar artwork.

Warning

Color images are trickier to scan than grayscale graphics, primarily because, in most cases, reproducing the relative color balance and rendition of the original is as important as accurately representing the detail within the image. Even slight bluish or greenish casts to human skin look atrocious (although you can often get away with inaccurate color if it leans in a warmer direction such as red or magenta). So, factors such as color balance and fidelity come into play when scanning color images.

Color transparencies are a special case, although these days only professional graphics workers and serious photo hobbyists need to scan color slides frequently. Color transparencies are challenging. First of all, few personal scanners are set up to handle them (most require a separate scanning attachment, and you can also purchase dedicated slide scanners, which have higher resolutions and are built specifically for scanning transparencies).

Second, transparencies have the longest dynamic range of any artwork a scanner encounters. Reflective art, such as photographs, are strictly limited in the number of tones they can include: the whitest white is determined by the reflectivity of the paper, plastic material, or substrate on which the photograph is printed, while the darkest black can be no darker than the maximum density produced by the fully exposed and developed emulsion on the substrate. The scanner's illumination reflects off the whitest and darkest portions of the print, producing a long, but still limited dynamic range.

Cross-Reference

You'll find more information about getting great color scans in Chapter 10, "Optimizing Color," and you'll get lots of practice applying your new knowledge in the projects in Part II of this book.

Transparencies, in contrast, are illuminated by light pumped through the film itself, potentially presenting much more detailed light and dark areas when compared to prints. If you think 30- and 36-bit scanners do a great job capturing long-scale color and grayscale prints, they are unmatched when it comes to grabbing transparency images faithfully.

Cross-Reference

Chapter 9, "Getting Better Scans," also looks at transparency scanning.

Moving On

In this chapter, we looked at some of the nuts and bolts that make scanners work. While you don't need to understand electricity to use a toaster, it's nice to know enough to avoid sticking a fork inside to retrieve an errant slice. In the next chapter, we're going to show you ten things (or more) that you probably don't know about scanner installation.

Installation Tips

Ninety percent of the time, installing a scanner is a simple procedure that works without a hitch. You may be reading this chapter because you find yourself in the 10 percent bracket. Perhaps you're an extra-cautious new scanner owner who wants to know what can go wrong in advance, or a frustrated owner not yet willing to brave the technical support line queues of your scanner vendor. In either case, you'll find the answers you need in this chapter. Even if you're a member of the majority and have no trouble installing a scanner, you'll want to read this chapter anyway. Understanding how a scanner is connected to a computer can help you troubleshoot problems and come to the aid of less fortunate friends and colleagues.

In the Windows world, Intel-standard computers are actually a motley collection of components, using two or three different interface systems — ISA, PCI, and Advanced Graphics Port (AGP) — plus others, such as universal serial bus (USB). These components all must contend for the use of a limited number of distinct system resources, including interrupts (IRQs) and direct memory access (DMA) channels. When combined with a plug-and-play operating system (such as Windows 95, 98, or 2000) that may or may not mediate these disputes, scanner installation has some hidden pitfalls that vex a small minority.

Installation can be less of a problem in the Macintosh world because all Macs from the Mac Plus to the first G3 models included a SCSI interface. The iMac and later models have USB or similar connections. In most cases, installing a scanner on a Mac is just a case of connecting the two devices with the right cable. But even Mac users can encounter problems while installing scanners, however.

Setting Up Your Scanner

Your first question should be, "Where do I put my scanner?" Scanners used to be big, heavy devices that took up a great deal of desktop real estate. David's own older-model ScanJet occupies the top of a deep two-drawer file cabinet that's placed within easy reach of his keyboard.

Modern flatbed scanners are much smaller, often only a few inches wider and deeper than the largest original (for example, 8½ × 14-inch sheets) they can handle. Sheet-fed models are sometimes not much bigger than a rolling pin and can nestle between your monitor and keyboard. As a result, you have considerably more flexibility today for placing a scanner on or near your desktop. Keep in mind the following:

■ **Put your scanner close at hand.** This may seem obvious, but we've seen a few installations in which scanners were put a step or two away from the user's desk, rather than within reach. Such placement may be an acceptable solution for sheet-fed scanners or flatbeds with automatic document feeders (ADFs) frequently loaded with stacks of documents. In office environments, remote scanners linked to several users over a network are necessarily located a distance from some users' desks.

Such cases mean that you'll need to move to the scanner to load a new stack, clear a jammed sheet, or scan a document not suitable for the document feeder. For flatbed scanners, a location even a few steps away is rarely acceptable, unless you commonly scan only one sheet in a session. Put your scanner within arm's reach, even if you have to move other equipment to do so. Can't your computer's system unit reside on the floor? Often a computer can sit beside or under a desk, and still be conveniently reached to turn it on or insert a CD-ROM disk. Perhaps you can move your printer to make room? A willingness to stretch a little to retrieve hard copies from your printer can make room on your desk for a compact scanner.

■ **Avoid sources of vibration.** Today's lightweight scanners are potentially more subject to blurriness caused by vibration during a scan because they lack what one imaginative car company called in the mid-'70s "road-hugging weight." Even lightweight, well-designed units suffer from this vibration problem, although less than flimsier, bargain-basement scanners. Even so, don't put your scanner on top of a system unit (the fan and CD-ROM drive can cause vibration), or too near a printer (particularly an inkjet unit with a carriage that goes back and forth). In the unlikely event you live or work near a subway line or other external vibration source that really rattles your office at intervals, consider putting your scanner on top of a bed of foam rubber to dampen the shaking.

■ **Avoid environmental extremes.** Don't put a scanner near your room's heat source or directly in front of an air conditioner or humidifier. It's improbable that the heat, cold, or moisture found in an office or home will damage your scanner, but you should never subject sensitive electronic equipment to avoidable environmental extremes.

■ **Give your scanner a safe power source.** In most cases, a safe power source means plugging the scanner into a quality surge protector. An uninterruptible power source (UPS) isn't usually necessary, as a scanner won't be harmed by a power blackout, and you won't lose any work if a scan is interrupted unexpectedly. However, power surges can damage a scanner, so a surge protector is a good investment. Keep in mind that the electronics in these devices eventually wear out after protecting your equipment from a certain number of surges (even small spikes can cause wear and tear on a surge protector). Follow your vendor's guidelines and replace surge protectors when recommended. In addition, these protectors vary in the amount of "surge" they can protect you from. For the highest degree of safety, get a good quality surge protector (rather than one of those power-strip cheapies) and unplug your scanner and computer from its power source when a really vicious thunderstorm is buffeting your home or office.

■ **Always use a scanner's carriage lock.** When setting up or moving a scanner, and especially when shipping a scanner, remember to use the carriage lock to fix the scanner's most fragile moving part in place. You'll usually have to shut off the scanner to position the carriage for locking; then either flip a switch or insert a locking screw to hold the component tight for moving.

A scanner's carriage can be easily damaged by rough treatment, even for something as simple as turning over the scanner to check its underside. Figure 3.1 shows the carriage lock of a typical scanner.

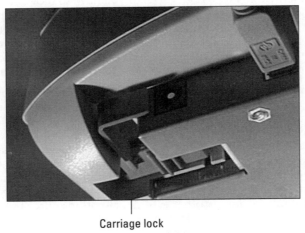

Carriage lock

Figure 3.1 A scanner's carriage lock should be used to protect the moving parts.

Installation Step-by-Step

With the latest scanners, installation can be a breeze. With some models, recent Hewlett-Packard offerings in particular, the first step in any installation is to install the scanner software. That puts the software components, or drivers, that recognize your scanner in place so the scanner can be identified and configured automatically when you plug it in. The best bet is to follow the directions that come in the installation manual.

After that, you can connect your scanner physically to your computer, as described later in this chapter. You'll probably be linking your scanner through a universal serial bus (USB) connection, but may need to use another interface, such as a SCSI or parallel port. We'll explain some of the pitfalls of these interfaces.

The last step in installing your scanner may be configuring your computer with the software needed to control the scanner, as not all scanner models do this setup before the scanner is physically connected. Even so, this should be an automated process, taken care of by the vendor's installation program. It will copy the controller software to your hard disk, including any special interface drivers (such as TWAIN) needed to let your scanner speak to the vendor's software or other programs, such as Adobe Photoshop.

Software and Drivers

As we mentioned, newer HP scanners let you install the software before you connect the scanner. Just insert the CD-ROM that came with the scanner and follow the instructions to copy the software. There's not much to be concerned about. But, here are a few things to keep in mind when installing and using your scanner software:

- Be sure to close all other running programs before installing your software. Some programs can interfere with setup applications. You may even have to reboot your computer to allow the installation to finish.

- Windows 95/98/Me/NT/2000 may have several TWAIN drivers installed at once: one supplied by your scanner vendor; another that may also work with your scanner supplied by a third party, such as Corel Corporation; and individual drivers for other image capture devices you may have, such as digital cameras. If you're working within a program like Photoshop, you'll need to select each TWAIN source separately as you require it. (In Photoshop 5.5 and earlier versions, the choice is made using File ⇨ Import ⇨ Select Twain_32 Source. With Photoshop 6.0 and later, you can select the driver directly from the File ⇨ Import menu.)

- If you're using Linux, you'll probably find that connecting a scanner can be more than a little problematic. Linux support for USB has been spotty, so you'll probably have to stick with scanners that use a SCSI interface. Few scanners ship with drivers for Linux. There are some third-party drivers, such as the software known as SANE. If you're not an experienced Linux user, your best bet is to locate a compassionate colleague who already has a scanner working under the operating system, and rely on his or her help.

Scanner Interfaces Made Easy

As you learned in Chapter 2, there are many different ways of connecting a scanner to a PC or Macintosh. Today, however, only four of these options are in common use: serial connection, parallel port, SCSI, and USB. This next section outlines the procedures you'll need to follow, and offers some caveats to keep in mind when hooking up a scanner through each procedure.

USB

Universal Serial Bus connections are probably the easiest of all scanner interfaces to set up. Most recent PCs, as well as Macintosh systems starting with the iMac, have USB ports already included. You can also buy adapters to put USB ports in later computers; these adapters cost about $50 and use an internal slot. Figure 3.2 shows a USB connector.

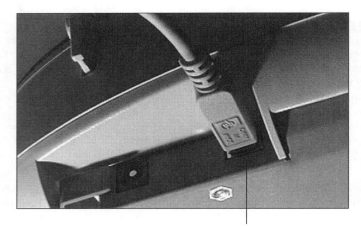

USB Connector

Figure 3.2 A USB connector

If you don't have any other USB devices, just plug your scanner into your computer using the supplied cable and hook up the power supply. Although the universal serial bus can provide up to 500 milliamps of power (enough for small devices, such as modems), a scanner's motor and light source require more juice. You'll need the external power connector that comes with your scanner. You don't have to worry about IRQs, IDs, or other settings with a USB device. Up to 127 peripherals can be connected and operating at the same time — although you can expect such a heavy load to have an impact on the speed or performance of the devices.

Multiple USB devices need to be connected through a device called a *hub*. The hub links to one USB port and supplies two to four (or more) new USB ports for additional devices. Hubs are inexpensive (around $50) and some devices have built-in hubs, making it possible to plug in other units in a daisy-chain-like fashion.

Tip

If you are buying a hub, you may want to consider a "powered" hub. A powered hub has a power supply connected and provides power to downstream USB devices. If you have a non-powered hub, you may find that some devices plugged into it do not work.

Once you've connected your USB device, install the scanner software. You're ready to rip.

Warning

Microsoft Windows NT 4.0 does not include support for USB devices. Don't purchase a USB-style scanner if you want to use it under Windows NT. Instead, use Windows 98 or Me (Millennium Edition). If you are using NT, consider upgrading to Windows 2000. We're currently using Windows 2000 Professional with a USB scanner and having no problems. Also, keep in mind that while Windows 95 had USB support grafted on near the end of its run, many users report problems using USB under that operating system. Upgrade!

USB 2.0

A new version of USB, called USB 2, will be showing up in computers soon – and scanners using that interface will likely soon follow (or lead the way). The nice thing about USB 2.0 is that it is much faster than the current version of USB, and it is compatible with existing USB devices. USB 2.0 can rival SCSI and FireWire in real life applications.

Serial Connection

Very few scanners use serial connections these days, but we're providing this short section on making serial connections in case you inherit one, or buy a used scanner that requires this interface.

On Windows machines, the serial connections are called the COM ports, which are usually given numbers like COM1, COM2, COM3, or COM4. This kind of connection is also called RS-232 — derived from the designation the port received in the early days of computing. COM ports are usually used for mice, modems, digital cameras, and a few other devices.

Macs up to the iMac also have conventional serial ports — again called the RS-422 designation. However, these have generally been used for modems and printers because Macintosh mice are connected through the same Apple Desktop Bus (ADB) port used by the keyboard (again, the iMac and later systems don't work this way).

A few scanners connect to PCs through a serial connection, but I don't know of any Macintosh scanners with this configuration. Some non-USB serial scanners are all-in-one multifunction devices that link to the PC through both a parallel port (for printing) and serial port (for scanning and communications). Using a standard serial connection has some distinct disadvantages, and this method has fallen into disfavor, which is why you see very few serial scanners anymore.

The main problem is that each serial port requires its own IRQ, and PCs have only 16 of them available — more than half of those dedicated to the system itself and the main peripherals such as the floppy disk drive, clock, and a pair of hard disk interfaces. Most of those IRQ assignments are fixed and cannot be changed. The others that can be modified may as well be fixed: IRQ3 and IRQ4 are almost always assigned to COM2 and COM1 (in that order), with IRQ5 set aside for a sound card and IRQ7 for the parallel port.

These assignments mean that if you have a serial mouse and modem attached to COM1 and COM2, it may be difficult to find a free interrupt for a third COM port. On most Windows machines, COM3 and COM4 share the same IRQs as COM1 and COM2, and devices attached to them can't be used at the same time. While plug-and-play operating systems are supposed to provide dynamic allocation of IRQs and device sharing, at present using more than two serial devices on a Windows machine is still an iffy proposition. If you absolutely must connect a scanner or other device to a serial port, here are some possible solutions, in descending order of desirability:

■ Switch to a PS/2 style mouse if your system has a PS/2 port. This port uses its own IRQ, often IRQ12, leaving one of your two COM ports free for the scanner.

■ Buy an add-on input/output (I/O) card. These devices, costing less than $50, provide additional serial ports and instructions for setting them to a free interrupt. Your PC's COM ports may be limited to IRQs smaller than 8, while add-on cards frequently support the "upper" IRQs, such as 10, 11, or 12, that may be available if your system isn't jam-packed.

■ Use an external modem and a serial switch. If you use an external modem, you can plug it into an external switchbox (often available for $15 or less) and flip between the modem and your scanner. You still can't use both at the same time, but the switch eliminates the possibility of one device conflicting with another. Even so, you may have problems with this solution if you try to access a scanner before you switch to it. Windows may require that you reboot.

Parallel Port Connection

The parallel port has become more popular as a scanner interface for Windows machines for several reasons: It's a guaranteed part of every PC, suffers from fewer conflicts than the serial port, and is inherently faster. (A parallel port exchanges 8 bits of information with your computer at a time, compared to 1 bit at a time with a serial connection.) Still, there are some things you need to know to use a parallel port successfully.

First, you might need a newer PC. Fortunately, only very old PCs are equipped with plain-vanilla parallel ports. These ports were designed for "talking" to a printer, with data going mostly from the PC to the printer, and little or no information coming back to the computer other than a few error codes for power-off or out-of-paper conditions.

All newer PCs have some kind of fully bidirectional parallel port, with one of these three designations: bidirectional, enhanced parallel port (EPP), or enhanced (or extended) capabilities port (ECP). These three designations are not identical, and while some scanners can use any of them, a few devices require one or the other. You'll want to check your documentation to make sure your system has the correct kind, and use your CMOS setup program to switch to the proper configuration.

Note

The CMOS setup program is the utility you can access when your computer starts up, usually by pressing a special key such as F2 or DEL before the operating system starts to load. Look under Peripheral Setup or a similar menu, and find the Parallel Port setup section to confirm that your computer is configured for the proper kind of parallel port required by your scanner.

Warning

Use only a new bidirectional parallel printer cable. This is often called a "data cable" and it should meet the IEEE-1284 specification. Cables labeled "IEEE-1284" compatible may not be fully IEEE-1284 compliant. Older cables don't always have wires connected for all the signals that need to pass between your computer and scanner. If your scanner is furnished with a cable, it will be the right kind.

Second, you may find yourself immersed in tricky multiple-device configurations. The parallel port has been attractive because, traditionally, only a printer was attached to it, and printers often work smoothly with other devices using the same port. So, a parallel-port scanner probably has a "pass-through" connection you can use to connect your printer: plug the scanner into the computer's parallel port and then plug the printer into the pass-through.

Unfortunately, many of us have several parallel-port devices, such as Iomega Zip drives. Daisy-chaining more than two parallel-port devices is likely to cause problems. If you really want to use a parallel-port scanner, find an alternative connection for your other devices. Zip drives, for example, now come in ATAPI (EIDE) and SCSI varieties that are faster than the parallel-port version to boot. Although David has a parallel port Zip drive, we use it chiefly as a traveling companion for use when we encounter a computer that doesn't have its own Zip drive. Our everyday Zip drives include a Zip 100 connected through the same SCSI connection used for a ScanJet 4c, and a Zip 250 daisy-chained with a more recent HP scanner through the USB port. (Yes! You can have more than one scanner connected to a computer at once.) It's also good to know that many HP scanners have more than one interface, such as both USB and parallel port, or USB and SCSI, giving you a choice of how to connect your scanner.

SCSI Connection

The SCSI bus was the favorite of scanner vendors for over a decade. Capable of transmitting more information in a second than the fastest scanner can generate, the SCSI is fast. A SCSI interface can handle multiple (up to seven) devices without conflicts and can exchange data among these devices simultaneously. SCSI host cards are also relatively inexpensive, especially for scanner vendors who were able to provide cheap "crippled" versions that didn't fully implement the SCSI specification, but worked just fine with a scanner. Not to take a negative tone — SCSI is a great interface, especially for experienced users (or anyone with a compatible Mac) — but there are many disadvantages to SCSI of which you should be aware. This longish section will explain how to overcome them. Points to ponder include:

- **Few new Windows machines are furnished with them.** A SCSI interface is almost always an add-on for those who don't already have fast SCSI disk drives or SCSI CD-ROM devices.

- **Adding a SCSI card means opening the computer.** While there are parallel-to-SCSI adapters, most SCSI add-ons require opening the computer and installing the interface in a free slot, which assumes the user knows how to do this operation and actually has a free slot. And parallel-to-SCSI adapters can be problematic — adding the challenges of SCSI to the challenges of parallel.

- **SCSI cards require an IRQ.** In most cases, a free IRQ will have to be found for the SCSI host adapter. This situation can be problematic for some scanner owners with machines already stuffed full of accessories.

- **SCSI devices can be tricky to set up if you're not familiar with them.** Each device requires its own "ID" number, and a component called a *terminator* must be placed at each end of the SCSI chain. We'll look at this requirement later in this chapter.

Note

Interrupts are the signals sent to the microprocessor that tell the microprocessor hat there is some additional work for it to complete. Ordinarily, the microprocessor continues to work at the task at hand. At intervals, however, it polls to see if an interrupt signal has been sent since it last checked. Each kind of interrupt has a unique number assigned to it. All you really need to know to avoid conflicts is which interrupts are used by which add-on boards in your system. The Windows 95/98 Device Manager can help. Use the Control Panel to access the System control panel. Choose Device Manager and click the Computer icon at the top of the list, and then the Properties button to see a list of IRQs assigned by your system. For older, non-plug-and-play-compatible devices, the manual that came with your device might tell you, or you may have to look on the interface board itself, on which there are usually jumpers that are clearly labeled. The jumper may be installed on a set of pins labeled IRQ11, with the pins next to them labeled IRQ12, and so forth.

Using SCSI

SCSI is a system-level interface; that is, an interface that conveys information to the CPU in logical terms. In contrast, the so-called device level interface sends information along dedicated wires or lines (your serial and parallel ports are an example of device level interfaces). Because each device on a SCSI interface does-n't require its own set of dedicated lines, the devices are able to share a single bus in parallel fashion. More intelligence is required in the device itself, as the device must interpret or decode requests from the computer and decide that the signal is in fact meant for it and not one of the other devices on the connection.

Each SCSI device must have circuitry on-board that receives requests for information from the computer and intelligently handles (in the case of a hard disk) finding the data: retrieving it, decoding it, and passing it along to the computer on the data lines common to all the SCSI devices in the chain. A scanner must be able to receive commands from the computer and convey scanned information (converted from analog to digital form, as discussed in Chapter 2, "How Scanners Work") back to the computer.

Because the computer doesn't have to be concerned with the nuts and bolts of operating the peripheral, a SCSI device can be a hard disk, tape drive, CD-ROM, CD-R, CD-RW device, printer, or scanner. The bus is easily fast enough to handle a scanner's information.

Up to eight devices can be attached to a SCSI bus, but one of them is always your computer, which leaves you seven connections for your peripherals. SCSI devices contained in your computer (whether it's a PC or a Mac) are attached to a single cable with multiple connections on it. External devices are daisy-chained together: that is, you plug a cable into your computer and then into the first device on the chain. To add a second device, plug an additional cable into a connector on the first peripheral and then into your new device. Connectors for a SCSI daisy chain are shown in Figure 3.3.

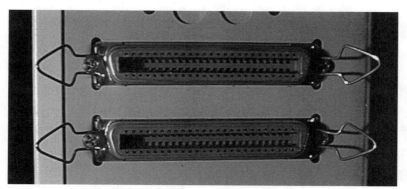

Figure 3.3 Connectors for a SCSI daisy chain, using the old SCSI-I interface

Each device in the chain has an address number from 0 to 7; the higher the number, the higher the priority of device. When the computer has information coming in from more than one SCSI device at once, the one with the higher address priority can be handled first. The computer itself always has the SCSI address of 7 and, therefore, is given the highest priority in the chain. A bootable SCSI device (one that can be used to start up your computer), such as a hard drive, is usually given a SCSI address of 0. The numbers from 1 through 6 are commonly available to scanners and other devices.

The SCSI address assignment does not have to relate to the order of the devices on the chain, nor do you need to use them in any particular order. An external hard disk closest to the computer may be Device 5, while a scanner that follows it on the chain may be Device 2 or 6. It doesn't matter. What does matter is how many and which devices are equipped with a feature called a terminator, which tells the computer the SCSI chain beginning and end locations. We'll look at terminators shortly.

A number of utility programs can "read" the SCSI bus and tell you what devices are present, and many scanners, including Hewlett-Packard scanners that use a SCSI interface, are furnished with such a utility. Figure 3.4 shows a display for a typical SCSI bus utility. The program can interrogate the devices to retrieve information about them. The manufacturer puts the model name and number of the device in its internal memory to make this data available, if so desired.

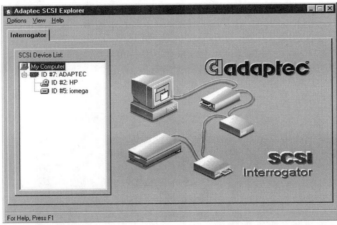

Figure 3.4 A SCSI utility can show which devices are connected to a computer.

Connecting SCSI Devices

Once you've gotten your SCSI interface connected (or, if you use a Mac already furnished with a SCSI port), you can connect the scanner to your computer. External SCSI connectors come in three varieties and two genders. Macs and some PC SCSI cards have a female 25-pin connector at the computer, which resembles the D-shaped connector used for a PC's parallel port. It's more common to see a female SCSI-II connector on a PC these days. The scanner itself may have either of these two connectors, or a larger 50-pin connector. All three types of connectors are shown in Figure 3.5.

Figure 3.5 Top to bottom: 25-pin Mac-style SCSI connector; SCSI-II connector; 50-Pin "Centronics"-style SCSI connector

Each of these female connectors are mated with male versions of the same connector contained in the SCSI cables furnished with your scanner, or purchased separately. Many different varieties are available with different combinations of connectors and genders. You may need a male-25-pin-to-male-SCSI-II cable to link a Mac with a device having a SCSI-II connector, or a male 50 pin/male 50 pin to daisy-chain two other devices. If your scanner doesn't have the exact cable combination required, your best alternative is to carefully examine your computer and the devices you'll be connecting, and then write down what combinations of connectors you need. Gender changers, which change a female connector into a male connector (and vice versa), and 50 pin/SCSI-II conversion adapters can help you modify the connection at one end of a cable without having to buy a whole new cable.

Setting Addresses

Next, set a unique SCSI ID for each device connected to your SCSI interface. If you have external SCSI devices in addition to the scanner, you'll usually find a set of switches or another indicator that shows the current SCSI ID for that device and allows changing to some other ID if there is a conflict. If you also have internal SCSI devices (such as a hard disk or CD-ROM writer), you may have to use a SCSI bus utility program to determine the current ID of the internal devices. In most cases, you'll be able to use the factory ID setting for your scanner. If not, choose an unused address.

The Terminator

It's not commonly known, but Arnold Schwartzenegger used his tagline "I'll be back!" in many films other than "The Terminator." When the movie strongman invokes the term, the other characters usually have no inkling of how much trouble his promised return will cause. Similarly, you don't want signals to come back in a SCSI chain either, unless you're looking for trouble of a different kind. On the SCSI bus, a terminator is a device that absorbs SCSI signals at the end of the chain to keep them from bouncing back to produce electrical noise that can lead to errors.

Generally, your SCSI bus should have two terminators: one at the beginning and one at the end of the chain. If your computer has an internal hard disk, it should have a terminator. If your scanner is the only external device on the SCSI bus, it should have a terminator, too.

Things get only a little more complicated when you connect an internal hard disk and two or more external SCSI devices — say an external disk and a scanner. In that case, any device in the middle doesn't need a terminator, but the device at the end of the chain does. Scanners and other external devices such as Zip or Jaz drives usually have a switch or other clearly marked setting to turn termination on or off. A few older devices don't have this feature. They require something called an external terminator, which is plugged into one of the SCSI connectors on the device. It's usually easiest to just put this kind of device in the middle of the chain and use a more easily terminated device at the end. Remember that only the device at the end of the chain requires termination.

Setting a device number for your scanner that doesn't conflict isn't especially difficult, even though various systems are used by various devices. Some devices, such as hard disks, use a jumper to specify a SCSI address. A typical jumper is shown in Figure 3.6. In a hard disk, the SCSI jumper is often located on the back of the disk, near the cable connector. Other devices, including scanners and some external hard disks, use a more convenient scheme: either a rotary switch on the back of the unit, which can be set using a small screwdriver, or a pushbutton device that cycles through each address as you press it one or more times. In both cases, it isn't necessary to open the device to set the SCSI address.

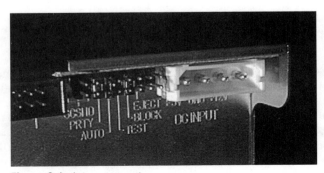

Figure 3.6 A jumper setting

Although setting up a SCSI device can be complicated if you use several devices, it's a one-time operation.

Moving On

Although most scanners come with good instructions to help you get them installed and running, the information in this chapter can help you get over the rough spots. Now it's time to show you how to get great scans. The next chapter concentrates on resolution, interpolation, and how to get sharp images.

Resolution, Interpolation, and Sharp Images

What resolution do I need? That's the number one question posed by scanner neophytes, scanner veterans, and even those who are just considering purchasing a scanner. Everyone wants to know what resolution they should look for in a scanner they are buying, and then, after the image grabber is set up and operating, how to select the resolution for a particular scan.

The short answer is: Don't sweat the small stuff! With modern scanners, resolution is not only small stuff, it's not even the stuff you should be worried about. As you learned in earlier chapters, many other factors, such as the scanner's sensor itself and the optics used to focus a scanned image onto the sensor can have much more of a bearing on how sharp your final image looks. While this chapter clears up some of the myths associated with resolution, we're also going to cover how you should work with various types of art, and we introduce a significant new technology that brings intelligence to many scanning operations.

However, it's easy to see why desktop scanner users can quickly become confused over the topic of resolution. The issue is clouded by widely held misconceptions about "true" resolution, interpolation, and sharpness. In truth, the quality of a finished scan is affected by much more than the number of samples per inch claimed by your scanner or the number you actually use for your scan. As we noted, the optical quality of the scanner and the intended final application for the image are more important than the previous factors. As a result, "higher" resolutions often aren't useful; they actually capture nothing but extra time, as well as hard disk space you could have used for another purpose.

As mentioned briefly in Chapter 1, selecting a desktop scanner on the basis of resolution alone can be like opting for a barely street-legal 190 mph sports car over a more refined motor car capable of "only" 150 mph, when neither will ever be driven much over the legal speed limit. The extra horsepower that you can't use may come at the expense of riding comfort, reliability, or other important factors.

In addition, reliance on scanner resolution figures alone is unwise because there is no standard way of measuring or representing these capabilities. A scanner with true 600 spi resolution may capture more information and provide sharper scans than one marketed as an 800 spi scanner. The latter may actually be a 400 spi device that uses special mathematical routines to manufacture the extra pixels and simulate the higher figure.

Moreover, there are different kinds of resolution to consider: the resolution of the scanner that grabs the image; the resolution of the display device that shows the image as it is edited; and the resolution of the output device, such as a printer or imagesetter. All these need to be taken into consideration at some point.

In practice, higher resolutions in the scanner aren't necessarily of any real use. A setting of 150 to 200 spi may capture all the available information in many types of originals. Higher resolutions may give you nothing more than a sharper look at the grain of a photograph. However, there are some applications in which resolution is important, and some of the following background material should make this easier to understand. But first, we'll give you the bottom line in the next section. If you want to know why the following recommendations are true, you'll find the answers in the rest of the chapter.

The Bottom Line

For standard work, the following rules of thumb work quite well for scanning line art, black-and-white or color photos, and text captured with an optical character recognition (OCR) program:

Line Art

This type of original includes black-and-white or color drawings that include only solid lines, dots, or other strokes, with no shading. Previously halftoned artwork, such as photos clipped from publications, also qualify as line art — but watch out for copyright issues when reusing published material! For such art, you should scan at the same resolution used for final output. If an image is destined for a 600 dpi laser printer, then 600 spi is your best choice. This arrangement allows a one-to-one correlation between scanned pixels and printed dots, and reduces the likelihood of jaggies — the stairstepping effect discussed in Chapter 2.

With the new 1200 spi scanners, you may be tempted to scan at 1200 spi for your printer. In most cases, that is not really needed — you may find more detail captured, but you will typically find that your file is four times larger and the printing times longer, with no gain in final image quality. In practice, most original line art does not have detail small enough to warrant 1200 spi — so you may not see any difference between 600 spi and 1200 spi — except a much slower printout! The biggest advantage of higher spi is to allow the scanner to enlarge small originals. You'll need this top setting only if you're scanning something postage stamp-sized (like postage stamps!) and want to preserve tiny details.

Tip

When checking scan quality, people tend to zoom way in on the image. Remember, no matter how high the resolution setting you use to scan, if you zoom in enough when looking at the image, you will see jaggies, defects, and noise. In short, you can make any image look bad if you try hard enough. The best bet when examining scanned images is to look at them at the same magnification and size you will use in the final product.

Black-and-White or Color Photos

When scanning photos you should choose the resolution based upon two factors: what you plan to do with the photo, and whether you plan on enlarging it. For instance, if you are printing the image, you should scan at 150 to 200 samples per printed inch. If you are scanning for a Web page, you would want to used something like 72 or 75 spi.

In times past, scanner users had to worry about halftone frequencies (the number of lines per inch in the dot "screen" used to produce the halftone), but with modern printers, halftone and image rendition is handled by the printer and printer driver, so you don't have to be concerned with such issues. Finally, if you are enlarging an image, you need to scan at a higher spi, and in many cases you can let the scanner handle that for you.

For example, with newer Hewlett-Packard scanners, the scanner and software will recognize the type of image you are scanning, and your destination (printer, Web page, and so forth) and pick the right spi for you. If you are enlarging, you should use the scaling function, which will, in effect, operate the scanner at a higher or lower spi to automatically give you the right result at the right size. Gone are the days when you needed to worry about spi.

Optical Character Recognition

Modern HP scanners provide integrated OCR and some high-end models have drag-and-drop — so you don't need to worry about spi. Just select the scanned text or page from the scanning software and copy and paste it to your word processor, or, with models supporting drag-and-drop, drag the text to your word processor document. However, if you do decide to use an external OCR package, such as Caere Corporation's OmniPage, you may need to set the resolution.

In those cases, the resolution best used for optical character recognition (OCR) also involves tradeoffs. The higher the resolution, the more information with which the OCR software has to work — but the longer it will take to process the data. Consequently, higher resolutions are not always the best answer. As a rule of thumb, scanning at a setting as low as 300 spi will provide enough detail to allow the OCR software to reliably differentiate 10 point or larger typefaces. If you are scanning material with smaller type, 400 to 600 spi (up to the maximum optical resolution of the scanner) can be useful. Don't bother with interpolated resolutions for OCR — interpolation slows down the OCR process and provides little benefit.

What Is Resolution?

Resolution is measured differently for each kind of device. Printer and imagesetter resolution is measured in *dots per inch,* the number of actual spots that the device is able to place on a piece of paper or film. Even if the device is able to vary the size of the dots, the number of them in a linear inch remains the same at a given resolution. These dots are usually round or oval in shape.

Your computer display's resolution is measured in *pixels per inch,* the number of picture elements that can be shown on the screen. Pixels are square, as you can see in Figure 4.1, which shows a close-up view of a grayscale image.

As you'll learn in the following sections on halftoning, the halftone patterns used to represent photographic images are measured in spots and lines. Spots are the dots (elliptical, round, square, or some other shape) that make up the picture information. Lines are the number of rows of these spots in an inch that determine a halftone screen ruling (the number of lines per inch).

Figure 4.1 A close-up of a grayscale image

Scanner resolution is measured in samples (not dots) per inch. As you discovered in Chapter 2, all desktop flatbed scanners use the same basic principles to capture images. An original piece of artwork is placed facedown on a glass platen and held in place by a cover. A bar with a moving light source and mirror reflects an image of the original, line by line, to a sensor. So far, this sounds a lot like a traditional office copier. However, desktop scanners, as well as the latest digital copiers, convert the analog information to digital format for manipulation and storage by a microprocessor — your computer, in this case.

The resolution in the X dimension — the width of the scanned image — is determined by the number of sensors available to capture each line of the image. The most popular desktop flatbed scanners today have 600 to 1200 of these sensors per inch, providing, at best, a true horizontal resolution of no more than 1200 spi.

Recall that the resolution in the Y dimension — the length of the scanned image — is determined by the distance the sensor moves (the stepping increment) between lines. A scanner that can capture an image in $\frac{1}{800}$-inch steps in this direction doesn't necessarily resolve 800 lines per inch. Instead, the finer increments can be used to provide a smoother image, particularly with line art.

The optics used to focus the image, the spot size and shape on the sensor, the amount of overlap in the y-direction of the pixels, and other factors also contribute to the true resolution of a scanner. In fact, today, the spi rating of a scanner is, like bit-depth, often more about numbers hype than reality.

Scanner manufacturers use this information in designing equipment. It may be useful to trade off some sharpness in the blue channel in exchange for a much higher modulation transfer function (MTF) rating in the green channel, if the end result is an improved overall image.

Note

Scientists refer to something called a *modulation transfer function* (MTF) to measure the real sharpness of an image. MTF is a way of representing the response of the system to different colors, or frequencies of light. In color scanning, MTF becomes more complex because optics have a different focus for each of the primary colors of light (as you'll learn about in Chapter 10) — red, green, and blue. In addition, the amount of each color used to make up an image is not evenly distributed: 60 percent is derived from the green light, 30 percent from the red, and 10 percent from the blue.

A new standard under final development by the ISO provides a standard measurement for the real resolving power of a scanner. This standard, ISO 16067, measures something called spatial frequency response, and will provide truer measurement for "resolution" and help combat the spi specification inflation that is prevalent.

As a result of these many factors, two 600 spi scanners may produce very different results. One 600 spi scanner may actually provide higher resolution than another scanner with the same nominal specifications.

What Is Interpolation?

Interpolation is a process used when changing an image's size (up or down) or color depth to something other than its original size or color depth when captured. Interpolation shouldn't be confused with simple scaling. When an image is scaled up without interpolation, each pixel is duplicated a specific number of times. This enlargement will eventually produce jaggies or rough edges, which are especially noticeable in diagonal lines. Figure 4.2 shows an example of a scaled-up image without interpolation.

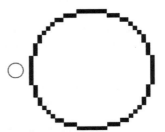

Figure 4.2 The original image is on the left; the image on the right has been scaled up 800 percent without interpolation.

Interpolation also produces images with more pixels, but the algorithms used to generate these pixels can be much more sophisticated. Instead of simply duplicating pixels, interpolation software looks at the pixels surrounding the new pixel and produces one with characteristics that closely match the transition between pixels. That is, if one pixel is dark gray and the next pixel is light gray, a medium gray pixel is created to insert between them. Figure 4.3 shows how the value of a new pixel is calculated from the values in the upper row to produce the new pixel in the bottom row.

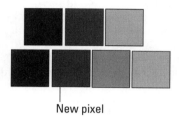

New pixel

Figure 4.3 Top row: original pixels. Bottom row: new pixel calculated.

In this example, the pixel inserted between the second and third pixels from the left is assigned a tone halfway between the two adjacent pixels. In a pixel-doubling scaling scheme, one or the other of the pixels would simply be duplicated. The distribution of new pixels is also important: they can be evenly distributed or created in clumps that add unwanted objects or artifacts.

Well-implemented interpolation produces images that have useful information not found in the original scan because the algorithm more or less accurately calculates the pixels that would have been captured if the scanner had had the higher resolution. In years past, some machines marketed as 600 spi scanners were just 300 spi devices that used interpolation. That marketing ploy wasn't quite an accurate representation of the scanner's capabilities, of course. Fortunately, scanner vendors now generally describe their products in terms of true optical resolution. The maximum interpolated resolution is provided as a separate number.

Unfortunately, as spi specifications become more inflated, as pixels become smaller and scanners become cheaper, the quality of the lens and optics has become more important and less known. In other words, a higher spi scanner may not resolve small details better than lower spi. This has been true in the past, but it is becoming truer. The new, more accurate ISO SFR specification we described previously may help this in the future.

Some scanners interpolate in hardware on the fly, while others do it in software residing in the user's computer. Done properly, interpolation can be very useful — it will produce larger images of much better quality than those simply scaled up by duplicating pixels blindly. A very small, detail-filled line art image, such as some postage stamps or a steel engraving, can be effectively scanned at higher interpolated resolutions. But for most work, interpolation produces no new information and isn't even necessary.

In many ways, *downsampling* is the opposite of interpolation. Whereas the latter creates new pixels for a larger image by examining the pixels already present in an image, downsampling is used to reduce the size of an image by intelligently removing and changing pixels in the final image, rather than just discarding them.

In practice, downsampling happens a lot, particularly with higher spi scanners. For instance, if you have a 1200 spi scanner, it cannot scan at 300 spi, but *must* downsample to 300 from the 1200 raw capture. How well it does this is *very* important and varies from model to model.

Image editors use one of three resampling algorithms: Nearest Neighbor, Bilinear, and Bicubic. With the Nearest Neighbor method, the application calculates pixels by examining the nearest pixel in the position where the new pixel will go. This method works best with line art, but doesn't take into account the fine gradations found in photographs. The Bilinear method bases its calculations on the values of the pixels on either side and produces better quality images than the first method. The preferred method for resampling is Bicubic, which uses sophisticated formulas to calculate the new pixel based on the surrounding pixels (above, below, and to either side). While this procedure produces the best quality, it is also the slowest of the three algorithms.

Some of the scaling routines used in the latest Hewlett-Packard scanners produce results that are as good as or better than bicubic interpolation. These scanners use particularly complex sharpening and blurring routines that dynamically change the amount of sharpening based upon the noise, lightness, and detail in the image. In short, the scanner takes many, many factors into account when creating new pixels through interpolation. For that reason, your best bet, with HP scanners, is to allow the scanner system (hardware and software) to perform interpolation or downsampling.

What Is Sharpening?

Sharpening is another way to enhance apparent resolution. This is a software technique in which blocks of pixels, say 3×3 or 5×5 pixels square, are examined. The center pixel may be altered, depending on the values of the other pixels in the square, to enhance the contrast. Sharpening can therefore make the edges of lines more distinct, as borderline pixels are darkened or lightened. The process can also be carried out in reverse to blur an image and hide unwanted detail. Figure 4.4 is a close-up of an image before and after sharpening.

Sharpening techniques can produce real gains in resolution by making details that are present in the original image stand out more strongly. With binary (black-and-white) scans, it is easy to measure the gains that can be produced by sharpening techniques. Sharpening is also useful for continuous tone grayscale and color scans, but can be carried only so far because of the increase in contrast.

Sharpening can also have negative effects — increasing the apparent noise or graininess in the image. More sophisticated sharpening systems, such as those found in HP ScanJet Scanners, actually take into account the amount of image noise, detail, and the lightness and darkness of the image as well as the local features around a pixel in the image.

Figure 4.4 Left, unsharpened. Right, sharpened.

Understanding Grayscales and Continuous Tone

Rules of thumb are great for getting started, but knowing the reasoning behind them can help you when you encounter artwork that doesn't respond well to rule-of-thumb treatment. We'll start with a look at how grayscale and color images are captured and converted for output on your printer or an offset press. This discussion will help you understand why such images don't require high resolutions.

Black-and-white and color photos are reproduced in books, magazines, and other publications using a process called halftoning, which we'll explain in more detail later in this chapter. The halftoning process, which reduces an image to a series of dots of different sizes, is the reason why higher resolutions aren't necessarily better when scanning photos. Some detail is lost in reducing the image to dots, so any extra resolution is actually wasted.

A grayscale scan is a bitmap (a representation of the pixels in row and column format) in which each pixel of the image represents the density of that pixel in the original artwork. Figure 4.1 showed a close-up of a grayscale image, enlarged enough that you can see the individual pixels. Note that the pixels are square — this is one of the reasons why the term "dots per inch" doesn't apply to scanned images; the picture elements are not dots.

The original image can theoretically include black, white, and an infinite range of tones in between, although in practice nothing of the sort occurs. A scanner divides this infinite range into a set of gray tones, usually 256 different shades from pure black (0) to pure white (255).

Note

In a black-and-white print, the blackest black (called *D-max*, for maximum density) is limited because the paper always reflects some light; nothing this side of a black hole absorbs all the light that falls on it. Similarly, the whitest white (called *D-min*) is limited to the maximum amount the white paper can reflect.

A scan of a full-color image such as a photograph is actually three different grayscale images. Each color layer represents the density of a particular primary color — red, green, or blue — in the image. Figure 4.5 shows a grayscale version of a color image, accompanied by the grayscale representations of each of its color layers. You can see the different color channels (a channel is a layer representing red, green, or blue) in the figure. It's important to know that even color images contain grayscale information because this underlying nature affects how we choose the resolution for a scan.

Figure 4.5 Clockwise from upper left: A grayscale version of a color image; the red, green, and blue versions of the same image

Printing Grayscale and Color Images

For a long time, computer printers did a poor job of reproducing a continuous range of grayscale or color tones. They were able to print only solid dots of the particular shades of ink available to them or a few mixtures of the colors — to achieve hundreds or thousands of colors, but not the millions and billions contained in scanned images. To simulate continuous tones, techniques called *dithering* (representing tones by black-and-white patterns) and *halftoning* (representing tones by a collection of dots) have been used. However, this situation has changed with newer HP printers, both inkjet and laser, which can print variable dot sizes and overlay primary colors to produce more than just a few hundred colors or tones. A short discussion of how halftoning works may serve to illustrate how important this capability is.

To create a dithered image or a halftone in the traditional way, the image is divided into cells. Each cell contains an appropriate mixture of black and white space or, in the case of a color image, the individual color and surrounding white space. The eye blends the black or color dots together with the white space to simulate lighter tones. Several colors printed very close to each other create intermediate colors on the page. Figure 4.6 shows how dots can be arranged to create gray tones. If you look at a newspaper halftone with a magnifier, you'll see that large and small black dots make up the gray tones in black-and-white photos, and colored dots create the color images.

Figure 4.6 Dots arranged to simulate a range of tones

Because we can print only black or colored pixels, we must use them as building blocks to construct the various sized dots or printer cells needed to reproduce a continuous range of tones. The fewer printer dots used to make up one of these super-dots, the fewer the different tones of gray available.

For example, a cell that measures two printer dots on a side offers five different combinations of tone, including black and white. A cell measuring four dots on a side provides 16 different combinations, plus white, as you can see in Figure 4.7.

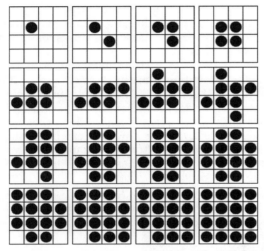

Figure 4.7 Combinations possible with a four-dot cell

As we use up printer dots to create cells, something else happens. With a four-dot square cell, a 600×600 dpi printer actually becomes a 150-cell-per-inch output device because four dots in the horizontal and vertical directions are required to produce a particular cell. However, 16 different shades, plus white, aren't enough to reproduce a 256-tone image. A printer needs to use either larger cells (reducing the printer's resolution further) or change the size of the printer dots, allowing more combinations within a fixed cell size. Modern printers can do both to give us realistic grayscale images, even at 600 dpi. Some color printers also use additional colors of ink (black, plus three "strong," or dark, and three "weak," or diluted, colored inks) to increase the number of tones available.

The use of more than four ink colors, plus the capability to create different sized dots in the latest inkjet and laser printers, vastly expands the number of colors available so that these printers can generate full color images that include thousands of different shades and hues.

In all cases, however, because of the need to construct printer cells from the available printer dots, the effective resolution of the printer used to reproduce a grayscale or color image is somewhat lower than its rated resolution. That's why you don't need to scan an image that will be reproduced on a 600-dpi printer at 600 dpi: much of the information will be discarded when the image undergoes the dithering or halftoning process.

The other reason is that the original — the photograph — does not have any detail that you need this high a resolution to capture. The photographic process cannot reproduce printed detail this fine. So scanning at 150–200 spi (for one-to-one reproduction) captures everything of interest in the image.

Why is it important to have 256 different density values? You already know that images with only a few different levels look poster-like and unrealistic, as you can see in Figure 4.8. This is particularly true of subjects that have large expanses of tone that change gradually from one shade to the next. Pictures with sky, water, or walls typically require more tones for accurate representation. If a sufficient number of tones are not available, the image will be divided into objectionable bands.

Figure 4.8 Left, 256-tone image. Right, banding produced by an insufficient number of tones.

But do we really need as many as 256 different density levels? Studies have shown that the human eye can differentiate only about 30 to 60 different gray levels. A highly detailed subject with no large gradated areas can sometimes be represented by as few as 16 gray levels. Why do we need more?

The answer is more obvious when you consider the nature of most images. Those 64 or so levels we can discern aren't always spread evenly along the entire gray spectrum. In a photo of a wooded scene, like the one shown in Figure 4.9, there's a lot of detail in both the highlights (the water in the stream) and the shadows (the leaves cloaked in shade). All the tones that make up the detail in the stream are compressed into one end of the spectrum — the lighter end. But, if we distributed 64 tones equally, we might have only 16 tones to represent all the nuances of the water.

Figure 4.9 A scene with detail in both highlights and shadows

However, there's more to this scene than the stream. There's a lot of detail in the trees and rocks next to the stream. These details are partially illuminated by the softer light that bounces off the surrounding surfaces. If your eyes become accustomed to the reduced illumination, you'll find that there is a wealth of detail in these shadow images. Certainly, there is more information than can be represented by, say, 16 tones.

With 256 tones you get extra information, which you can then distribute as you wish to adjust the reproduction of an image. Even though they are evenly distributed along the spectrum, 256 different levels still give you sufficient highlight and shadow tones from which to choose. Image editing can further refine the way the tones are distributed by "clumping" them in areas of the scale that have the most detail.

So, we've arrived at two conclusions: a scanner must capture a sufficient number of tones to represent an image accurately, and the resolution only has to be high enough to accommodate the natural loss of detail when the image is converted to a halftone.

Where Should Halftoning Be Done?

In times past, there were as many as three different points in the scanning/printing process in which halftoning could be performed. Scanners sometimes performed this task for you. If you knew the size at which your image would be reproduced, you could specify a halftone pattern through your scanner controller software.

When halftoning is done during the scanner process, the continuous tone information is discarded so you have no way to edit the image or scale it to another size later. And, because built-in dithering schemes are optimized modern printers devices, you are better off applying the halftone pattern later in the process, when you print. Halftoning within the scanner is no longer provided by most scanners because of these drawbacks.

The second place halftoning can be done is within image editing software, which often includes a broad selection of halftone or dithering schemes that can be applied. You can convert a grayscale or color image using one of these and preview it onscreen before sending the file to your printer. This strategy may be your best choice if an image will be scaled, or output on a high-resolution device.

However, the third and best place for halftoning to occur is the printer or printer driver. Today modern printers provide much more sophisticated dithering capabilities than in the past. For nearly all purposes, you should just work with grayscale or full color images in your editor, and let the printer take care of applying halftones.

More on OCR

Before reading this chapter, if you had been asked what the best scanning resolution to use for optical character recognition was, you might have said "the highest available" without stopping to think about the answer. By now, you know that optimum resolution is not as simple a choice as you may have thought previously. As with line art and photos, the speed and accuracy of OCR is dependent on more factors than just resolution.

Indeed, the most advanced scanners on the market include sophisticated page decomposition tools and can make on-the-fly adjustments for colored papers, stains, and other potential roadblocks. Such a scanner may provide much better recognition and speed at a true 200 to 400 spi than another model that is supposedly capable of 600 spi resolution.

OCR accuracy and speed are important for many scanner users, as optical character recognition has become an essential tool in law offices, education, and a variety of document management applications. OCR enables you to convert the text on virtually any paper document into an electronic form that can be edited and reprinted, or stored in a database for rapid retrieval. For organizations or individuals buried under stacks of paperwork, this capability can be a godsend.

An OCR system must handle a wide variety of typestyles and fonts, paper of different colors, and other variations. Typewritten text can vary widely from machine to machine; a worn ribbon, broken or overlapping characters, and other defects are difficult to interpret. Computer-generated, laser-printed text is somewhat easier for an OCR program to "read," but still can contain stylized fonts, tables, and graphics.

To interpret text, an OCR program must have a clear "picture" of each individual character. Then, techniques such as *pattern matching* (a character's bitmap is compared with a library of fonts to find the closest match) or *feature extraction* (for example, two diagonal lines that meet at the top, with a crossbar, is an A) identify individual characters. Other tools, including built-in dictionaries and a set of context-defining rules (a 1 surrounded by numbers is probably the number one, rather than the letter *l*) also are brought into play. Figure 4.10 shows some of the different characters an OCR program can recognize through feature extraction.

Figure 4.10 Although all of these characters have different shapes, an OCR program can recognize them as the letter A through feature extraction.

However, the original text must be captured at a high enough resolution to provide the OCR software with enough information. Too much information, though, is not necessarily a good thing.

The higher the resolution, the more time the OCR software must spend analyzing the bitmaps. An 18-point *M,* for example, occupies a square measuring one-quarter inch per side; at 400 spi, that's 40,000 pixels of information. OCR software would not need so much data to analyze such a large typeface, if printed clearly. At 100 spi and 2,500 pixels, a system should be able to analyze the same character as much as 16 times faster, if everything else is equal.

So, with large, clear typefaces, lower scan resolutions produce better performance with no sacrifice in accuracy. For 10- or 12-point type, 200 spi is often quite enough resolution to enable fast OCR interpretation. Smaller sizes or difficult originals can benefit from higher resolutions.

However, OCR scanning rarely requires a resolution higher than 400 spi, and few OCR packages work well with such settings. More important to accuracy is how flexibly the scanner is able to read a page.

Intelligent Scanning Technology and OCR

Hewlett-Packard's scanners include a feature called Intelligent Scanning Technology that helps produce readable images from the most complex and difficult documents. Most scanners enable you to set only a single "threshold" per page. Much like the lightness/darkness settings on a copier, this control specifies how light or dark text on a page will be seen. If a page contains both light and dark text or, as is common, regular text plus text that is printed on a colored background or obscured by a stain, the OCR software will be unable to interpret both in a single scan.

By contrast, Intelligent Scanning Technology provides sophisticated processing of the page that goes beyond simple thresholding or even variable thresholding, providing complex page analysis that separates images, drawings, and text and provides the most optimal processing for each type.

Simple, single-column typewritten pages are no problem for most OCR systems, but more complex pages may contain multiple, snaking columns. Several news articles, plus advertisements, photographs, and graphics can appear on a single page. Intelligent Scanning Technology is able to sort out related material and place it in the proper order. It can recognize tables so that the columns can be retained in the translated document. Some graphics can be ignored while text printed on colored or shaded backgrounds (which other OCR systems might misread or treat as graphics) can be correctly interpreted.

 Cross-Reference

You'll find a more complete discussion of Intelligent Scanning Technology in Chapter 6, "Using One-Button Features and Software."

Moving On

This chapter has offered a general introduction to resolution, interpolation, and sharpness as they apply to various kinds of scanned originals. In later chapters, you'll learn how to improve your scans. But first, we'll look at the latest generation of Hewlett-Packard scanners.

The Latest Generation of Scanners

One of the best things about the latest generation of scanners is that there is a broad selection of models, each built with exactly the features required for certain kinds of scanning jobs. That wasn't always the case. Not too many years ago it was common for each scanner vendor to offer just a single one-size-fits-all model. When scanners cost $1,500 to $2,500 and few PC and Mac owners could afford them, that approach made a lot of sense. When scanners weren't sold in the huge numbers they are today, there was little need to provide a variety of models.

And given the expense, it wasn't practical to leave off a feature here or there to create a custom-tailored scanner because it really didn't provide much in the way of savings. (Trimming a $100 feature from a $1,500 scanner didn't amount to much of a price reduction.) Conceivably, a proliferating product line when sales volumes were lower could end up costing a vendor more because of the cost of supporting multiple models.

So, for many years, the only optional features available for scanners were components such as an automatic document feeder or perhaps a transparency adapter. All other capabilities came standard, and you paid for them, whether you needed them or not. Today, that's not the case. Scanners are selling by the millions, and the cost to produce them has dropped sharply. It makes perfect economic sense for vendors such as Hewlett-Packard to configure models that provide the exact performance and features you need.

Fortunately, choosing the right scanner from among the wide range of options is fairly easy. They've been divided into (in HP's case), four different categories: entry level (such as the HP 3000 Series), intermediate (including the HP 4000 Series), business scanners (such as the HP 5000 Series), and professional models (all the scanners in the HP 6000 Series). One of these should be a good fit for the tasks you want to do. This chapter provides an overview of the latest Hewlett-Packard scanners so you can go shopping armed with the information you need to make an informed choice.

The following sections will describe only the main models in each category. Hewlett-Packard offers three different "packages" within many series, and the difference between them generally is only the software that's provided. The three subcategories are:

- **C.** This designation denotes the basic scanner in a series. This package always includes software for capturing and editing images, making direct copies with your printer, and translating documents into editable text using optical character recognition. The exact software bundle is different for each series, and each scanner is provided with software suited for its intended users.

- **Cse.** These scanners have the same hardware specifications as other models in the series but include additional software for personal and home applications, such as creating greeting cards.

- **Cxi.** The top-of-the-line models within each series come with all the software provided with the C and Cse models, plus additional business-oriented applications.

We're going to concentrate here on the hardware itself, rather than the different software applications bundled with the scanners. That's because the same or similar software may be included with several different scanner series. This chapter will detail your hardware choices and provide a brief discussion of the bundled software's capabilities.

Cross-Reference

If you want more information on the software packages and how to use them, turn to Chapter 6, "Using One-Button Features and Software," Chapter 7, "Capturing Formatted Documents with Optical Character Recognition," and Chapter 8, "Scanning to a Destination."

ScanJet 3000 Series

The Hewlett-Packard 3000 Series scanners are intended as low-cost, entry-level models, although the latest 3400c is a cut above most starter scanners. These units provide basic scanning capabilities without sacrificing speed and quality. They are aimed squarely at new scanner users who want to grab some images but may not have much experience working with graphics (you know who you are!). These scanners make it easy to slap an original down on the glass, push a button, and end up with a captured image or hard copy printout.

Entry-level scanners are an excellent choice for those who are new to scanning and don't know yet exactly how much scanning they'll be doing. (Typically, after you've used a scanner for a short time, you'll come up with dozens of new things to do with it that you didn't even think of before!) These low-cost units provide a risk-free entrée to the scanning world, and are simple enough to use that you don't need any experience with scanning to get to work right away. After you've got some scanning under your belt, you may chomp at the bit for a more sophisticated unit that can handle more demanding jobs. Your entry-level model can then be passed along to the kids or kept as a backup. While the 3000 Series scanners are all 600 spi models, as you learned earlier, resolution alone doesn't control your final image quality. They have the high-quality sensors and optics you really need for the best end results.

Cross-Reference

For information on resolution and how it affects scans, see Chapter 4, "Resolution, Interpolation, and Sharp Images."

Two models, the ScanJet 3200c (still available in many stores) and the ScanJet 3300c that replaced it, are small, compact units that can have you scanning in minutes effortlessly. These scanners are for the entire family. The HP software guides you through creating impressive letters, reports, and cards for work, school, or other activities. They can optimize pictures automatically and, used with a color printer, can make vivid color copies. There are only two buttons on the front of these scanners: one launches the PrecisionScan LT scanning software, while the other activates the HP Copy Utility.

The older 3200c connects to your computer with a parallel port connection, while the 3300c links through a universal serial bus (USB) connection. (An enormously helpful set-up poster provides easy instructions for getting your scanner installed and running.) Although not as fast as more expensive models, they can still capture a 4×6-inch color photo in less than 90 seconds, or convert a full page of text to a word processing file in a little more than 2.5 minutes. These scanners are perfect for many imaging tyros.

 ### Cross-Reference

See Chapter 3, "Installation Tips," for a discussion of scanner interfaces.

The latest model in the 3000 Series is the smart, new ScanJet 3400c, shown in Figure 5.1. With a stylish blue top and translucent lid, it's outfitted for fast operation with three push-and-go buttons. One button activates the new PrecisionScan LTX scanning software, for fast action when you need to grab an image and store it on your computer (for example, to embed in a document or presentation). The PrecisionScan application simplifies capturing images but also has advanced tools for exposure adjustment, color adjustment, and dimensioning images.

Figure 5.1 The Hewlett-Packard ScanJet 3400c is a highly capable entry-level scanner.

A second button launches the HP Copy Utility. Place a document on the scanner's glass, press the Copy button, and your computer and its printer function as a handy copy machine. You may never need to run to the copy shop again, and once you've made a color copy, black-and-white duplicates of color originals will never look the same. The third button is something new. It scans images that you can send directly to your e-mail software, making it very easy to share images with friends, relatives, and colleagues.

About 50 percent faster than its series-mates (scanning a 4×6-inch photo in about 60 seconds), the 3400c is furnished with both USB and parallel cables, giving you a choice of interfacing configurations.

ScanJet 4000 Series

Intermediate scanners are the choice for anyone looking for additional features and more flexibility for just a little more money. A typical user will be someone who's creating Web graphics, perhaps grabbing some images for online auctions, converting photographic prints to digital files, or doing a lot of optical character recognition (OCR).

The ScanJet 4300c, shown in Figure 5.2, is the latest Hewlett-Packard scanner in this category. Like the 3400c, it's a three-button scanner you can use to activate many common tasks with a single press of a button. However, this model adds a nifty new control panel that makes the scanner more like a walk-up copier. You can select color or black-and-white copies, enter the number of copies you want (up to 99), and then press the Copy button to crank out your duplicates without interacting with your PC.

Figure 5.2 The HP ScanJet 4300c is a step up for those looking for an intermediate scanner.

It's also furnished with PrecisionScan LTX, the easy-to-use software, with additional options and more advanced image editing tools. For those who want to manipulate complex documents (say, a page with several columns of text as well as some pictures), this software will capture both types of content so you can work with them separately. The 4300c is furnished with both USB and parallel cables, so you can use it with the latest USB-compatible systems as well as older computers that have a parallel port but no USB connector.

ScanJet 5000 Series

The next step upward is a series of scanners intended for business use. These units are faster and have all the utilities required to scan, copy, attach images to e-mail, and send faxes. If you use a scanner throughout the day for business applications, you'll find that these models will help you work faster and get more done. With all their power, these scanners have enough automation and built-in intelligence to perform many tasks easily, even if you have little or no experience in image capture. Hewlett-Packard offers two models in this category: the HP ScanJet 5300c, and the ScanJet 5370c.

The HP ScanJet 5300c, shown in Figure 5.3, is a four-button scanner, for scanning, copying, e-mailing, and faxing. When you're ready to share an image or document electronically, just push a button to start scanning directly to your e-mail or Web application. HP's Intelligent Scanning Technology automatically optimizes your images for the Internet, so your images look their best online.

The software identifies text, line art, and color images and chooses the correct resolution, bit-depth, and file format for each element on the page. In addition to publishing Web pages or posting information online, you can produce an electronic brochure, e-mail detailed information to clients, forward proposals, or send multiple pages as an e-mail attachment or fax.

The 5300c scans 35mm slides using an optional adapter (called XPA). Also available is an automatic document feeder (ADF). Unlike most scanners that use these two add-ons, HP scanners that support the XPA and ADF accessories let you have both components plugged in and available for use at the same time.

Transparency scanning is one application for which higher resolution can be important, and the 5300c scans at 1200 spi to pull out extra detail from 35mm color slides. Even while capturing more samples per inch, this scanner is able to operate more quickly than the 3000- or 4000-series models, capturing a 4×6-inch color photo or capture using OCR a full page of text in less than 50 seconds. It can grab a full-page black-and-white drawing in less than 40 seconds. It can use both parallel and USB interfaces.

Figure 5.3 The HP ScanJet 5300 Series scanners are sophisticated image grabbers for business applications.

The ScanJet 5370c, shown in Figure 5.4, is a more powerful version of the 5300c, with 1200 spi resolution and 42-bit color depth (especially useful for color transparencies, which tend to have a lot of detail in both shadows and high-lights). This model is furnished with a 5×5-inch transparency adapter (so it can capture 4×5-inch transparencies as well as 35mm slides) and can be outfitted with an optional ADF. The document feeder lets you copy stacks of documents at a 2 pages-per-minute rate, making this unit the next best thing to an office photo-copier. (Actually, because it can scan, fax, and do other things, this scanner might not be "next best" to anything!)

Figure 5.4 The ScanJet 5370c is the first HP scanner that supports scanning color negatives.

It is the first HP scanner that supports scanning of both color slides and color negatives. Negatives are especially tricky to capture because of the orange mask built into the film. You can't just scan a negative as you would a transparency and then reverse the tones and colors. Some tricky algorithms must be used to optimize the scanned negative image.

The 5370c comes with HP's high-end scanning software, PrecisionScan Pro, which provides unparalleled ease of use with features such as drag-and-drop and advanced scan control, while including OCR and complex page scanning all bundled into one package. That's a definite plus, as you don't have to learn several different scanning software interfaces to do all your work. Learn PrecisionScan Pro's features, and you can do anything the scanner is capable of.

ScanJet 6000 Series

Yes, Virginia, there is a Santa Claus, and he's brought us all some professional-quality scanners for pro graphics workers and businesses that want high-speed, high-quality scans with optional manual control over key functions. Scanners of this sophistication used to cost well over $1,000 and couldn't do half as much as the latest generation of top-of-the-line units.

The three top-drawer units are the ScanJet 6300c, 6350c, and 6390c, all based on the same scanner "platform." All three offer 1200 spi, 36-bit scanning, but boast two (count them) scanning lamps, which allow the units to capture images faster. You can link these scanners to your computer through a USB connection, but they can also be used with an optional SCSI card (which makes these scanners practical for those still using Windows NT 4.0, which does not support USB).

 Cross-Reference

You'll find more information about SCSI and USB interfaces in Chapter 3, "Installation Tips."

Five front-panel buttons automate tasks when you're in a hurry. At the press of a button, you can scan, copy, e-mail, fax, or capture as a file any original you put on the scanning bed without fussing with intermediate steps. Advanced on-board image processing hardware optimizes your scans before they are sent onward to your computer, so the scans these models produce are exceptional.

If you've ever waited in frustration for the scanner lamp to warm up when you needed a quick scan, this series is furnished with a utility that allows turning the lamps on automatically at a particular time of day to avoid warm-up delays. That's important because these scanners can be fast: you can grab a 4×6-inch color photo in less than nine seconds. In other words, by the time you've selected the next picture to scan, your 6300 Series scanner will already have captured the last one.

In addition, the 6300 Series includes advanced scanning capabilities such as Dual-Image Scanning and the capability to share a scanner across a local area network (LAN) so others in your office can use your scanner from their own desktops.

The 6350c adds the automatic document feeder and the 6390c, shown in Figure 5.5, is bundled with both the 25-page ADF and transparency adapter. With the ADF, hands-free copies can be made at a zippy 5 pages per minute, assuming, as is likely, that your printer can crank sheets out that quickly. Those designing Web sites will find the additional software furnished with the 6300 Series models especially useful. Included is Adobe's easy-to-use PageMill Web site creation software, and HP Intelligent Assistants to help guide you through scanning for Web authoring and e-mail.

Figure 5.5 The ScanJet 6390c is the top-of-the-line unit with a 25-page automatic document feeder and transparency adapter included.

Other HP ScanJets

The scanners listed above include those offered by HP at the time this book was written. Several older HP ScanJets are still in wide use. Here is a brief discussion of some of those scanners.

Note

Many of the older HP models use versions of the software discussed in later chapters.

Older HP scanners:

- The ScanJet, ScanJet Plus, and ScanJet 3p were the earliest HP scanners. They were 300 ppi black-and-white scanners and shipped with Scanning Gallery and DeskScan.

- The ScanJet IIc and IIcx were 400 spi, 24-bit color scanners with legal-size scan beds. The first and second color scanners offered by HP, they supported a 50-page ADF, and the IIcx supported a full $8\frac{1}{2} \times 11$ XPA. They shipped with DeskScan II scanning software on the PC and used SCSI interfaces.

- The ScanJet 3c and 4c were 600 ppi, 30-bit color scanners that shipped with DeskScan II and supported a 50-page ADF and full-sized XPA.

- The ScanJet 4p and 5p were lower-cost color scanners from HP. The 4p was a legal-sized, 300 ppi, 24-bit color scanner. The 5p, smaller and faster, was a 300 ppi 30-bit color scanner that was the first to sport a button to launch the scanning software. The 4p shipped with PictureScan, and the 5p with PrecisionScan.

Older 4000 Series scanners:

- ScanJet 4100c was a 300 ppi 36-bit color scanner that shipped with PrecisionScan.

- ScanJet 4200c was a step up to 600 ppi.

Older 5000 Series scanners:

- ScanJet 5100c was a version of the 5p that used a parallel rather than SCSI interface. It was a 300 ppi, 30-bit scanner and featured a fast-on Xenon lamp. It shipped with PrecisionScan.

- ScanJet 5200c was a step up to 600 ppi and 36-bit. It came with a newer version of PrecisionScan.

Older 6000 Series scanners:

- ScanJet 6100c was the last in the series of HP Trichromatic Beam Splitter Scanners — the 6100c replaced the 4c. It was 600 ppi and 30 bits per pixel.

- ScanJet 6200c featured new image processing hardware and increased bit depth. This scanner shipped with the PrecisionScan Pro software and was 600 ppi and 36 bits per pixel.

While the above scanners are no longer sold new, they are still widely used and popular.

Moving On

Hewlett-Packard's latest generation of scanners provides something for everyone: basic, entry-level scanning for those looking to get their feet wet; intermediate scanning for anyone looking for more advanced image capture capabilities; business scanners that help you work faster and more productively; and professional scanners for the most demanding imaging applications. In the next three chapters, we'll look at how to use the software that is furnished with these scanners.

Using One-Button Features and Software

Scanning has never been easier! In the past, using a scanner could be a complicated and tedious process, involving a cryptic software interface with dozens of controls. That wasn't much of a problem when scanners cost thousands of dollars and were used by relatively small numbers of people. Early scanner users knew they'd have to develop their skills to put their hefty hardware investments to work most efficiently.

Today, anyone can afford a scanner, not just graphics professionals. Any home or office user who wants to capture some text, grab an image, or send a fax can justify the purchase of one of these handy tools. However, most of us don't want to do a lot of fiddling with controls and making complex adjustments. After all, a scanner looks and operates quite a bit like a walk-up copier. Is there any reason it can't be as easy to use?

No, there's not! Whether you're a casual user who just wants to make an occasional scan, or a busy scanner aficionado who'd like to capture images quickly and productively, you'll find the newest scanners are tailored specifically to your needs. In most cases, you can scan an image, make a copy, or send a fax just by placing a document on the scanner glass and pressing a button.

This chapter, and the two that follow, will serve as your introduction to using the features of the latest generation of Hewlett-Packard scanners. In this chapter, we'll look at using one-button features for performing simple scanning tasks in seconds. Chapter 7 provides more information about capturing documents with optical character recognition. Then, in Chapter 8, you'll learn how to use more advanced software features to scan to specific "destinations" (such as fax, Web pages, or desktop publishing).

Why Buttons?

Until recently, scanners were used in a non-intuitive way. The first step was to open the cover and place the original to be scanned down on the scanner glass. But which way? Face up? Face down? With the top edge of the original at the end of the scanner closest to the cover hinge, or "upside down" with the top edge closest to you? And that was the easy part.

Then, it was necessary to turn your attention back to the computer and locate the software that was used to make the scanner actually do something. The average new user would be asking themselves such questions as: Where is the software? Do I need to load my image editor first? I want to scan text into my word processor; can I do it from there? What if I want to send a fax? Should I use my fax software to scan? Suppose I want to do several unrelated tasks in succession; do I need to switch back and forth between my image editor, fax program, and word processor?

As you might guess, that's not a very logical way to use a scanner. When new scanner owners approach a scanner, they are looking to the scanner itself as the place to initiate the scanning process. They walk up with an original and place it on the scanner — and then expect something to happen. What doesn't make sense to them is going back to the computer and "launching" some software.

So, Hewlett-Packard introduced buttons on its scanners, starting with the HP ScanJet 5p. The button interface — walk up to the scanner, place an original on it, and press a button — makes a lot of sense. However, a single button is not enough because the scanner owner may want to do different things.

Some scanners do, in fact, have only a single button, forcing the user to select an application back at their computer. Often, the application to be chosen depends on the task (image editing, faxing, text recognition), and is not clear. The idea of going back to the computer to identify what to do with the button you just pressed is pretty silly — the point of the button is to avoid that!

Current HP scanners come with three to five buttons, like the arrangement shown in Figure 6.1, but all configurations achieve the same purpose — causing the scanner to do something with the original. The section that follows is an overview of the things that happen when you press a button on an HP scanner.

Figure 6.1 Buttons can trigger a series of functions with a single press.

Pressing the Right Buttons

Let's look at each of the typical scanner buttons one at a time, starting with the most common. If your scanner doesn't have the button discussed, that doesn't mean you can't do a particular function with your scanner — it just means you will have to interact with the scanning software and maybe other software on your system a little more.

Scan Button

The Scan button kicks off the scanning process by grabbing a preview scan of anything you place on the scanner glass. The button, which usually has an icon representing a scanner with an open cover (as shown at left in Figure 6.1), automatically launches the main scanning software, which may be PrecisionScan LT, Precision Scan LTX, PrecisionScan, or PrecisionScan Pro, depending on which scanner you own. (We'll look at each of these different products later in this chapter.)

Pressing this single button does four things automatically:

- **AutoSelection.** The scanner examines the document preview image and locates the boundaries of the image-containing area for a final scan. You can reselect the scan area manually, but in most cases, the AutoSelection feature will do a good job for you.

- **AutoType.** The scanner looks at the kind of image and tries to determine what type it is: text, text and image, black-and-white drawing, color drawing, black-and-white photo, or color photo. Choosing the right type of image is important because the scanner will process each type of image differently during the final scan. If the scanner guesses wrong, you can correct its selection manually.

- **AutoExposure.** Using the area chosen by the AutoSelection feature and the type of image determined by AutoType, the scanner then sets a recommended exposure, which determines brightness and contrast of the final image. If you don't like what you see in the preview image, you can change it before making the final scan.

- **Auto Color Balance.** The scanner examines the area selected and adjusts the color to ensure whites are white and colors are colorful.

Other settings are made for you, behind the scenes, so to speak. For example, based on the type of original you appear to be working with, the scanner will automatically select the best resolution for the job. It will use default values that you've specified, such as scanning to the same size as the original (rather than making the final image larger or smaller) or automatically sharpening images during the scan.

Because the scanner will choose the correct settings in the vast majority of cases, grabbing a scan will be one-button easy. Press the Scan button on your scanner, preview the image, and then click the "final scan" button (the name of the button varies depending on the software you're using) to finish the task. What could be easier than that?

Copy Button

Another frequent job for your scanner is to make a quick copy of a document. An office copier is little more than a scanner and a printer housed in a single case, anyway, so your own PC, printer, and scanner can do the same jobs easily. With the Copy button, you can make those duplicates just by placing the original down on the scanner glass and pressing the button.

The Copy button is generally marked with an icon, like the one in the center in Figure 6.1, shaped like a printer with a piece of paper feeding into/out of it. (It's hard to tell which, since most printers and copiers don't work this way any more.) When you press the button, the HP ScanJet Copy Utility will be launched, and a copy of your original made using the default settings you've specified. You can also change the default settings to, say, increase the number of copies produced or to enlarge or reduce the duplicate. The whole process works quite a bit like a real photocopier. One neat thing is that with your low cost color printer and scanner, you can get color copies that rival expensive color copy machines!

With the ScanJet 4300, the process works a lot more like a real photocopier. The single Copy button found on other scanners has been expanded to an array of three buttons in the middle front edge of the scanner, augmented by a small, but highly readable LCD display. This button array is shown in Figure 6.2. These controls enable you to specify the number of copies and color or black-and-white copying. (Of course, your computer must be switched on to use your scanner/printer as a copier!)

Figure 6.2 The buttons on the ScanJet 4300 enable you to use the scanner as if it were a walk-up photocopier.

Here's a short discussion of those copying controls, and how to use them:

■ **LCD Display.** In the center of the front panel, you'll find an LCD display measuring about $\frac{3}{4} \times \frac{1}{2}$ inch with large, easily read numbers representing the current number of copies to be printed. The default value is 01, of course.

■ **Number of Copies.** To the left and a little below the LCD display is a peanut-shaped button used to specify the number of copies you want. There are two round bumps on the button, labeled minus (–) and plus (+). Press the minus button to decrease the number of copies, and the plus button to increase the number of copies. Up to 99 copies can be selected.

Tip

If you have more than 50 copies to make, it's quicker to count down to the number you want, rather than count up. With the LCD display at 01, press the minus button. The display will decrement down to 99, 98, 97, and so forth until you reach the number of copies desired.

- **Color/Black-and-White.** To the right and a little below the LCD display are a pair of yellow-green LEDs labeled with a red/green/blue triad of dots, and a pair of dark and light gray dots. Beneath them is a button. As you press the button, the LEDs are illuminated alternately; when the upper light is on your copies will be printed in full color (assuming you have a color printer, of course!). When the bottom light is illuminated, the copies will be in black and white.

- **Copy.** The Copy button is located below the LCD display. Press it to activate the copying process. If all you want is one copy, just put your original on the scanner and press this button. Or, specify the number of copies and color/black-and-white mode first.

E-mail Button

One task that has grown tremendously in popularity is sending documents and images via e-mail. The E-mail button — represented with an icon resembling an envelope zipping through space, shown in Figure 6.1 on the right — captures a document or image and sends it on to your e-mail software. Later in this chapter, we'll explain in greater detail how this button can be used, and you can find additional information in Chapter 8, "Scanning to a Destination."

Often what people want to do with scanned images, be they photos or complete documents, is e-mail them. The preview is done, the image analyzed and optimized, the type selected, and the output destination of e-mail selected.

Fax Button

A scanner turns your one-way, receive-only fax modem into a two-way fax machine! If you have something to fax, just drop it on the scanner glass, press the fax button (which is found on some, but not all HP scanners) and the image will be captured at fax resolution and sent on to your fax software for delivery. If you don't have fax software, the file will be formatted and saved in a format that is appropriate for faxing at a later date. You could, for example, copy the saved file to another computer that is equipped with fax software and send it from there. The Fax button, shown in Figure 6.3, is usually represented by an icon of a dedicated fax machine, complete with telephone handset.

Figure 6.3 The fax button can start your fax on its way.

Document Management Button

The HP 6300 series scanners have a fifth button, used to summon document management functions. If you press the document management button (6300 series), the page you placed on the scanner will be send to the document management software installed on your computer. The 6300 series comes with Caere Page-Keeper Standard, shown in Figure 6.4. Document management software like PageKeeper gives you a central place to store, search, and view documents and images you've captured with your scanner. Handy buttons within the software make it simple to access other applications available on your computer, such as Microsoft Word, WinFax, or Photoshop, and to drag-and-drop images to them.

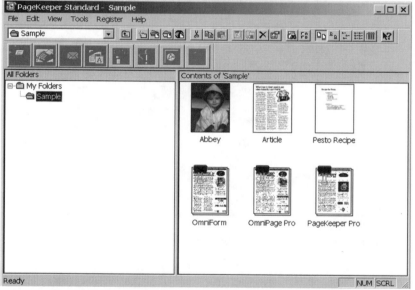

Figure 6.4 PageKeeper can be used to manage all your documents and images.

Customizing Buttons

The installer program that sets up your software does a good job of configuring your scanner and its buttons for you. You can also fine-tune what your buttons do, choosing, for example, which applications are connected to which button. The amount of customization you can do is determined by which scanner you have. This section will show you how to customize your buttons.

Defining Buttons with the Control Panel

Some of the settings you'll want to make can be set using the Windows Control Panel. Just follow these steps to provide initial configuration of your buttons:

1. Choose Start ➪ Settings ➪ Control Panel to produce the Windows Control Panel. The Windows 2000 version is shown in Figure 6.5.

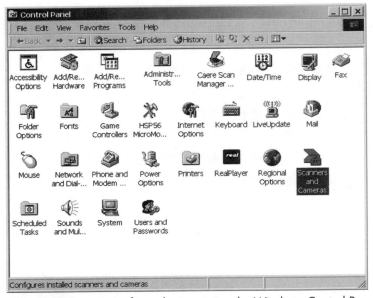

Figure 6.5 You can configure buttons using the Windows Control Panel.

2. Click the Scanners and Cameras icon to access the Scanners and Cameras Properties dialog box shown in Figure 6.6.

3. Select the scanner you want to configure in the Devices window, and click the Properties button. The Properties dialog box for your scanner, like the one shown in Figure 6.7, appears.

4. Click the Events tab to view the scanner events (buttons, actually) you can define in this dialog box.

5. Choose the button you want to customize from the drop-down list, and put a check mark next to the application you want to associate (configure the software to use) with that button in the Send To This Application list. Notice that only generic fax and e-mail applications are available. You must define the exact application for those tasks separately, as you'll see shortly.

6. Click OK to apply your change.

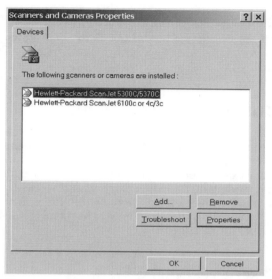

Figure 6.6 Choose the scanner you want to customize in this control panel.

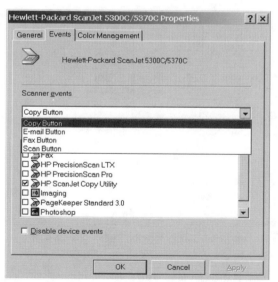

Figure 6.7 Select which application will be associated with a button.

Note

If you want to "turn off" or disable your buttons entirely for some reason (say, your toddler is sending too many faxes when your back is turned), mark the Disable Device Events checkbox.

Defining Buttons with Button Settings

Customizing buttons for your fax and e-mail tasks requires an extra step because there are additional parameters you can set. Just follow these steps:

1. Access the Scanner Button Settings dialog box, shown in Figure 6.8. Its location varies depending on the particular scanner software you're using. You'll find it either in a Settings menu within the scanning application itself, or under ScanJet Utilities when you navigate to the Start ⇨ Programs ⇨ ScanJet Software menu.

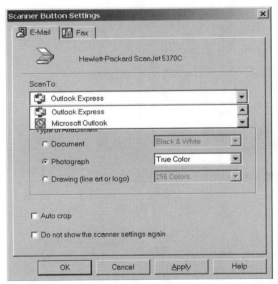

Figure 6.8 Set E-mail and Fax button settings in this dialog box.

2. Click the E-Mail tab, if the tab is not already displayed, and choose your e-mail application from the drop-down list in the Scan To area. Some computers will have only one e-mail application configured; others may have several, such as Outlook Express, Outlook, and Netscape Mail.

3. In the Type of Attachment area, click each of the radio buttons for the Document, Photograph, and Drawing types in turn, and then select options appropriate to each, as follows:

- For documents (text-only items such as letters, or text/graphics items such as newsletters), choose whether you want the document to be scanned in black and white or true color. Black-and-white attachments are smaller and faster to e-mail, but color attachments better represent the image of your original document.

- For photographs, you can choose either true color or grayscale representations. Again, grayscale attachments are faster to e-mail than color attachments. In addition, you can check the Auto crop box at the lower-left corner of the dialog box to tell your scanner to automatically crop images being attached to e-mail to eliminate extraneous material.

- For drawings or line art, such as logos, you can choose 256 colors or black and white (for the same reason described above), and select AutoCrop if you want your scanner to trim your image for you.

4. Next, click the Fax tab (if your scanner has fax capabilities) to access the dialog box shown in Figure 6.9.

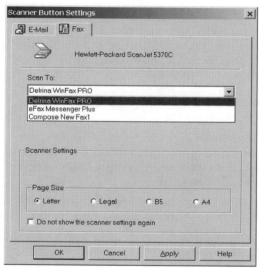

Figure 6.9 Configure your fax settings with this dialog box.

5. As you did with the e-mail configuration in Step 2, choose the application you want to direct your fax scans to. You may have the eFax Messenger Plus software, furnished with many HP scanners, or a third-party program such as WinFax Pro.

6. Choose the size you want your faxes sent as, either legal or letter size (for the U.S.) or their European equivalents, B4 and A4.

7. Click the Apply button to make your modifications.

Your Scanner Software

You'll learn how to use your scanner software in more detail in Chapter 8, "Scanning to a Destination." The following section provides an overview of the packages currently shipping with Hewlett-Packard scanners, and what they can do. In addition to the scanner software itself, HP scanners are furnished with a wide variety of other useful applications for image editing, faxing, document management, OCR, and other functions. Four different software packages are available: PrecisionScan LT and LTX for entry-level and intermediate scanners, and PrecisionScan and PrecisionScan Pro for business and professional applications. In practice you'll probably be using PrecisionScan LTX or PrecisionScan Pro. The other two packages are available only with a limited number of older scanners. Here's a quick rundown of the four packages:

PrecisionScan Pro

PrecisionScan Pro is focused at the more advanced user who wants quick, automated scanning available at the press of a button, but wants to retain control over many scanner functions. Some of the key characteristics of PrecisionScan Pro, shown in Figure 6.10, are as follows:

■ It's designed to take advantage of the scanning capabilities of more advanced scanners to provide the best possible image quality.

■ The PrecisionScan Pro interface includes many of the image processing functions that professional graphic artists look for, such as tools for fine-tuning color before a final scan, or removing a halftone screen from original images that have already been screened.

■ PrecisionScan Pro provides a fast, low-resolution preview for quick evaluation of an image and follows that with a final, high-quality scan.

■ It provides support for transparency scanning with a transparency adapter and, with the HP 5370, support for scanning color negatives.

■ PrecisionScan Pro offers more choices for scanning an entire page and saving in a format that preserves the document formatting, such as Adobe Portable Document Format (PDF). These choices appear in the following situations:

 • When the user selects a page, selects nothing, or selects a portion of the page and the image type selected is "text and image"

- When the user saves as "whole page" (both text and all graphics) — or scans to mixed formats such as PDF in text and image mode

- When the Automatic Document Feeder is used in whole page mode

Figure 6.10 PrecisionScan Pro is HP's most advanced scanning software.

Using PrecisionScan Pro is easy. It operates in a traditional preview/final image mode. First the page is scanned and a preview shown on the screen. The preview is analyzed by the scanner and, if AutoSelect and AutoType features are turned on (the default), then the primary component found on the page (the main text area, or main picture area, depending on what is dominant, or the single component if you are scanning something like a photograph) is selected, auto-typed, auto-exposed, color balanced, and the result presented to the user.

In most cases, this auto selection is just what the user wanted, so you can send the image to a final destination (software application, or a device such as a printer) in a number of ways, which will be discussed in more detail in Chapter 8. You can select Send To from the menu or button bar, and direct the image to the application of your choice. You can also drag the image directly into any open application that supports drag-and-drop. You can scan the image to a file. You can "copy" the image to the Windows clipboard. In any of these cases, the scanner will do a final scan with all the settings applied to the image.

After the preview, if you want to change the image or the automatic settings, you can do this using the preview image. For instance, you can change a color photo to a black-and-white photo. You can adjust the color saturation, or adjust the exposure. You can change the dimensions of the output scan (how big the image will be when printed or displayed), change the sharpening, zoom in for a closer look, and so on. Once you have a preview of the image as you want it, then you again send, drag-and-drop, copy, or save the scan and the scanner will perform the final scan, with all the settings you have made.

You should always do as much of the image manipulation as you can in the scanning software. That's because the final scan performed by the scanner with PrecisionScan Pro will apply the manipulations you specify using the full bit depth and full available resolution of the hardware to give you the best results possible. You'll get better results, faster, if you do this fine-tuning with the scanner rather than later in an image editor. Of course, there are times when the image editor is essential — there are some things you cannot do in the scanning software (like remove a scratch). But don't assume you need to adjust exposure, scaling, and so on in an image editor. You will get better results if you use the scanner to do this whenever possible.

One of the most common things people forget to do when scanning is to set the size they want the output image to be. For instance, if you are scanning a 35mm slide, you probably want to enlarge it so that it prints out bigger than a 35mm slide actually is. PrecisionScanPro on the 5370 will even warn you with a Smart Friend if you are scanning a 35mm slide or negative and you have not enlarged the image. Setting the output size through enlargement or reduction is one of the most important kinds of image manipulation that you can perform in the scanner. The results will generally be much better if you let the scanner enlarge the image than if you try to enlarge it afterward.

Cross-Reference

For more information on image editor modifications, see Chapter 10, "Optimizing Color," and Chapter 11, "Image Editing."

Note

With HP ScanJets, the software (whether it is PrecisionScan Pro or one of the other versions) is optimized, individually, to work in concert with your ScanJet hardware, and to provide the very best scans the hardware can offer. For instance, Precision Scan Pro will operate a ScanJet 6300 differently than a ScanJet 5370 — because the hardware is different. This does not mean one scanner is necessarily better than the other for a particular task (although a more expensive scanner will generally provide higher performance), but it does mean you are getting optimized results with each unit.

One of the key features of PrecisionScan Pro is that many of the automatic functions can be turned off. For instance, you can disable AutoType and AutoExposure if you wish. You can also create a set of "settings" (dimensions, exposure settings, selection areas, and so forth) and save those setting for repeated use later. This is useful for applications in which you do the same type of scan many times — such as photo IDs or newsletters.

PrecisionScan

The older PrecisionScan software provides a way to scan either simple items or complex pages quickly, accurately, and easily. Unlike PrecisionScan Pro, it operates in a slightly different manner, attempting to gather as much information from the scan during the "preview" as possible. In fact, the "preview" in PrecisionScan is not really a preview scan at all, but a limited "final" scan. In many cases — actually in every case possible — the final is never performed because the "preview" has already captured the information needed to complete the scan. That means the preview scan takes a bit more time, but you may save some time if a final scan isn't needed.

With PrecisionScan, when you press the scan button, a higher resolution scan of what is on the scan bed is performed. This high quality preview is analyzed to identify all the elements on the scanner bed. For instance, if there is a page with text, some photos, and a logo, each element is identified as its particular type, selected, auto-exposed and highlighted, and then the result is presented to the user as a set of blue selected regions. As you move the mouse over each region, you will see the cursor change, indicating what the region has been identified as — text, color photo, drawing, and so forth.

At this point, you can just accept the scan and all the regions will be processed and sent to your destination. Note that the term is *processed*, not *scanned*. That's because in many cases, all the information has been captured already and it is just sent on with no final scan necessary.

In many cases, no rescan is done and the final scan takes literally just a second or two. If any of the selections, areas, or changes you've made require a re-scan, the scanner will do that — automatically. The type or quantity of scans and re-scans will depend on the ScanJet hardware you are using — again, the software and hardware are optimized to work in concert.

PrecisionScan LT

PrecisionScan LT, available with older scanners, is designed for the user who is a beginner or just wants to get the scan done quickly and easily with little interaction. PrecisionScan LT leads the user along with an easy three-step interface that helps make sure you get what you want, easily and simply.

PrecisionScan LT, like PrecisionScan, performs a higher quality "preview" and selects the major element on the original artwork (instead of selecting all the different elements). For instance, if the page is mostly text, that is what is selected. If it is a photo, that is selected. Of course, you can change what is selected if you want. The user is led through the next steps — say enlarging or reducing the image — and when the user accepts, the result is sent to the destination, often with no re-scan. Again, if the scanner has the information already, then there is no need to re-scan.

PrecisionScan LTX

PrecisionScan LTX is a simpler version of PrecisionScan Pro. Like PrecisionScan LT it leads the user through the steps, but like PrecisionScan Pro the preview is a true preview and a final scan is always performed. Also, some of the imaging-specific tools for optimizing a scan, such as contrast and brightness adjustment, which we'll look at in later chapters, are provided in LTX — making it more focused on photography, which frequently requires image manipulation of this sort. PrecisionScan LTX is shown in Figure 6.11.

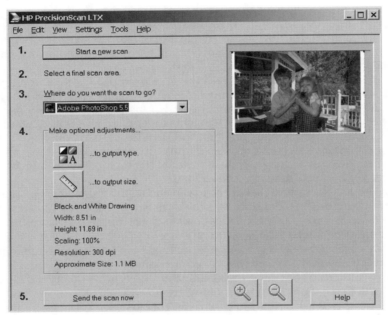

Figure 6.11 PrecisionScan LTX is easy to use, but has some fine-tuning features for more advanced scanner users.

More on Intelligent Scanning Technology

We described Hewlett-Packard's Intelligent Scanning Technology (IST) briefly in Chapter 3, "Installation Tips." IST is so powerful that a discussion of its features could fill a book. We'll conclude this chapter with an overview of just a few of the things this technology can do.

How your scanner uses HP Intelligent Scanning Technology depends on which ScanJet you are using and what kind of task you are working on. For instance, with HP Precision Scan Pro, you'll find tools for clicking and selecting things. For example, if you click on a photograph, HP Intelligent Scanning Technology will:

- Find the edges of the photo
- Determine if the photo is black and white or color
- Optimize the exposure
- Apply color optimization
- Set the appropriate scanning resolution, sharpening and filtering
- Present the result to you in the preview window

If you click on a paragraph of text, HP Intelligent Scanning Technology will:

- Find the edges of the paragraph
- Recognize this as text
- Set the image optimization for OCR
- Present the result in the preview window — indicating the image is "Text"

In both cases, if you then perform the final scan (by one of the methods discussed in Chapter 8, "Scanning to a Destination,") the final image will be scanned according to the settings, further processing such as OCR performed, and the result placed in your destination.

Cross-Reference

For more information on optical character recognition, see Chapter 7, "Capturing Formatted Documents with Optical Character Recognition."

The same type of processing is done in HP PrecisionScan. However, instead of the processing taking place when you click or select something, the entire scan bed is scanned and analyzed — and each different type of component on a page (say a photo, some text, and a drawing) is independently analyzed and optimized. In this case, you see a number of automatically defined regions in the preview display. You can select all or none of them, and then "accept" them and the appropriate processing will be performed.

When is a preview not a preview? As discussed in the earlier section on scanning software, you may notice that with some ScanJets, the "preview" scan is slower and includes automatic processing and optimization. This is true in PrecisionScan and PrecisionScan LT. In fact, as noted before, the scan being done here is not a preview scan but a much more complex analysis. You will notice that, in many cases, when you "accept" the scan, the scanner does not perform any more scans — but just sends the result to the application. Simply stated, if the information is already captured (say for a color or black-and white-photograph), the scanner has no need to re-scan.

Does this mean the slower preview makes the scanner slower? No! In fact, because no "final" scan is needed, often the entire task is much faster. Speed, to a real user, is more than just preview or final scan time; it includes final processing and transfer of the image to the application — even launching the scanning application and final application.

In the case of PrecisionScan, you may even "accept" many different regions and image types at once. For instance, if your page has a color photo, a black-and-white photo, and two columns of text, PrecisionScan allows you to send all of this to your destination application at one time. In this case, optimal processing will be performed on the color photo and the black-and-white photo and both sent to your application. The text will be processed by OCR and sent as editable text. In most scanners, this would require several scans and multiple scanning applications.

Note

Depending on your hardware, the multiple type of scan made possible by PrecisionScan will sometimes require a re-scan of part of the page, and sometimes not. In any case, it is automatically handled and processed.

Intelligent Scanning Technology can do things as simple as automatically choosing the best file type for your applications, or as complex as full decomposition and recomposition of a complex page containing text, graphics, photos, and formatting. The key is that you do not have to understand the intricacies of scanning different originals. You can use the scanner knowing that HP Intelligent Scanning Technology will provide the level of advanced functions you've chosen.

For example, all HP ScanJets support the new color standard called *sRGB*, which provides a more standardized way of representing colors than the plain old RGB system. (You'll find support for sRGB in image editors such as Photoshop.) In fact, HP was one of the driving forces behind development of sRGB to provide accurate, easy, and reproducible color scans.

Optimization of scanners for sRGB means that something called *colorimetry* (the spectral sensitivity, lamp spectral content, and HP patented color optimization hardware and software) are all optimized to used the sRGB color space. Images scanned on an HP ScanJet are automatically optimized to sRGB, which is the default color system now used by the Windows operating system, Photoshop, and printers such as those from Hewlett-Packard.

Another example of hardware HP Intelligent Scanning Technology is the optimization of the exposure control systems in the ScanJet 5370c Scanner to allow quality scanning of color negatives. If you've ever looked at a color negative, you know they don't really make sense to the human eye. A color negative is designed to work with color positive films and processes to produce nice photos and was never intended to be viewed directly. Negatives have an odd-looking orange tint, for example, that makes them difficult to examine by eye and extremely tricky to scan. The particular vagaries of color negatives mean that the exposure control systems in a scanner must be changed dramatically if you want to get a quality scan of a negative.

Changing a color negative to a color positive is not a simple reversal of tones (black to white, white to black, dark gray to light gray, and so forth) as with a black-and-white negative. It is a complex image-processing step that includes non-linear tonal modifications, optimized exposure, and specialized sharpening and smoothing. So, scanning software like that for the HP 5370c includes a special menu item for converting color negatives. Using the software's Invert button, which is intended for black-and-white negatives, won't give you good results.

Indeed, the hardware in the 5370c is designed to permit color negative scans. While some scanners claim the capability to scan "color negatives," few actually have the complex optimization and processing taken into account in the design of the hardware and software.

The underlying "intelligence" in PrecisionScan Pro, PrecisionScan, PrecisionScan LT, and PrecisionScan LTX is the same. However, the extent of the automation and the manner in which you interact with it is different. Also, in general, the more advanced and more expensive the scanner model, the more sophisticated and powerful the tools you have.

Moving On

This chapter provided an introduction to one-button scanning and Hewlett-Packard scanning software. In the next two chapters, you'll learn how to apply these capabilities to optical character recognition, and how to scan directly to "destination" applications, such as fax software.

Capturing Formatted Documents with Optical Character Recognition

IN THIS CHAPTER • Why OCR?

• Requirements for OCR

• How OCR works

• Getting the best quality

• Putting OCR to work with your HP scanner

In the last chapter, you learned the basics of how to use the one-button features and PrecisionScan software furnished with Hewlett-Packard scanners. We briefly discussed optical character recognition (OCR) — the conversion of documents into editable text (and graphics). In this chapter, we're going to look a little more deeply into how OCR works, and how you can use it to capture complex and formatted documents. Then, in Chapter 8, we'll bring everything together with a discussion of scanning to destinations, such as desktop published documents using OCR, Web pages, or fax.

Of all the things you can do with your scanner, optical character recognition may have the broadest applications, the greatest diversity in quality, and be the least understood among users. You can use OCR to capture text from a fax or from a hardcopy produced by a laser or inkjet printer. OCR can translate printed matter in books, magazines, or newspapers into text files you can edit (but make sure you have permission, first!).

The latest OCR systems can even preserve the layout of a document with text, pictures, and graphics, providing you with files you can refine in your desktop publishing software. As you might guess, nearly everyone has a use for OCR at one time or another, but in the past nobody really knew how to use it effectively. Effective OCR required a high-powered computer and optional software packages that cost $500 or more.

Today, the best scanners come bundled with everything you need to do optical character recognition, even with the least expensive scanner. For example, OCR is built right into HP's PrecisionScan software. If you're like most of us, the time you save using OCR will pay for your scanner all by itself!

Why OCR?

The reason OCR is important is simple: The arrival of the paperless office or paperless home computer room, predicted long ago, will probably coincide with the arrival of the paperless bathroom. Some 95 percent of the information we work with is still stored on paper. Even as we approach a computer density of one (or more!) units per desktop, business and personal activities continue to rely heavily on paper output.

At work, you can read paper reports anywhere, shuffle through stacks of them on your desk, make copies of them, and do lots of things that even the best desktop metaphor won't handle (although the PageKeeper software bundled with HP scanners comes very close to making a computer desktop practical).

At home, you may download Web pages of information, print out information from your online auctions, or discover an old treasure-trove of family information in typewritten form. That's a lot of paper!

And, if anything, personal computers have created more paper in the form of desktop publications and reports. High-speed laser printers make it as easy to generate 100 copies as five. How often have you printed out Web pages, or filed away a paper copy of a spreadsheet? You may give a presentation using a computer display or LCD projector, but you'll still want handouts to give to your audience.

Paper remains our most important source of information and our most popular way to exchange it with others. Yet, in its raw form, hard copy data is of absolutely no use to a computer. If you scan in a letter with no additional processing, all you have is a picture of a page. To the computer, the document is a collection of pixels and nothing more. The information must be captured and converted to the numeric codes that the computer can handle. That's where OCR comes in. Optical character recognition isn't a way of eliminating paper; it just helps you live with it and use it more effectively.

Requirements for OCR

Optical character recognition presents your scanner and computer with some of the stiffest challenges they may face. An OCR package must be able to recognize complicated pages, with a tremendous amount of graphics and a daunting array of type styles and sizes. Is this area a picture or a graph? Sometimes characters touch. Are the characters fi (often fused together in professional typesetting into something called a ligature) two characters, f and i, or is it an h? Is the word, then, handcuffing or handcufhng? Big difference, eh? The section that follows, "How OCR Works," will tell you a little about how your scanner and its software can tell the difference.

Of course, the page an OCR program is scanning may contain a lot more than simple text. There may be graphics that the program has to ignore (if only the text is important to you) or, more likely, capture and dump in a separate file. Text may be arranged in columns that snake around on a page. Good OCR programs recognize those columns and retain the format if you wish. They are smart enough to insert the correct formatting codes in the word processor of your choice. They can tell boldfaced text from ordinary text and even recognize many different type styles.

Today's intelligent scanners can do something very sophisticated that formerly required an expensive device called a compound document processor. They can easily differentiate between graphics and text in a single document. Within regions or zones containing graphics, your scanner functions as a bit-mapped graphics scanner, capturing the image-intensive information. It also recognizes text information and attempts to interpret the alphanumeric characters in a form the computer can use with OCR.

When doing OCR, you want a fast computer and a fast scanner. Any Pentium-class PC or Power Macintosh qualifies, as long as you have at least 32MB of RAM (64MB is better). As with any scanning application, you'll want to have plenty of hard disk space to store your efforts. A fast scanner completes the picture. The latest Hewlett-Packard scanners can translate a page in about a minute. Anything a lot slower than that can drive you crazy. Sixty additional seconds on top of the basic OCR capture time of a fast scanner may not sound like a lot of time, but when you multiply it by the 100 pages in some documents, you can look forward to a long wait.

If you are doing a fair amount of OCR work, you'll certainly want to consider a scanner that has an automatic document feeder. Strictly speaking, the scanner may not convert pages much faster with an ADF, but you won't care how long the process takes if you don't have to sit there watching it.

How OCR Works

The term "optical character recognition" is probably a misnomer today because OCR software does so much more than convert printed text into computer text files. The character recognition function is only one portion of the task. The others involving things like recognizing text, graphic, and picture components of a page and capturing them appropriately for reassembly in a file for your computer. That's a process known as page decomposition/recomposition. The document-to-word-processing function of OCR is best thought of as text recognition, and it's a very complicated process indeed.

Text Recognition

It's amazing how well scanners handle the job of text recognition. OCR is successful today because scanning packages have so many different tools at their disposal that, when used together, increase the speed and accuracy of the text recognition process. Speed is always important, of course, but most of us don't scan 100-page documents very often. Instead, the average OCR user values accuracy above all.

How accurate is accurate enough? How about a 95 percent accuracy rating? It sounds good on paper, but doesn't look good on the display screen. With a text-only page containing 2,000 characters, a 95 percent accuracy rate translates into 100 errors. Most of us can type in a page from scratch faster than we can find and correct 100 typos. Even spell checkers aren't much of a help with that volume of goof-ups. Today's OCR software can achieve accuracy levels well above 99 percent, so a page might have one or two errors, or none, depending on the complexity of the page and its clarity. (As you'll see, poor originals generate more errors.)

To recognize text that accurately, an OCR program can use any or all of three basic methods of identifying what characters the scanner is looking at. It can compare the characters it encounters with a set of patterns until it finds a match. It can also look at the individual elements that make up a character, deciding that two diagonal lines and a crossbar must be an uppercase A, regardless of how they are arranged. Or, it can use information about how words and sentences are put together to make educated guesses that can be confirmed or disproved by the other two methods. Here's a short discussion of each of the three techniques.

Pattern Matching

The earliest and simplest OCR programs used pattern matching, also called matrix matching or template matching. This method is very flexible simply because you can train the program to read new typefaces just by providing a new set of patterns to match against. Today, no OCR software relies on pattern matching alone to recognize text. It's simply another tool that may or may not be used.

Pattern-matching software divides each character into a matrix of blocks. The sample characters in its library are divided into a similar matrix. The software then compares the two to find a match. The number of congruent bits helps the software decide whether it has found a match. The system works because the number of possible matches for any given character is limited — typically 100 or so upper- and lowercase letters, symbols, and punctuation.

If a character scores significantly higher against one sample than another, odds are very good that it is, indeed, that character. Matrix matching can work very well with documents that contain only a few fonts, such as most computer-generated hard copies. Accuracy drops considerably when the OCR program must attempt to guess which pattern library to use and when it is trying to read a new text font that matches the existing libraries poorly. An example of pattern matching is shown in Figure 7.1.

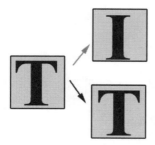

Figure 7.1 Pattern matching

Pattern matching is a fairly flexible scheme. Scanned characters don't have to match the ideal patterns exactly; they need only score high enough to allow the software to make a good guess. The most sophisticated algorithms can vary how much variation is allowed, so the system can be fine-tuned for high quality, low quality, and damaged originals.

Software can also check against several pattern libraries simultaneously, which is useful for fonts that don't quite match a specific type style and for pages that contain mixed type styles.

Pattern matching software can also be trained to recognize new typefaces, but fortunately this is rarely done these days because it is a tedious procedure that involves scanning a sample of the type style and then identifying each character individually. The process speeds up as the software gradually begins to recognize characters. You usually have to add several variations for each character to a given library to account for letters that aren't 100 percent uniform. In a few cases with older software, it was possible to fill up the available spaces in the library and be unable to add any new variations.

Feature Extraction

Topological feature extraction is a more advanced technique for interpreting characters on a page. Each symbol is broken down by the features that make up that symbol. That is, a letter A consists of a crossbar and two slanted lines joined at the top, as shown in Figure 7.2. As the scanner operates, built-in algorithms extract the features of the character being read and provide a match.

Figure 7.2 Feature extraction can identify all these different variations.

The chances of spotting an A, no matter what font happens to be used, are excellent. Feature extraction can even be used to interpret constrained handwriting — that is, characters printed with a modicum of care roughly on or inside a box printed on a form (in an ink invisible to the OCR).

Because no character has more than about 20 different features and because a long list of patterns does not have to be compared, feature extraction has the potential to be a very fast OCR method.

Other Techniques

Scanners can also use other techniques for identifying text, often using these processes to "break ties" when your OCR package isn't 100 percent positive what a particular character is.

Context checking is one method that is used to break ties. The characters that appear on either side of a questionable character can provide important information. A lowercase l or uppercase O found in the middle of a group of numbers is probably a numeral. Text that appears 5t. is probably the abbreviation St., while

8old has a good chance of being Bold, particularly if it appears at the beginning of a sentence. As you can see, some artificial intelligence techniques can be used to identify characters with greater certainty.

OCR programs can also use word lists and dictionaries. If no word can be found that matches a given set of characters, the OCR program can substitute characters for the most questionable ones in the group until a valid word is found. For example, since the letters a and s are frequently confused by OCR software, a check of a word list would tell a smart program that becsuae might be because.

Statistical modeling can also be used to improve guesses. That is, how often does the letter combination that would result from a given choice actually occur in English? An h follows a t a high percentage of the time; a k does not. So the software could easily differentiate between the somewhat similar h and k. In the future, expect to see OCR software that can develop statistical models for specific types of documents, such as medical records. That would help improve accuracy even when reading highly technical material containing jargon not found in standard dictionaries.

Another technique is called adaptive masking, which blanks out, or removes, blotches, dirt, and other non-character information before the software tries to evaluate a page.

Getting the Best Quality

To get the best results, you should focus on the quality of your scanned images. Make sure the glass platen on a flatbed scanner is clean and that your original is of the best quality. A tiny defect that you can ignore or retouch on a graphic image can cause an error that must be found and fixed in a text file.

You should know in advance that no OCR product reads text 100 percent error free. Some of them come close, however — especially when compared to the products available only a few years ago. Good quality original text can make all the difference.

Knowing just what elements of a page can give your OCR program trouble can help you avoid the jobs that won't save you much time. In some cases, you can make corrections ahead of time to make the scanning process go smoother. Listed here and shown, in part, in Figure 7.3, are the common OCR trouble spots:

- **Underlined text.** Underlining often causes descenders (the "tails" of letters such as g and y) to run into the line, which can confuse an OCR program.

- **Joined text.** Joined text is any text in which characters "bump up" against each other, such as the n and the i in Figure 7.3. This is especially common with ligatures, found in typeset text, which join two characters together to make them more readable to the human eye. They can cause problems for your OCR software, however. OCR packages can "learn" that ligatures are unique characters. Poor quality printing can also join characters in unfamiliar ways.

Underlined text
Joined text
Kerned text

Figure 7.3 These kinds of text can cause OCR problems.

- **Broken text.** If your text is fractured because of poor printing (especially found in a thermal fax or dot matrix printout), your OCR software may be unable to interpret a character or may see it as two characters. If the lowercase m is broken at the end of the first hump, it may be interpreted as an r followed by an n.

- **Kerned text.** Kerning is the adjustment of the space between letters so that pairs such as AV fit together more efficiently. However, tightly spaced material can usually be handled by software that uses feature extraction because it doesn't care how closely characters are spaced as long as they don't touch. With pattern matching, part of one character intrudes into the matrix of the next, confusing the program.

- **Boldfaced characters.** Doubling the line thickness of characters can cause them to run together, producing joined text that is difficult to read.

- **Italics.** Slanted letters can distort the features of a character enough to confuse some programs and join characters together enough to cause problems.

- **Photocopied text.** The inevitable quality losses that come with photocopying text can introduce faded areas, broken characters, and poor contrast. You may be able to adjust the photocopier's contrast to produce a better, more readable copy.

- **Dirt.** Any noise on the page causes problems with any OCR program. Dirty patches may look like characters to your software. If they touch a character, they can change an O into a Q or an F into an E. Use the cleanest original you can.

- **Fax.** All fax documents are sent as bitmaps that are reconstructed in the destination computer, or, perhaps, printed out directly with a dedicated fax machine. Resolution can be as low as 96 dpi, producing relatively fuzzy text compared to the 600 dpi (or better) output of the typical laser or inkjet printer. Faxes can be more difficult for OCR software to interpret.

To get the best quality, follow these steps:

Make Sure Your Page Is Aligned

Most software will read your text if the page is skewed slightly. Yet, accuracy can drop drastically if the page is tilted by more than 10 percent or perhaps 5 degrees. It's usually pretty easy to align perfectly square pages. Just butt the edges up against the guides on the scanner platen. An automatic document feeder will usually thread the pages through with excellent alignment.

However, pages that are not square can present a problem. You might encounter one of these as a photocopy that was made with the original itself skewed. Or, the text might have been deliberately printed at an angle. Since pages are placed face down on a flatbed scanner, you may find it default to align the page. You might need to draw a line on the back of the sheet corresponding with the baseline of the text. Then use that line to align with the guides on the scanner.

Make Sure Your Original Is of Top Quality

Repair tears and cover up serious blots that may confuse the OCR software. A touch of correction fluid may help. If you aren't able to alter the original, work on a photocopy. A copy can also improve the contrast of a poor original, although the scanner's built-in contrast controls will usually take care of this automatically.

Watch Out for Translucent Paper

Newsprint is particularly bad. Some characters from the reverse side can show through, confusing your scanner and its software. The fastest way to prevent this problem is to put a black piece of paper on the back side of the page. The black paper absorbs light that travels through the sheet and prevents it from bouncing back to the scanner sensor. If you're scanning a lot of translucent sheets, consider mounting a black sheet on the cover of your flatbed.

Use Your Word Processor's Spell Checker to Double-Check for "Bad" Words

Although OCR software may have a spell checker built in, your own word processor is likely to have its own proofing tools that have been customized with your own special dictionary. Run a text document through this check as a final quality control.

Putting OCR to Work with Your HP Scanner

There are various reasons why you may want to capture text from an original document. Perhaps you just want to reuse a paragraph of text. You may want to capture the entire document. You may, in fact, want to re-create the original with figures, images and columns. What you don't want to do is spend a lot of time doing it, by tediously retyping. With HP scanners, all of the above are supported, from OCRing a simple sentence to capturing a complex document accurately. This next section provides an overview of OCR scanning with HP scanners; you'll find more detail on your options in Chapter 8, "Scanning to a Destination."

Simple Text Scanning

Let's start with a simple text-scanning task:

1. Place a document with text on the scanner; click the preview button (as you learned in the last chapter) to view a pre-scan image of your page, as shown in Figure 7.4.

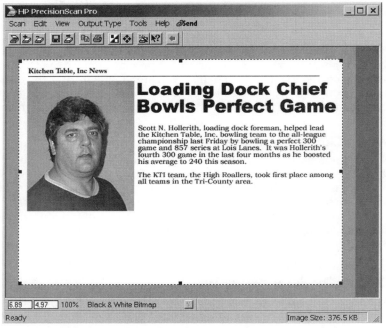

Figure 7.4 Viewing a preview scan

2. Within the preview window, click the mouse and drag to select some text. Notice that the type of scan shown in the Output Type menu changes to Text as the scanner automatically recognizes the selection as text. If there is a background image behind the text, it's possible the scanner won't recognize the text. In that case, just choose Text as the type from the Output Type menu. (HP scanners will often recognize and select the text for you.)

3. Send your text to a destination by clicking the Scan To button and choosing the destination from the drop-down list in the Destination dialog box, shown in Figure 7.5. Depending on what the destination is, different things will happen. If the destination, such as Microsoft Word, supports text, the page is converted into editable text and dropped automatically into the destination application. Or, if your scanner supports drag-and-drop (discussed in Chapter 6) you can just drag the selected text to the target application.

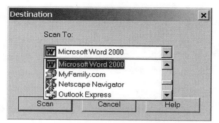

Figure 7.5 The Destination dialog box

Cross-Reference

You'll find more on scanning to a destination and drag-and-drop in Chapter 8, "Scanning to a Destination."

Of course, if the destination does not support text, then an image of the text will be sent — in some appropriate format such as TIF (for, say, Photoshop), depending on the application receiving the image.

Scanning Complex Pages

You can perform more complex scanning of pages that include both text and graphics by selecting Text and Image as the Output Type. In this case, the entire layout may be preserved, depending on how you have your scanning software set — and depending on the layout of the original. Follow these steps:

1. Place an original containing both text and graphics on the scanner, and click the Preview button.

2. Within the Preview window, click with the mouse and drag to select the document.

3. Choose your scanner's Settings or Preferences menu and choose a text output mode. For example, with PrecisionScan Pro, select Scan ➪ Preferences and click the Text tab, as shown in Figure 7.6. Then choose the text output mode, either Flowed Text or Framed Text, described in the paragraph that follows.

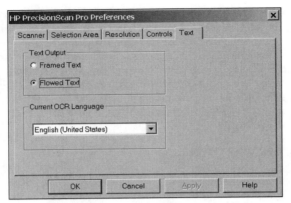

Figure 7.6 Choose Flowed Text or Framed Text.

4. Click the Scan To button and choose the destination for your captured
text and images.

There are two modes the scanner can use to handle text and images: Flowed
and Framed mode. If you pick Framed mode, the scanner will do its best to preserve exactly what you see on the page, including the relative layout of images,
text, columns, tables, and so on. For example, if your page has a picture, a column of text, a drawing, and a headline (like the page shown in Figure 7.4), the
scanner will attempt to create exactly the same page in your target destination
application, such as Microsoft Word. The image of the text would be converted
to a text file and placed in frames on the page in the same position as it appeared
on the original page.

The picture or drawing would be scanned as color or black and white, as
appropriate, and placed in its own frame. A line drawing would be scanned as a
drawing and, again, placed in its own frame. You'd end up with a page in Word
that looks very much like the original. The text and images are placed relative
to each other just like they were on the original, as you can see in Figure 7.7.

The advantage of this mode is that you have an editable version of nearly the
original document with format retained. If you wanted to just change a few words
and reprint, you've saved a lot of work. However, because the text is all confined
to frames, it doesn't "flow" from one place to another. That is, if you add text to a
frame, you may soon insert more text than the frame can contain. It won't automatically spill over to the next frame or page. Frame mode is not best when you
want to add a lot of text or edit heavily.

Instead, use the Flowed Text mode. In this case, the different components of
the original are still identified and scanned appropriately, but they are placed inline, or consecutively in the document. The images are included in the new document, but they are not placed in the proper positions on the page. In other
words, you've lost the original format. However, the text will flow together now
and you can edit it more readily, as shown in Figure 7.8. If you are planning to
edit heavily, you will find this format more useful.

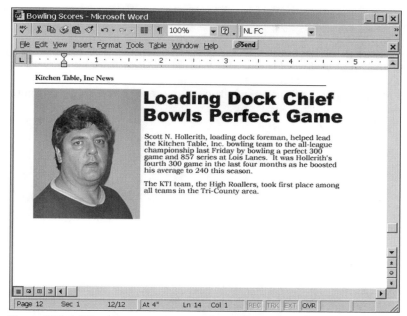

Figure 7.7 A Word document captured with Framed mode

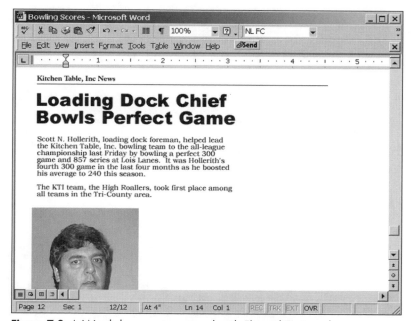

Figure 7.8 A Word document captured with Flowed Text mode

Moving On

This chapter provided some background information on optical character recognition, and an overview of the modes you can choose from when capturing text and text/picture documents. In the next chapter, you'll see how to direct your scans to their final destination, whether it's a word processing document, fax, or Web page.

Scanning to a Destination

The founder of one of the leading power tool companies once observed that consumers aren't really buying a tool as much as they're buying the capabilities it has. "People don't want a power drill, they want *holes*," he said.

In the same vein, Hewlett-Packard has recognized that, as popular as scanners have become, the hordes of new users aren't buying them because they've always wanted to own a scanner. What scanner owners really want are images for their Web pages, documents converted from hardcopies so they can edit them with their word processing software, or information that has been magically transported from their own desktops to other users over the phone lines using fax technology. When it comes right down to it, most of us don't care whether those feats are accomplished with a scanner or with a toaster. In fact, until recently you probably would have preferred the toaster because it was easier to use.

However, as we've seen, that's no longer the case. A scanner can be just as easy to use as a toaster, and is far less likely to burn your bread. HP's "one-button" scanning, discussed in Chapter 6, "Using One-Button Features and Software," makes scanning as easy as stuffing a pastry into a toaster slot.

The second part of the ease-of-use equation is that HP offers *scanning to a destination*. That means you can start your scan by pressing a button, and then direct the output to the destination of your choice. You can think of this technique as *pushing* an image from your scanner to the application that will use it, rather than the traditional technique of loading the application and then *pulling* the image into it through the scanner software interface. It's like putting something into a refrigerator rather than climbing onto the shelves and pulling it in after you. This makes a lot more sense.

Scanning to a Destination

As you learned in Chapter 6, "Using One-Button Features and Software," scanning to certain kinds of destinations such as fax, printer, or e-mail can be as easy as pressing a single button, provided your scanner is equipped with those particular buttons (not all HP scanners have all four buttons). However, within your scanning software you can direct a scan to any of those destinations, plus a lot more. Just activate a scan by pressing the Scan button on your scanner (every HP scanner has one of those!) and when the preview window appears, make any modifications you like. Then click the Scan To button (with PrecisionScan Pro, it's under the View menu, to the right of the floppy disk icon). The Scan To dialog box, shown in Figure 8.1, pops up. You can choose from the following destinations:

■ **ActiveShare.** Adobe's multifunction program that includes many of the destinations you'll want, plus other tools for modifying images and creating projects.

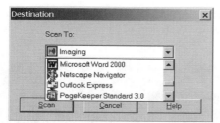

Figure 8.1 Select a destination from the Scan To dialog box.

- **Image Editor.** Any image editor you've installed on your computer will appear in the list (rather than the name "Image Editor"). For example, if you have Adobe Photoshop, Corel Photo-Paint, or PaintShop Pro, it will appear in the list. If you have more than one image editor, they all should have been detected when your scanning software was installed and they should appear in the list.

- **Word Processing.** Your word processing program as well as WordPad will be shown in the list, so you can scan to a destination compatible with OCR output.

- **Office Applications.** If you have Microsoft Office installed, its applications will appear in the list; you'll see Word, Excel, PowerPoint, Microsoft FrontPage, and so forth.

- **E-mail.** Your e-mail program, such as Microsoft Outlook or Outlook Express, will appear in the list.

- **Fax.** You have several fax options, including WinFax Pro (if you have it installed) and the eFax Messenger Plus software installed with many HP scanners.

- **Other Software** installed with the HP scanner will also appear in the list. These can include Corel Photo House, Corel Print House, Caere PageKeeper, Photo Fantasy 2000, and HP Graphics Desk. You'll want to refer to the documentation furnished with these programs to see all they can do.

When you select a destination and click the Scan button in the Destination dialog box, the scanner grabs the image and forwards it to the destination you specified, launching the application if it isn't already active on your computer. Let's look at a several destinations in more detail.

Scanning to ActiveShare

Adobe ActiveShare is the utility knife of your scanner toolkit. When you choose ActiveShare as a destination, your image is transported to the application with the futuristic interface shown in Figure 8.2. You'll notice lots of buttons in the ActiveShare window. Here's what they do:

Figure 8.2 Adobe ActiveShare is a multifunction program.

- **Importing images.** The pane in the upper-left corner contains icons for each of the scanner software packages you have installed. Usually you'll have just the one, but in Figure 8.2 there are three: DeskScan II 2.8 (for an older HP ScanJet 4c scanner), PrecisionScan LTX (for a ScanJet 4300c), and PrecisionScan Pro (for a ScanJet 5370c). Thanks to the miracle of a SCSI card and USB hub, the single computer used for the illustration had three different scanners attached at once, with no problems! In addition to the scanner software icons, you'll find one labeled Import that can be used to bring images into ActiveShare from other sources.

- **Album.** To the right of the image importing tools is an icon for the Albums you work with. You can create any number of albums and place your pictures in them for browsing and easy access.

- **Destinations.** At the far upper right are icons for four different destinations: Share on Web, E-mail, Create Postcard, and Fax. Click any of them to send the currently selected picture to that destination. We'll look at Share on Web, E-mail, and Fax later in this chapter. The fourth, Create Postcard, sends the photo to a mini-application that enables you to design and send your own postcard from your image.

■ **Viewing and managing images.** Beneath the Destinations panel on the right side of the ActiveShare window are icons and buttons for viewing and managing your images. The Plus and Minus buttons zoom in and out; you can also choose a particular magnification from the drop-down list below the zoom buttons. Below the zoom buttons are a pair of buttons for saving and closing the current picture. The horizontal panel in the lower right has buttons you can use to undo an action, search your albums for particular photos, create a new album, delete an album, make a duplicate of a photo, and delete a photo entirely.

■ **Your current photo.** In the center of the screen is an image of the currently selected photo. There's a caption underneath; type in the caption area to apply or change the caption for that photo.

■ **Access the Web.** In the far lower-left corner is a button you can click to access your ActiveShare images that have been stored on the Web. We'll look at scanning to the Web later in this chapter.

■ **Fix My Photo.** The Fix My Photo button produces the pop-up menu shown in Figure 8.3. You can click any of the choices to apply an instant, automated fix to common picture problems (too dark, too light, blurry, and so on); rotate the photo; trim or crop the picture; remove "red eye" glare from the irises of the eyes; and access additional correction tools for color and other parameters.

Figure 8.3 You can fix many photo problems automatically with these options.

■ **Photo Projects.** This button produces a pop-up menu like the one shown in Figure 8.4. You can choose from a variety of projects including assembling your photos into a slide show, creating wallpaper for your display screen, adding motion blur for a special effect, and other easy-to-do projects.

Figure 8.4 Create a slide show, generate wallpaper, or add motion blur to your images.

Scanning to the Web

One of the most exciting new capabilities to come to scanning is the capability to scan your images directly to a Web site, where they can be viewed by family and friends, business colleagues, or anyone else you'd like to share them with. The best thing about Scan to Web capabilities is the service is entirely free.

Anyone can use Scan to Web by downloading HP's Scan-to-Web software from the HP Web site (http://www.hp.com). Run the software, and sign up for one of the service providers who will host your images: Zing.com, Myfamily.com, or HPCartogra.com. If you don't have an account, the software will help you set one up (these services are all free!).Then, the Scan to Web choice will appear in your Scan To menu, and you can grab images and place them on your provider's Web space automatically. You'll be given URLs you can supply to your friends and associates so they can view your pictures.

You can also share images on the Web from within Adobe ActiveShare, using Adobe's eCircles image hosting service. To use eCircles, just click the Share on Web button within ActiveShare. Your browser will pop up. You should then jump to the eCircles Web page, and you'll be invited to sign up by choosing a logon name and password, and supplying some information such as your e-mail address. After that, sharing images by scanning to the Web is almost automatic.

Just select an image and click the Share on Web button. The dialog box shown in Figure 8.5 pops up so you can log into eCircles.

Figure 8.5 Log into eCircles.

Then, you'll be given the opportunity to save to a particular Circle and album, which you can consider to be an online album that you grant various individuals access to. You may then decide whether the image will be stored on the Web in viewing-only quality (for fast downloads by those accessing your images over the Internet) or in a higher printable quality that can be used for making hard-copies, greeting cards, and so forth. You'll make your choice from the dialog box shown in Figure 8.6.

Figure 8.6 Choose the album and quality level for your shared image.

After that, anyone can go the Web site and view your images. You can visit the site yourself and manage the images with your browser, as shown in Figure 8.7. Scanning to the Web is a great way to share your photos, or to put copies of them on the Internet for safekeeping (in case you lose the original file or the original hardcopy). Instead of sending out multiple e-mails with your vacation photos, you can post them online and let anyone view them at their leisure (or, if your photos are really boring, *not* view them and say they did).

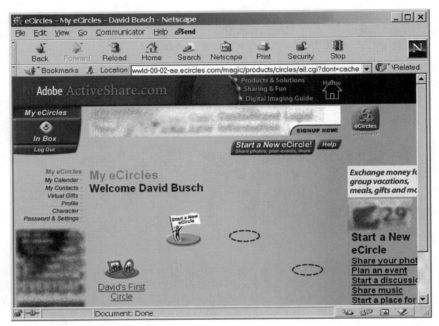

Figure 8.7 Manage your images from your browser.

Scanning to a Web Page Editor

When you scan to a Web page editor, such as Microsoft FrontPage, the scanner will capture the image, process it optimally for display on the Web, save it in JPEG format, and then put it directly into a Web page for you to work on. After each image is scanned, you'll be asked if you'd like to scan additional images so you can load up your Web page with several graphics before beginning to work on the page itself. An image scanned directly to Microsoft FrontPage is shown in Figure 8.8.

Scanning to a Web page editor streamlines your Web page editing. Instead of scanning pictures and loading them individually into your Web page, you can grab images for the page directly.

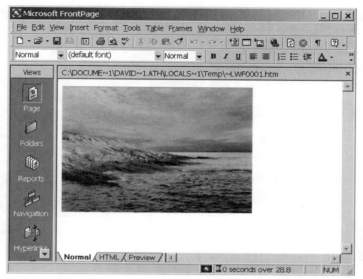

Figure 8.8 Scan directly to a Web page editor such as Microsoft FrontPage.

Scanning to Fax

When you scan to fax, the scanner will grab your image or document and send it to your fax software as shown in Figure 8.9. The cool part is that you'll be asked if you want to scan more pages so you can do multipage faxes with ease. You'll find this can be the fastest way to fax a document. In many cases, it's even faster than using your fax software's scan option because you don't even have to load the software first. Just scan (using your scanner's Fax button, or scan to the fax destination if it doesn't have one) and choose a recipient. What could be easier than that?

Scan to E-mail

When you scan to e-mail, your image will be directed to the e-mail program you set up in Chapter 6 as your default program for sending mail with attachments. (It's possible to have more than one e-mail program installed and used on a single computer.)

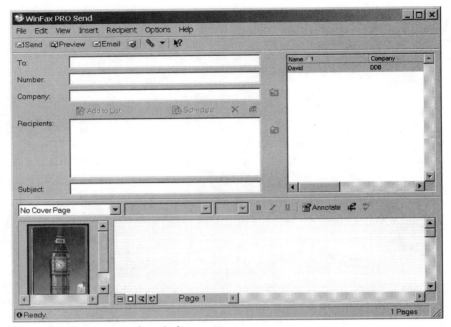

Figure 8.9 Fax images directly from your scanner.

Scan to Other Applications

You can also scan directly to any other application in the Scan To list, including PageKeeper (installed with many HP scanners), your word processing program, a desktop publishing program, and so forth. This feature is a real time-saver! Figure 8.10 shows an image scanned to PageKeeper.

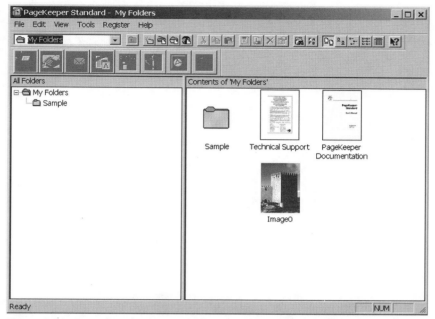

Figure 8.10 Scan directly into applications such as Caere PageKeeper.

Moving On

Now that you know how to grab images with the push of a button and scan to a destination quickly, you'll want to learn how to get better scans and optimize the color of your graphics. You can discover how to do both of these in the two chapters that follow.

Getting Better Scans

IN THIS CHAPTER
- Using scanner controls
- Setting preferences
- Previewing
- Choosing an image type manually
- Sharpening
- Choosing resolution
- Brightness and contrast
- Color adjustment

Getting the best possible scans doesn't have to be a lot of work. Modern scanners have automated features that simplify choosing scanner settings. In most cases, you won't have to select all or most of the options yourself. However, when you encounter that difficult piece of artwork, it's a good idea to understand how your scanner controls and options work so you can use your human judgment to fine-tune your scan. This chapter explores all the key scanner controls at your disposal and shows you how to get a better scan.

Choosing the Best Original

A good scan starts with a good original. Scanners can't capture information that doesn't exist so you should make sure that the original you'll be scanning is the best and most faithful photograph or artwork you can obtain.

If you're scanning a photograph and have a choice between scanning a 5×7-inch enlargement or a 3½×5-inch snapshot, choose the larger size. The enlargement will frequently have more detail than the smaller print. Note that you'll soon reach a point of diminishing returns. An 11×14-inch enlargement from a 35mm negative will not necessarily contain any more information than an 8×10-inch print. You'll probably find that the grain of the film (actually dye clumps in color negative films) will be bigger and more noticeable, and any lack of sharpness in the camera lens will be readily apparent.

If you're scanning text for OCR, use an original document rather than a photocopy. If you must scan a fax, make sure it has been sent to you in Fine rather than Standard mode. Ask the person sending you the fax to use a larger type size to make the text easier for the OCR software to interpret.

You'll save yourself some extra work if you learn which defects matter, and which don't. Experience is the best teacher, as there are no hard and fast rules. For example, you'll discover that a few dust spots in a photograph don't mean you must have the picture reprinted — just take a few minutes to retouch the dust spots out of the scanned print. You'll also find that a slight amount of blurriness can be easily compensated by some sharpening during the scan. The amount of dust or blurriness that is acceptable is something you have to learn for yourself.

Using Scanner Controls

The following section details each of the key controls of your scanner and gives you the information you need to set them properly. Keep in mind that while many of these controls, such as brightness and contrast, are also available in your image editor, it's almost always preferable to have the settings as correct as possible when you make the scan. Image editors can't add information: they can only change the pixels already in the scan. It's better to make some slight adjustments in an image editor to fine-tune a well-scanned image than to try to make wholesale changes after the scan. We'll use PrecisionScan Pro as the representative scanning program because it has all the features of PrecisionScan LTX, and more.

Setting Preferences

You can set many of the preferences your scanner will use in the Preferences or Options dialog boxes of your scanning software. The PrecisionScan Pro Preferences dialog box (accessed from the Scan menu) appears in Figure 9.1. The following section describes each of the options you can set.

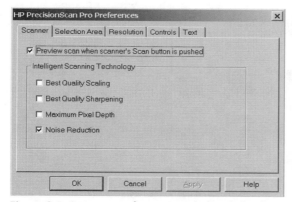

Figure 9.1 Set your preferences with this dialog box.

Scanner

The Scanner tab of the Preferences dialog box has five checkboxes you can mark or unmark to enable or disable a feature. These include:

- **Preview scan when scanner's Scan button is pushed.** Automatically creates a preview when you press the Scan button on your scanner. You'll generally want to have this option enabled.

- **Best Quality Scaling.** This option applies the highest quality scaling to the final scan, but can result in longer scan times.

- **Best Quality Sharpening.** This option gives you the best sharpness in your final scan. As with the preceding option, it can increase scan times, but if you scan many images at maximum resolution, checking this box and the Best Quality Scaling box can help you avoid specifying these qualities manually.

■ **Maximum Pixel Depth.** This is another top-quality parameter, telling the scanner to always use the highest pixel depth available when making a final scan. It doesn't hurt to have this option enabled at all times, but you'll particularly want to use it with images that have a long *dynamic range* (details in both shadows and highlights) because using the maximum pixel depth provides extra information the scanner can use to preserve these details.

■ **Noise Reduction.** This option tells the scanner to apply special algorithms that reduce the amount of random artifacts (noise) in a scan. The default setting is marked. There's not much reason for you to change this.

Selection Area

There are four options on this tab (see Figure 9.2), which enable you to control how the scanner selects an area for a final scan from the preview, and what it does with that selection. You can choose any or all of these:

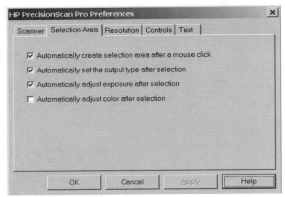

Figure 9.2 Choose how your selection area is set with this dialog box.

■ **Automatically create selection area after a mouse click.** The scanner searches the preview area and determines the scan area when you click in the preview. For instance, if you click on a photo, the photo is selected. If you click on text, the paragraph is selected. You will find it is much easier just to click on a photo than to "select" it manually. However, if you always make manual selections, you can turn this capability off. You can manually make another selection if you like.

- **Automatically set the output type after selection.** The scanner examines the selected area and determines what type of graphic, text, or text/graphic subject it is. Usually the scanner does an excellent job, so you'll want to leave this capability enabled. If you frequently select an output type different from the one the scanner would select, you can turn this option off. For example, if you regularly scan color originals but want the scans to be grayscale (like a black-and-white photo), you may want to turn this off. It will be easier than resetting the output type to Black & White Photo every time because the scanner will otherwise continue to recognize the photo as a color photo (that's what it is!).

- **Automatically adjust exposure after selection.** The scanner makes corrections for exposure automatically. Again, you'll want to leave this enabled in virtually all cases because you can always override the automatic exposure settings — and they give you an excellent place to start in those few cases in which the automatic exposure is not all you want.

- **Automatically adjust color after selection.** When this box is checked, the scanner corrects the color of your selection. If you scan a great many originals that you don't want the scanner to color correct, disable this option

Remember that even if you have the all the automatic preferences described above turned on, you can always override them on a case-by-case basis. The only time you will probably want to turn them off is if you regularly scan something that needs manual adjustment.

Resolution

The Resolution tab offers a list of the available resolutions that have been defined by the software designers for your scanner, although the scanner, of course, can use any other resolution that you prefer. The available resolutions are shown in the Resolution List. At the right side of the dialog box, the tab shows the default resolution (the resolution that's been built into the software as the best for that type of artwork) that will be used for photographs (continuous tone) images, and for B&W Bitmaps (line art). If you click the Add button, a dialog box appears with a space for you to type in any resolution you want from 12 to 999,999 samples per inch. As we pointed out in earlier chapters, in virtually all cases you shouldn't need to choose
a resolution, but if you feel you must select a resolution, the capability is there. (Resolutions other than the scanner's real optical resolution are interpolated, of

course.) Resolutions above 1,200 spi are useful for enlarging very small selections but produce massive file sizes for any selection of larger dimensions.

The Resolution tab is shown in Figure 9.3.

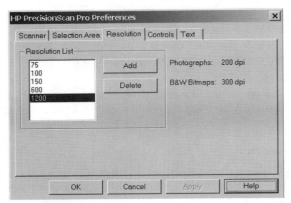

Figure 9.3 Add or remove resolution options with this dialog box.

Controls

Graphics professionals are the only ones who really have a need for the Controls tab, shown in Figure 9.4, which modifies the fineness of the controls in the Tools menu for adjusting gamma and exposure correction, shadow detail, and black-and-white threshold parameters. The higher the number of the bit readout, the more increments available for making fine adjustments. The 8-bit readout gives a range of 0 to 255 bits; the 10-bit readout gives a range of 0 to 1,023 bits; and the 12-bit readout gives a range of 0 to 4,095 bits in the sliders of the Exposure Adjustment and Black & White Threshold tools, shown in Figure 9.5. After you've set the parameters shown in Figure 9.4, the slider increments shown in Figure 9.5 reflect your changes the next time you use the Exposure Adjustment tool.

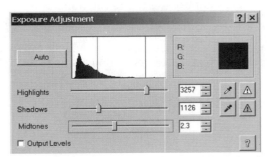

Figure 9.4 Set the fineness of your Exposure Adjustment and Black & White Threshold controls with this dialog box.

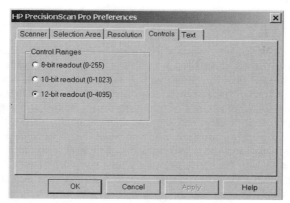

Figure 9.5 The Exposure Adjustment tool's slider increments are determined by the Controls tab settings.

Text

The Text tab, shown in Figure 9.6, enables you to set Text Output to Framed Text or Flowed Text, and specify the language used for OCR functions from a list of more than two dozen.

Cross-Reference

For more information on OCR functions, including a discussion of framed and flowed text options, see Chapter 7, "Capturing Documents with Optical Character Recognition."

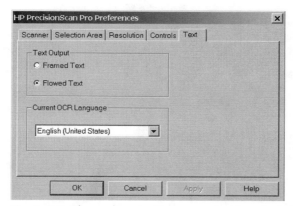

Figure 9.6 Choose how text is captured with optical character recognition with this dialog box.

Previewing

A preview scan is an excellent way to evaluate an image prior to the final capture. You can crop the preview to select the exact portion of the image to be scanned and make some decisions, based on the preview, of how much you may need to adjust the brightness, contrast, or other image parameters. HP PrecisionScan Pro enables you to make real-time adjustments of these parameters and see the results immediately in the preview. While a preview scan generally shows the entire scanner bed (for example, if your artwork is smaller than the scanner glass, blank white space will show around the artwork in the preview), you can also zoom in on a preview by clicking the Zoom button. This capability is especially helpful if you're scanning a small original. Figure 9.7 shows a preview scan.

If you don't like the automatic selection area chosen by the software, click outside the selection with the mouse and then click in one corner of the area you want to select and drag to draw a selection rectangle around the area you want to capture, or, you can adjust the edges by moving the mouse over the border or a corner (the cursor will turn into a arrow symbol) and then clicking and dragging the border to where you want it.

Figure 9.7 Preview scans give you an idea of what the final scan will look like.

Choosing an Image Type Manually

Obviously, scanner settings can vary depending on whether you're capturing a black-and-white drawing, a grayscale photograph, a color drawing, or a color photograph. For example, if you're grabbing an image of a line drawing, a higher contrast setting that wouldn't be acceptable for a grayscale photograph is okay. Many scanner control applications, such as PrecisionScan Pro and PrecisionScan LTX, can examine an image during a preview scan and make an excellent guess about the kind of image with which you're working. Sometimes, you'll want to set this control yourself: when you want to capture a color image in black-and-white, or when the scanner software chooses the wrong image type.

With PrecisionScan Pro, the image type is selected automatically or can be chosen from a drop-down list, shown in Figure 9.8. You can choose from these types:

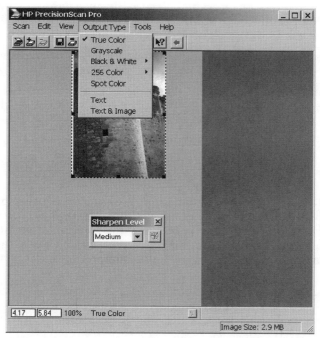

Figure 9.8 You can choose an image output type manually.

- **True Color.** A full color image — such as a color photograph.
- **Grayscale.** A monochrome image such as a black-and-white photo. Select this one if you want a color photo to be scanned in black and white for a non-color printer.

- **Black & White.** You can select from two types of black-and-white images, bitmap (line art, or raster image) and scalable (vector) image. In the latter case, the scanner software automatically traces the edges of the image, providing scalable objects that can be manipulated in drawing programs such as CorelDRAW. Scalable is also nice for drawings you will include in documents because you can enlarge and reduce them without losing quality.

- **256 Color.** This choice has three different selections: Web Palette, which uses the 216 colors that can be displayed by all browsers; System Palette, which uses the 240 colors set aside by Windows; and Optimized Palette, which creates the best set of 256 colors to represent your image from the millions available with a true color scan. This is useful when you want to scan to a Web page and want the image to appear nicely on the Web when viewed with limited computers. It also reduces the file size.

- **Spot Color.** A spot color scan captures a limited range of colors, as when you're producing a spot color printed piece with only a few extra hues. Spot color is very useful when scanning things such as logos or business graphics. Solid colors will be recognized as a single color.

- **Text.** Use this choice when your original contains only text. The scanner software converts the text image to editable text using OCR.

- **Text & Image.** Use this choice when your original contains both text and graphics. The scanner will scan each type of image separately, saving the graphics in image files and the text as editable text using OCR.

Sharpening

Sharpening can help fix fuzzy photos by increasing the contrast between pixels at the boundaries between image areas. Keep in mind that sharpening controls can't work miracles: a really blurry picture can't be made razor-sharp. Also remember that sharpening makes everything sharper. If your picture has dust or scratches, these imperfections will become more evident after sharpening is applied.

Tip

Sharpening increases the contrast of an image so you may want to lower the contrast using the contrast controls (described under "Brightness and Contrast") whenever you apply extra sharpening.

Some scanner software has sharpening controls available in the main dialog box. Because PrecisionScan defaults to applying a normal amount of sharpening, you probably won't have to make any adjustments. If you do, you'll find that the controls are tucked away in a floating dialog box like the one shown in Figure 9.9. You can make this dialog box appear by checking the Sharpen Level menu item in the Tools menu. If you find you want to use the Sharpening control a lot, it, like the resolution control, can be "clicked" onto the top or bottom border of the Precision Scan Pro window.

Your choices range from None and Low sharpening through High and Extreme. You can evaluate the amount of sharpening best with a Zoomed preview, which you can obtain by clicking the Zoom button. At the right side of the Sharpen Level dialog box is the Auto Sharpen button, which sets the degree of sharpening to the optimal level for the particular Output Type selected for the original.

Figure 9.9 Choose the amount of sharpening and output resolution with these floating dialog boxes.

Choosing Resolution

Some scanner software have sliders or dialog box settings for specifying resolution. (Chapter 2, "How Scanners Work," and Chapter 4, "Resolution, Interpolation, and Sharp Images," explain the basics of resolution.) As you learned in those chapters, resolution isn't really a critical issue in most cases. The scanner software, such as PrecisionScan Pro, will automatically choose an ideal resolution for the Output Type you're working with. However, if you really must set resolution yourself, here's a recap of the "ideal" resolutions. PrecisionScan Pro has a floating

Output Resolution dialog box, which like the Sharpen Level dialog box, can be shown or hidden from the tools menu, and has an AutoResolution button at the right side for choosing the best resolution for a given Output Type. The Output Resolution dialog box appears in Figure 9.9.

- For text and line drawings, resolutions should be set to the dpi of the printer, up to no more than 600 spi.

- For photographs, a resolution of 100 to 200 samples per inch should be sufficient.

When you're scanning transparencies, you should still set the output resolution at about 200 spi (the default) — but be sure to use the dimension tool to enlarge the image. In fact, the scanner will operate at a higher spi than you specify, but the image will be "saved" as 200 spi and the appropriate size. For instance, if you want to enlarge something 2x, or 200 percent, the scanner will actually operate at 400 spi, but the image will be saved as 2x bigger. If you scanned at 400 spi and 100 percent scaling, your image would appear in your destination at the original size, not bigger — and then you would have to scale it up.

Brightness and Contrast

As with the other user-adjustable parameters, you'll find that your scanner will usually choose the optimal brightness and contrast for your image for you. Sometimes, you'll want to use a different setting for a special effect. With PrecisionScan Pro, these adjustments are made from the Exposure Adjustment dialog box, shown in Figure 9.10. It has three sliders you can use to adjust highlights, shadows, and midtones separately, as well as an Auto button to let the software do it for you.

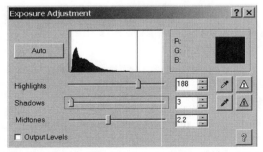

Figure 9.10 Set the brightness of Shadows, Highlights, and Midtones separately with this dialog box.

Color Adjustment

Your scanner software should capture the best color automatically. Fine-tuning color may also be done in your image editing software, as outlined in Chapter 10, "Optimizing Color." However, most scanner software, including PrecisionScan Pro, allows changes to color rendition before carrying out a scan. The control, available from the Tools menu, and shown in Figure 9.11, is called Color Adjustment.

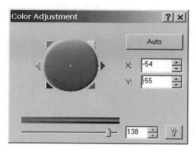

Figure 9.11 Adjust the saturation and color balance of your images with this dialog box.

It includes a slider for modifying the overall saturation (color "richness") of the image (to produce more vivid colors), a color "wheel" with buttons you can click to add cyan, magenta, yellow, blue, red, or green, and an Auto button to let the software adjust the color for you. If you want to use these tools, read the description of color optimization in Chapter 10. You can apply what you learn to these controls.

Moving On

Getting better scans is only half the work. Once you have a scan in your computer, you may want to improve it by adjusting the color or by performing some image-editing transformations. We'll look at both of these functions in the next two chapters.

→ Optimizing Color

As you've seen in previous chapters, the latest HP scanners include technology that takes most of the pain out of getting good color right out of the scanning experience. You can slap an original down on your scanner, grab an image, and then view it, with reasonable expectations that your results will look very much like what you started out with. In addition, with some HP scanners you can adjust the color (increase or decrease saturation and modify hue) right in the scanning software. You may want to try to adjust this in the scanner first to save some time. However, there are times when you might want to tweak color a bit in your image editor. Or, perhaps you're using an older scanner that doesn't provide these amazing capabilities. This chapter tells you what you need to know to correct color the old-fashioned way and provides you with some background information so you'll know exactly what's happening with your colors.

What's Optimization?

The idea of optimizing color can take on several meanings, depending on how you plan to use your finished scan. If you've scanned a piece of artwork, such as a painting, you probably want the colors to match the original as closely as possible so the artist's vision is echoed in the finished scan. Something from Picasso's "Blue Period" should probably not come out with a magenta cast. Advertising artwork must also be scanned with a high degree of accuracy so the colors of the product are faithfully shown. If a green dress is portrayed as if it had just come out of a swamp, it's likely that the designer will find few buyers.

On the other hand, if your image was a scenic photo taken on a slightly overcast day, you'd probably be pleased with richer, more saturated greens in the foliage and deeper blues in the sky than in real life. Indeed, photographers often select the films they use as carefully as an artist puts daubs of pigment on a palette. Certain films are known for providing brighter, more saturated colors, while other provide a more realistic tone.

For images of human faces, optimized color rendition is even more complicated. While we all have a firm picture in our minds of how human flesh should appear, we'll readily accept flesh tones that are slightly redder or more magenta than in real life. However, even a minimal blue or green cast in a portrait can give your subject a deathly pallor. "Daylight" fluorescent lights were developed specifically because consumers were repelled by the sickly look earlier fluorescent lights produced.

"Good" color varies in other ways. If you plan to use an image on a Web page, you must sometimes compress the hues into the 256 colors that can be viewed by visitors to your page using a video card set to 8 bits. (Actually, it's safest to use only the 216 standard colors that most browsers can show with an 8-bit display.) Fortunately, that stricture is less common today because virtually everyone browsing the Web can use browsers at settings higher than 256 colors. HP scanners include the capability to create Web optimized images as you scan, but you may not want to degrade a scan (by converting to fewer colors) in the scanner. This is particularly true if you want to have a high-quality version as well as a

"Web optimized" version of the image. In this case, either saving two scans (one in each mode) or scanning only a high-quality version and creating a lower color-depth one in the image editor may be the best option.

The next few sections give you everything you need to know to understand how color is produced, and how to fine-tune your color scans for your intended application. We also discover how the most common color models differ, and offer tips for calibrating your scanner, video display, and printer so they work together.

How Colors Are Produced

You probably learned in high school science class that our eyes are able to detect only a relatively narrow band of wavelengths of light. These range from 400 nanometers (4 ten-millionths of an inch) at the short (violet) end of the visible spectrum to 700 nanometers (7 ten-millionths of an inch) at the long (red) end. We see certain frequencies as violet/blue, while longer wavelengths are perceived as red. All the colors in between have wavelengths that are shorter than red, but longer than blue — a continuous spectrum of hues.

Note

We don't really see a continuous spectrum of color. Our color vision comes from the three different types of cone cells in our eyes, each of which responds to different wavelengths of light. (Other cells, called rods, are used for detail and black-and-white vision when there is not much light.) Artificial color systems, which include computer scanners, monitors, printers, and other peripherals, attempt to reproduce, or model, the colors that we see. If the model is a good one, all the colors we are capable of detecting are defined by the model. The colors within the definition of each model are called the model's color space. Because nearly all color spaces use three different parameters, we can plot them as x, y, and z coordinates to produce a three-dimensional shape that represents the color gamut (color range) of the model.

The response to light of the cones and rods in our eyes is different than that of the filters in a scanner. That means that sometimes the scanner will "see" a color differently than you do. In addition, the scanner always uses the light that is built in, whereas you view colors under a wide variety of lights. To put it simply, sometimes the scanner will simply see a different color than you. The error is called metamerism and it is similar to the effect of not being able to see the color of cars in a parking lot at night when the only light is the street lights. The only way to fix metamerism would be to design scanners with filters that match the response of the human visual system — which is very expensive and not really needed. Metamerism exists, but it is not a major problem for well-designed scanners.

A scientific model that defines all the colors that humans see was defined in 1931 by the Commission Internationale L'Eclairage (CIE). However, computer color systems use one of three or four other color models that are more practical because they are based on the actual hardware systems used to reproduce the colors. One of the simplest ways to envision color is through the use of a color wheel, shown in Figure 10.1. This wheel shows the relationships of the primary colors and the intermediate colors located between each primary. Colors directly opposite each other are known as complements; that is, the complement of blue is yellow, and vice versa. You'll see that the illustration doesn't say which are the primary colors and which are secondary. You'll learn why in the sections that follow.

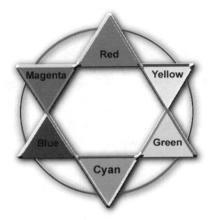

Figure 10.1 A color wheel is a simple way of showing the relationships between primary colors and intermediate colors.

Additive Color

One way to generate color is to use beams of colored light, generated by a light source such as a color television or computer display screen. All the colors we see in this way are produced by mixing the primary colors of light — red, green, and blue — in various combinations. Color monitors produce color by aiming three electronic guns at sets of red, green, and blue phosphors (compounds that give off photons when struck by beams of electrons), coated on the screen of your display. The guns excite the phosphors in proportion to the amount of red, green, or blue light in a given pixel of the image. The phosphors glow, and our eyes add their illumination together, perceiving a color image. If none of the phosphors glows, we see a black pixel. If all three glow in equal proportions, we see a neutral color — gray or white, depending on the intensity.

Colors other than black, gray, or white result when the red, green, and blue phosphors are used in uneven amounts. To produce pure red, green, or blue color, those hues of light can be used alone. Mixing red and blue together produces the reddish-blue color magenta. Blue-green is called cyan, while red and green mixed together produce yellow (this is the most difficult combination to understand; red and green don't seem like they ought to produce yellow, but they do). Because these colors are added together, they are referred to as the additive primary colors of light, and this color model is known as RGB.

Figure 10.2 shows a simplified representation of this color model. The largest circles represent beams of light in red, green, and blue. Where the beams overlap, they produce other colors. For example, red and green combine to produce yellow. Red and blue add up to magenta, and green and blue produce cyan. The center portion, in which all three colors overlap, is white.

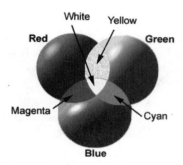

Figure 10.2 A simplified two-dimensional rendition of the RGB color model

Scanners and monitors must be calibrated in some way (either at the factory, or on your desktop), or adjusted for accuracy, because no scanner sensor or display actually sees or produces pure red, green, or blue light. Only lasers, which output one single frequency of light, generate absolutely pure wavelengths, and they aren't practical for display devices — although they are used for expensive, professional scanners. (In fact, a laser-based scanner would work well for scanning a specific type of original — but not for a wide variety of originals or natural objects.) Color representations on monitors or scanners differ from brand to brand and even from one device to another within the same brand. Fortunately, the industry is moving toward more standardized models so typical users have to spend less and less time "correcting" their devices.

Moreover, the characteristics of a device can change as it ages. For example, the phosphors in a monitor can "wear out," with some colors, particularly hues, changing in intensity at a different rate than others. So, identical information rarely produces identical images. From time to time, you may have to provide something called gamma correction, which was first mentioned in Chapter 2.

What's Gamma?

Just when you've learned about hue, saturation, and brightness, your image editor or scanner's instruction manual throws the term gamma at you. What is gamma, anyway? Gamma correction is needed because hardware systems used to reproduce colors, particularly color monitors, don't respond to colors in a linear way.

That is, given 256 shades of a particular color, a value of 0 should represent no color, 64 should represent 25 percent intensity, 128 should represent 50 percent intensity, and so forth. However, in real life, this linear scale doesn't apply. You'll quickly find that a value of 64 is usually not exactly half of 128. The relationship of the actual representation to the ideal is known as a gamma curve.

Scanners do happen to conform to the ideal rather closely, but CRTs and printers tend to vary. If you know the gamma curve of a particular device, however, you can correct it. For example, if you know that with a certain device a value of 64 produces an intensity only 90 percent of what it should be in order to be linear, you can boost that value by an appropriate amount whenever it occurs.

This process is completed by building a gamma correction table that includes a value for each of the levels used in a system. The correction values are automatically used by the scanning software to produce an accurate response when the image is printed or displayed.

Because scanners respond to reflected light in a more linear way than printers or monitors, gamma correction is critical. In HP scanners, the gamma used by default is a gamma of 2.2 (1.8 or 2.2 on Macintosh). This gamma is the correct one for the new standard sRGB color system. This standard has eliminated the need for special print path calibration (a system of color matching provided for earlier HP scanners) in the vast majority of cases.

Tip

If you are using an HP scanner that includes the Exposure Adjustment tool, you can adjust the gamma applied by adjusting the midtones value. Setting the midtones to 1.0 results in a linear response. If you look at the preview image with gamma of 1.0 you will see the image looks too dark and muddy. This is a good illustration of why you need gamma!

Subtractive Color

Colors can also be produced by reflection, as when we view an image of a printed sheet of paper. If you think about it, you'll see why red, green, and blue can't be used to represent all colors — although they work just fine when used alone (not overlapped) to provide what are called "spot" colors.

You can't overlap red and green pigment to produce their intermediate color, yellow. Red pigment reflects only red light; green pigment reflects only green light. When they overlap, the red pigment absorbs the green, and the green absorbs the red, so no light is reflected and we see black. Similarly, it is impossible to generate magenta from overlapping red and blue, or cyan by overlapping blue and green.

Instead, we use the RGB intermediate colors — cyan, magenta, and yellow — as our inks and pigments. Each of these absorbs or subtracts certain colors from the light, and reflects the remainder toward our eyes. For example, magenta ink on a white piece of paper absorbs some green light, reflecting the red and blue and producing the magenta color we see.

Similarly, yellow ink absorbs blue light and reflects red and green, while cyan ink absorbs red light and reflects blue and green. In each of these simplified cases, one RGB primary color is subtracted and we see the color produced by the two that remain in the reflected light. For that reason, cyan, magenta, and yellow are referred to as the subtractive primary colors, and one version of this color model is called CMY. Figure 10.3 shows a simplified rendition of this model.

As with the additive color model, real-world imperfections mean that mixtures of the three colors (in the form of ink, toner, or pigment) don't always produce the color you expect. Equal amounts of cyan, magenta, and yellow ink usually generate a muddy brown rather than a true gray or black.

Note

Composite black is the term applied to a "black" image produced using nothing but cyan, magenta, and yellow pigments.

So, when printing full-color images, a fourth "color," black, is added. Black can fill in areas that are supposed to be black and add detail to other areas of an image. The black pigment can replace equal amounts of the other three colors to produce the same effect with less ink and at a lower cost. This is especially true in the case of portions of an image that are usually nothing but black, such as text. Because B has already been applied to the RGB primary color blue, black is represented by its terminal letter, K, and the color model is known as CMYK.

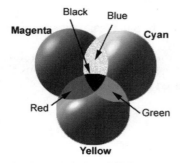

Figure 10.3 A simplified representation of the subtractive color model

Additive Versus Subtractive Color

When you view color images on your CRT during image editing, the colors in the image file are always converted to additive (RGB) colors for display — regardless of the color model used to represent the actual image. However, and this is important, the color model used for the actual file remains the same, unless you change modes and then save the file.

For example, if you load a file that has been saved using the CMYK color model (even though it was produced using RGB, like virtually all scanned images), a program such as Photoshop may let you work on it in CMYK mode, even though the colors must be converted to RGB for viewing.

You may also convert from CMYK to RGB mode, and back again. However, because CMYK can represent some colors that are outside the RGB gamut — and vice versa — you lose some hues each time. You'll usually want to stay with RGB until it's time to convert a file for the printer. Stick with CMYK only if that's the mode to which your file was converted, especially if you will be outputting to a printer or color separation system that expects to work with CMYK colors. That way, you'll avoid creating RGB colors that cannot be reproduced by the CMYK output system.

Other Color Models

Other color models include HSB (hue-saturation-brightness), HLS (hue-lightness-saturation), HSV (hue-saturation-value), and Lab color, which was developed
by the CIE as a device-independent international standard. CIELab colors look exactly the same when output to different, but correctly calibrated, monitors and printers. Some image-editing programs, including Photoshop, support this mode. The CIELab acronym comes from the three channels used to represent all colors in this model. The L* channel refers to luminance, while the a* and b* channels represent the colors from green to magenta and blue to yellow, respectively.

Because all the colors that can be represented in CMYK and RGB color models can be reproduced by CIELab, you can convert from CMYK or RGB to CIELab and then back again without altering any color values. This characteristic makes CiELab a perfect mode to use to perform certain operations that can't be done with one of the alternative models, and Photoshop makes extensive use of this model.

A particularly nice thing about CIELab is that changes in L*, a*, and b* can be related to how much difference people see in the color. That means that when the difference between two colors is measured in CIELab, you have some idea if a person will see the difference.

Color Correction Basics

Even if your scanner does a great job of correcting color automatically, sometimes, however, you won't be 100 percent satisfied with the image. You'll encounter horrid-looking images that are off-color because the originals were off-color. Instead of reproducing them faithfully, you may prefer to adjust or correct them.

Color rendition is the relationship between the colors used to produce your image — most often red, green, and blue. You need to worry only about three different factors: the balance between the colors, how pure or saturated the colors are, and their relative darkness or lightness.

Color balance is the easiest to understand. If you have too much red, an image will appear too red. If you have too much green, it will look too green. Extra blue will make an image look as if it were created under a full moon at midnight at the North Pole. Other color casts are produced by too much of two primary colors, when compared to the remaining hue. That is, too much red and green produces a yellowish cast; red and blue tilt things toward magenta, and blue and green create a cyan bias.

The saturation of each color involves how much of the hue is composed of the pure color itself, and how much is diluted by a neutral color, such as white or black. Think of a can of red paint and white paint. Pure red paint is fully saturated. As you add white paint, the color becomes less saturated until you reach various shades of pink. Color can also become desaturated by adding black paint, making it darker. Your image editor can help you adjust the saturation of a color by removing these neutral white or black components.

You can also adjust hue and saturation in some scanning software. If your scanning software does provide color correction controls, this approach is often the best choice because the scanner has the most information from which to work, and some image editors furnished with scanners, such as Adobe PhotoDeluxe, don't have sophisticated hue/saturation correction tools.

Brightness and contrast refer to the relative lightness/darkness of each color and the number of different tones available. If, say, there are only 12 different red tones in an image, ranging from very light to very dark, with only a few tones in between, then the red portion of the image can be said to have a high contrast. The brightness is determined by whether the available tones are clustered at the denser or lighter areas of the image. Pros use histograms to represent these relationships, but you don't need to bother with those for now.

What Went Wrong?

Why do we even encounter images that need correction in the first place? The major sources of bad color include the following:

- **Incorrect light sources.** Films intended for daylight shooting that were exposed indoors, or special films (usually purchased only by professional photographers) balanced for indoor lighting exposed outdoors will have an imperfect color balance. Fluorescent light sources introduce their own color problems. Sometimes, but not always, this bad color can be corrected at the photofinisher.

- **Incorrect photofinishing.** The equipment used to make prints from color negatives is highly automated, and usually can differentiate between different picture-taking situations. If not, you end up with off-color prints, or those that are too light or dark.

- **Maltreated film.** If you regularly store a camera in the hot glove compartment of your car, or take a year or more to finish a roll of film, expect to end up with prints that are off-color. If your prints have a nasty purple cast or rainbow-hued flares, your negatives probably suffered this indignity. Film damaged in this way often cannot be corrected by scanning and image editing.

- **Mixed light sources.** A picture taken indoors with illumination from both tungsten lamps and window illumination will have shadows and highlights with color casts from the mixed light sources. This problem, too, is difficult to rectify.

- **Faded colors.** Dyes used in color prints and slides will change when exposed to strong light or heat for periods as short as one to five years, or even when kept in a cool, dark place for longer periods (up to 20 years). If you can't make a new print from the original negative, the second-best remedy is to try correcting the image in your image editor.

Easy Color Correction with Image Editors

If you don't correct color using the scanner software (which, as previously mentioned, is often the best choice), most image editors provide as many as six ways to correct color. This section describes the easiest methods of correcting color with an image editor. You can practice them and find which method you're most comfortable with.

Warning

Keep in mind that no color correction method can add detail or color that doesn't exist. All techniques work well with photographs that have too much of one hue or another. The extra color can be removed, or you can beef up the other colors, so they are in balance once again. However, removing one color, or changing some colors to another color doesn't add any color to your image: either way, you're taking color out. So, if you have a photograph that is hopelessly and overpoweringly green, you're out of luck. When you remove all the green, there may be no color left behind. Or, you can add magenta until your subject's face turns blue, and you'll just end up with a darker photo. You must start with a reasonable image; color correction is better suited for fine-tuning than major overhaul.

Image Editor Color Balance Controls

The first way to color-correct an image is using the color balance controls of your image editing program. This method is oriented toward brute force, and may be a little complicated for the beginner. If you're using Photoshop, look under the Image Menu, choose Adjust, and then Color Balance (or just press Ctrl+B if you're in a hurry). The dialog box will look more or less like the one shown in Figure 10.4.

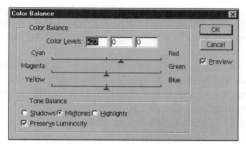

Figure 10.4 A color balancing dialog box

Photoshop lets you set color balance separately for shadows, midtones, and highlights. The color sliders let you adjust the proportions of a particular color, from 0 percent to 100 percent. In the case of Photoshop, you can either add one color, or subtract its two component colors (the colors on either side of it on the color wheel). For example, moving the Cyan/Red slider to +20 (sliding it toward the red end) has the exact same effect as moving the Magenta/Green and Yellow/Red sliders both to the –20 position (toward the left).

Which should you choose? If you want to add pure red (or green or blue), you can move the relevant control to the right. If your needs lean a little more toward one of the component colors than the other, move those sliders to the left instead. To summarize, then, reduce a color cast by:

- Adding the color opposite it on the color wheel
- Subtracting the color itself
- Subtracting equal amounts of the adjacent colors on the color wheel
- Adding equal amounts of the other two colors on its color wheel triangle

If you keep the color wheel in mind, you won't find it difficult to know how to add or subtract one color from an image, whether you are working with RGB or CMY color models.

Tip

The biggest challenge in correcting color may be deciding in exactly which direction you need to add/subtract color. Magenta may look a lot like red, and it's difficult to tell cyan from green. You may need some correction of both red and magenta, or you may be working with a slightly cyanish-green. You may find it easier to use a color ring-around approach, such as Photoshop's Variations mode, described in the following section.

You can also color-correct an image using the Hue/Saturation/Lightness or (Brightness) controls found in most image editors. The advantage of correcting color this way is that you can change the saturation of individual colors or all the colors in an image without modifying the hue or lightness/darkness of those colors. The Color Balance method changes only the relationships between the colors.

The hue/saturation/lightness dialog box of most image editors, like the Hue/Saturation dialog box shown in Figure 10.5, lets you change the richness of the colors in an image without modifying the individual colors, if you prefer. Apply Saturation changes to the main, or Master channel or layer, of an image. You can also increase just one color (say, to make your reds more saturated).

The Hue control allows changing the overall balance of the image (or one individual color layer, if you wish) by rotating the palette one direction or another around the periphery of the color wheel.

Figure 10.5 A hue/saturation/lightness dialog box

Variations

You can play with the color balance of an image for hours at a time, never quite achieving what you want. There's no guarantee that, after a lot of work, you may decide that an earlier version really did look better, after all.

Image editors often have a color ring-around, samples swatches, or variations mode. In this mode, the software itself generates several versions of an image, arranged in a circle or other array so you can view a small copy of each one and compare them. Photoshop's Variations mode is especially useful.

With Photoshop, you can generate a color ring-around by choosing the Image Menu from the main menu bar, selecting Adjust, and then choosing Variations from the submenu. The Variations window is shown in Figure 10.6.

This window has several components. In the upper-left corner, you'll find thumbnail images of your original image paired with a preview with the changes you've made applied. As you apply corrections, the Current Pick thumbnail changes. Immediately underneath is another panel with the current pick surrounded by six different versions, each biased toward a different color: green, yellow, red, magenta, blue, and cyan. These versions show what your current pick would look like with each type of correction added. You can click any of them to apply that correction to the current pick.

To the right of this ring-around is a panel with three sample images: the Current Pick in the center with a lighter version above and a darker version below. In the upper-right corner of this window is a group of controls that modify how the other samples are displayed.

The radio buttons determine whether the correction options are applied to the shadows, midtones, or highlights of the image — or only to saturation characteristics. You must make adjustments for each of these separately.

The Fine/Coarse scale determines the increment used for each of the variations displayed in the two lower panels. If you select a finer increment, the differences between the Current Pick and each of the options will be much smaller. A coarser increment will provide grosser changes with each variation. You may need these to correct an original that is badly off-color. Because fine increments are difficult to detect onscreen, and coarse increments are often too drastic for tight control, keep the pointer in the center of the scale.

The Show Clipping box tells the program to show you in neon colors which areas will be converted to pure white or pure black if you apply a particular adjustment to highlight or shadow areas (midtones aren't clipped).

You may Load or Save the adjustments you've made in a session so they can be applied to the image at any later time. You can use this option to create a file of settings that can be used with several similarly balanced images, thereby correcting all of them efficiently.

While you may most frequently start work only with the midtones, in most cases, the shadows, midtones, and highlights will need roughly the same amount of correction. In other cases, however, the shadows or highlights may have picked up a color cast of their own (say, reflected from an object off-camera). Variations enables you to correct these separately if necessary.

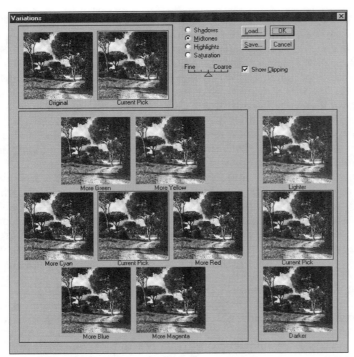

Figure 10.6 Variations-type dialog boxes enable you to pick and choose from various possible corrections.

Optimizing Color for the Web

Correcting color for printing and correcting color for use on a Web page are two different projects entirely. While the former involves producing an image that will look its best on the printed sheet, output in CMYK form, the latter deals with converting your scanned images to a form that will shine on the Web, as an RGB graphic. As you've learned in this chapter, RGB and CMYK are two very different animals.

Web graphics have another complication: some users (fewer all the time, fortunately) cannot view them using a 16-bit or 24-bit color display. So, to be absolutely, positively safe, you'll need to create images that still look best when viewed on an 8-bit, 256-color screen. Because 40 colors are reserved by your Windows or Mac operating systems for display of menus, icons, and so forth, there are actually just 216 colors known as "browser-safe" hues. Luckily, image editors such as PhotoImpact and Photoshop have built-in features to help you convert images to this useful color depth. Figure 10.7 shows one useful tool, which calculates the best color palette for Web display of images. (You can also create Web-optimized colors directly in some scanning software).

Figure 10.7 A Web-oriented color reduction tool

Web-Friendly File Formats

If your experience with images on the World Wide Web has mostly been from the outside looking in, you may be puzzled about which file formats to use for the graphics in your own HTML pages. The picture is not as cloudy as you might think. Two formats, both previously discussed in this book, dominate among current browsers. Here's a recap that will help you choose.

GIF

The Graphics Interchange Format, originally developed for use on the CompuServe Information Network, is a universal graphics format on the Web. All graphics-capable browsers can display GIF images inline with text. The chief advantage of GIF images is that they can be interleaved — alternating lines of the image can be downloaded from your page first, giving the browser a coarse preview of the final image, which then gradually becomes sharper and more detailed as the rest of the GIF data is received. Interleaved GIF images can grab a visitor's eye long enough to lure him or her further into your page.

Of course, the interleaved images are a virtual necessity because GIF files can be relatively large (at least, when compared to JPEG images) and take longer to download. GIFs can also be made transparent; that is, you can select one color to be replaced by the background color seen by the user's browser, so an image can be made to "float" on a page, rather than appear in a solid-color box. As a Web page designer, you will need one of any widely available utilities to create transparent GIFs.

GIF images can have no more than 256 colors, but can use any specialized color sets (or palettes) needed for a particular image. For example, if your image has only 124 unique colors, you can create a GIF with a 124-color palette, resulting in a significant savings in file size.

JPEG

JPEG, developed by the Joint Photographic Experts Group from which it got its name, can squeeze images down to more downloadable sizes. Some image quality may be lost, but the amount of compression and degradation are selectable; the Web builder gets to decide how much sharpness to compromise in the name of speed and viewer friendliness. Usually, when saving a JPEG file, you can select a quality level using a slider.

JPEG encodes files as 24-bit images, so if you have a full-color image that absolutely requires more than 256 colors (and you don't care about visitors who can't handle more hues), this format offers what you need.

The verdict? Consider the following points.

Use GIF When:

- You have an image that already has 256 colors or fewer.

- Your image ends up smaller as a GIF (sometimes the only way to find out which will happen is to save in both GIF and JPEG and compare the file sizes). You'll find that the fewer the colors, the smaller the file. A 16-color GIF can easily be smaller than a JPEG file of the same dimensions, so don't automatically assume you must use a JPEG for the smallest file size.

- You need the sharpest possible image, particularly with a line drawing or map. GIF uses a lossless compression scheme that packs an image down only a little, say, 15 to 20 percent, so the file can be reconstituted perfectly on your visitor's computer.

- You need a transparent or interlaced image.

- You're scanning a photo. (GIF is not usually the best choice for photos.)

Use JPEG When:

- You have an image that demands more than 256 colors.

- Your image is dramatically smaller as a JPEG image. GIF files grow in size as the number of colors increases, while JPEG files always use 24-bit color, and are compressed by discarding some information. Most often, images with many colors are smaller in this format.

- You are working with a photograph that can be compressed using JPEG's lossy compression scheme without much visible deterioration of quality. JPEG is best suited for photographic images rather than line art, for which sharpness is important.

PDF

Adobe's Portable Document Format (PDF) can be used as a Web format when you're presenting documents. PDF preserves the formatting of the document, and PDF files can be viewed directly in a browser that has the Adobe PDF helper file associated with files of that type. HP scanners can produce PDF files directly.

Converting to Browser-Friendly Palettes

This section deals with creating 256 (or fewer) color images, and so, by definition, it applies only to creating GIF files. You may be surprised that many of your color images don't really need 24-bit color. After all, a Web image measuring 64× 64 pixels has only 4,096 different pixels. Even if every one of them were a different color (which is unlikely), you'd need only 4,096 colors to represent that image accurately. In many cases, colors in the 256-hue neighborhood will be quite enough, particularly if you are careful when making the conversion After all, humans can differentiate between only about 250,000 different colors, and a 24-bit image can contain any of more than 16.8 million hues.

A palette is the set of colors used to reproduce an image. You'll want to create an optimized palette that includes only the colors in the image, or colors that are close enough that the image can be represented fairly accurately. In most cases, you don't want an equal representation of all the colors in the spectrum. Think of a portrait of a man wearing a blue suit and a solid red tie. You may need only 10–20 different reds to portray all the subtle shades of red in the tie. Another 40 or so blues may be needed for the suit. Only a few greens, yellows, or other hues would be needed. Or, the bulk of your tones may fall into the pinks or browns that make up flesh tones. By carefully selecting the most frequently used 256 tones in an image, you can often accurately show a 24-bit file using 8-bit color.

The latest versions of scanning software, such as HP PrecisionScan, can create optimized color palettes automatically. Image editors usually offer you a choice of methods in choosing the palette for converting an image to indexed color. Figure 10.8 shows Photoshop's Indexed Color dialog box. The parameters with which you have to work are described in the sections that follow.

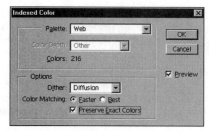

Figure 10.8 Photoshop's Indexed Color dialog box

Warning

Your software may not let you convert from CYMK to Indexed Color. Make sure you are working in RGB mode before trying to convert colors.

Palette

If your image already contains 256 colors or fewer, choose Exact to get a perfect rendition of the image. Otherwise, you'll probably want to select Web and convert the image to a palette using the 216 browser-safe colors.

You can try other choices if you like, but they will probably be less useful to you. An Adaptive palette uses frequently used colors in an image, and produces the best possible image for uses other than Web use, but such images cannot be declared browser-safe. System (Macintosh) or System (Windows) creates a palette that is evenly distributed among all the RGB colors. You probably won't want to use this choice, except for images with an even distribution of color. The Custom choice enables you to load a previously saved palette so you can share color palettes between similar images. Previous applies the last custom palette you used in this session (and is available only if you had used the Custom command earlier).

Color Depth

This is the number of colors in your palette, and is available only if you're converting an image with 256 or more colors. You can select the number of colors you want by choosing the bits per pixel from the drop-down list. If you're converting from a full-color 24-bit image, most often this value will be the maximum — 256 colors — selected by choosing the 8 bits/pixel selection. If your image has 128 colors or fewer, it will use a 7-bit palette; 64 colors or fewer, a 6-bit palette; and so forth. The Other choice allows you to choose an exact number of colors or you can specify fewer than 256. If your image has fewer than 256 colors, you'll be able to convert it precisely, retaining all the colors in the original.

Dither

This parameter tells the software how to simulate colors that don't have a direct equivalent in the palette that is built. Choose None, and the software selects the closest color in the palette for a particular pixel. Pattern uses geometric shapes of colored pixels to simulate colors. You may like the special effects that result, but avoid this choice if you're looking for realistic color. Your best choice is usually Diffusion, which distributes the extra colors randomly and naturally.

Some image editors, such as PhotoImpact, include automated modules that optimize both JPEG and GIF images for you. While these modules take you out of the loop, they can often provide better quality than neophytes can achieve on their own.

Moving On

This chapter provided tips on understanding and correcting color, and preparing color images for display on your monitor, for printing, or for showcasing on the World Wide Web. The next chapter shows you how to select an image editor for making these changes as well as many other enhancements to your pictures.

Image Editing Software

IN THIS CHAPTER • Selecting the right software

• Selecting an image editor

• Full-featured image editors

• Other tools

Scanners and image editing applications such as Adobe Photoshop have brought magic into the realm of any computer user. As recently as 160 years ago — before the invention of photography — seeing was believing. The skills of a magician, artist, or criminal were necessary to falsify what we thought we saw with our eyes.

Photography eventually shattered our trust in visual information. The first moving picture audiences were reported to have fled in terror from black-and-white images of oncoming trains, and to have ducked beneath their seats to avoid silver screen gunfire. Thanks to camera and scanner tricks, airborne hub-caps became flying saucers; movie stars who have never met have been shown in secret rendezvous on the covers of tabloids. National Geographic managed to move the Great Pyramid a few hundred yards to make a better cover illustration.

Things are no longer what they seem. A digital image can be manipulated in ways that are impossible to detect, which is usually for the better when your motives are to improve or enhance a picture rather than simply deceive. As Chapter 10 demonstrates, you can adjust the color of an event so it appears to take place at dusk instead of high noon. You can correct off-color hues to give a bad picture more pleasing colors. You can add or remove a person from a group picture — or you may simply want to remove some dust spots or obscure a dis-tracting background object. Scanner and image-editing magic can improve your pictures or turn them into something entirely different, depending on what you need. This chapter examines some of your options for editing, fine-tuning, and manipulating scanned photographs with image editing software.

Note

Starting with a quality original can minimize the time you spend "fixing" defects in the scanned image. Also, good scanners do many of the manipulations automatically with high-quality results. Processes previously completed in image processing software, such as gamma correction and exposure adjustment, or even color correction, are now done automatically by HP scanners. In higher-end scanners, some of the color changes can be achieved in the scanner at the time of scanning. Most often, you will not need to use an image editor.

Selecting the Right Software

This section will help you choose the right software for image editing. However, most of this chapter will deal with capabilities such as retouching, compositing (combining several images into one), and fine-tuning techniques that work with any software. First, let's review the tools at your disposal.

Selection Tools

The ability to select a portion of a scanned image for manipulation is a key capabil-ity, and most image editing software provides several methods for this process.

Selections enable you to apply changes — such as adding color, moving pixels, or sharpening — to a specific area of an image.

Possible options for selected areas vary by program. Each program allows you to move the selected area to another portion of your image, duplicate the area, and cut an area out of an image entirely. You may also be able to copy the area to a disk file, flip it horizontally or vertically, rotate it, slant it, or elongate it in one direction or another to produce a squashed or stretched image.

Other common functions include applying filters that blur, sharpen, add brush strokes, or perform texturizing effects to an image. You can also modify the color and color balance of a selection, reversing its tones to produce a negative image, or shrink or grow the selected area to make it larger or smaller.

A selection does not have to be one continuous area in your image. You can select one part of an image and then add another section somewhere else in the image to the selection, usually by holding down the Shift key. Here are the key selection tools:

Selection Rectangle/Circle

This type of tool enables you to define a square, rectangular, or oval area of the image for manipulation. You position the mouse at one corner of the area and click, and then drag the outline until you've defined the other boundary. Thereafter, you can carry out various functions on the portion of the image within that area, or invert the selection and make your changes only on the area of the image outside your original selection. Figure 11.1 shows an area selected with the circular selection tool.

Figure 11.1 A circular selection

Lasso

The second way of defining an area is with a tool often called a lasso. This tool lets you create a freehand line to select an irregular area. Most image editors have several variations on the basic lasso. One variation lets you click at points around the boundaries of the area being selected, so you can, with a little care, follow the edges of a portion of an image fairly closely. A more recent innovation is "magnetic" lasso, which examines the contrast between areas of an image and automatically "hugs" the edges of an object as you draw your selection boundary.

Magic Wand

The magic wand tool selects adjacent pixels based on their relative brightness using an adjustable "tolerance" level. For example, if you set the tolerance to a value of 1 and then click on a pixel, the magic wand selects all adjacent pixels with that exact same level of brightness. The selected pixels must touch each other, so if you click on a white area inside a black square, only the white pixels inside the square are selected. White pixels outside the square, being nonadjacent, are not selected.

Increasing the tolerance increases the range of pixels that can be selected. A setting of 32, for example, tells the magic wand to grab pixels either 16 values lighter or darker than the pixel you originally clicked. Variations on the magic wand include tools that select pixels based on color, as well as options to select pixels of a similar brightness range to the selection that exist anywhere in the image. Figure 11.2 shows a magic wand selection.

Figure 11.2 A magic wand can be used to select areas by brightness.

Tip

To expand the magic wand's selection in Photoshop, hold down the Shift key and click elsewhere in the image.

Masking

Because selections can protect (or expose) areas of an image to manipulations, they are sometimes called masks. Image editors may allow you to create selection masks by painting the area you want to select. This function is called Quick Mask in Photoshop. Painted masks are great when you want to define an area or several areas precisely to be selected. The mask color you've painted makes it easy to see exactly which areas will be selected. You can correct the selection by erasing portions of the mask, and blur the edges of the selection by feathering the mask boundaries, much as you would with an airbrush that fades out at its edges.

Selection Shapes

Some image editors have tools that enable you to select an area of a specific shape, such as a 1-pixel-wide (or tall) slice of the image, or a selection in the shape of text that you enter (so you can immediately fill the text-shaped selection or perform other manipulations on it).

Warning

In Photoshop, when you enter text using the Text tool, it is placed in its own layer. When you create a text selection, however, it is placed in the active layer. Keep that in mind before you perform a modification on the text selection that you didn't want to apply it to the current layer.

Vectors to Selections

As you learned in Chapter 2, vector images are composed of lines, rather than pixels. Image editors include a "pen" tool that lets you draw these lines and adjust them smoothly to create complex shapes. You can, for example, create a smooth curve that follows the contour of a portion of your image; with vectors, this process is much easier than trying to paint the curve with pixels. You can also convert these shapes into selections.

Selection Options

Selection tools have a wealth of options that make it easier to define exactly the area you want to select. These options include feathering the edges of a selection so the selected area blends into the surrounding portions of the image, and expanding, contracting, or smoothing a selection. You can also save selections to use them repeatedly. For example, once you've outlined a shape, you can save the selection that defines the shape and load it at any time to manipulate that area.

Painting Tools

Painting tools enable you to add or change the tones of an image, either by adding color or simply by changing the lightness or darkness of an area. We like to group a broad range of tools under the painting category, including pencils, brushes, erasers, and cloning (image area duplicating) tools because they all use a brush-tip metaphor.

Paint tools share other attributes. You can specify the opacity of the tool (using features with names such as opacity, pressure, or something similar), so the paint you apply can be laid down with varying degrees of transparency. Painting tools can be configured to apply only to certain kinds of pixels, such as only those that are lighter or darker than the tone being applied. The chief painting tools you'll need to learn are the following:

- **Pencils/Brushes:** Pencils and brushes can draw hard-edged or soft-edged lines using a tone or color you select. The brush tip can be varied in size from 1 pixel wide to a 64-pixel (or larger) circle, oval, rectangle, or irregular shape. You may even define your own brush tips using patterns, logos, or other shapes. Airbrushes are a specific kind of brush tool that feather the edges of the stroke as the "paint" thins out.

- **Erasers:** Erasers use the same brushes as other painting tools but remove areas of an image rather than add tone to it. Image editors can include specialized erasers, including those that "erase" the current image and restore it to its previous state when you last stored it on your hard disk or took a "snapshot."

- **Toning Tools:** Toning tools go by names such as Dodge, Burn, Lighten, Darken, or Sponge. These tools enable you to use brushes to lighten or darken areas of an image, or to soak up some of the color. Figure 11.3 shows lightening of an image area using the Dodge tool in Photoshop.

- **Rubber Stamp/Cloning Tools:** The rubber stamp/cloning tools are among the most important image editing features you'll need to master. These tools enable you to use brushes of your choice to paint over one area of an image with the image found in another area. So, you can fix up a background marred by dust spots by painting similar areas of the background over the dust spot. Cloning can be used to remove objects from images, duplicate objects from one portion to another area (for example, you can add a window by copying one from another portion of a building). Figure 11.4 shows how an image can be duplicated using the Clone tool in Photoshop.

- **Smudging/Blurring/Sharpening Tools:** These tools enable you to use brushes to smear areas of an image together, blur portions, or sharpen part of an image. Although blurring and sharpening, in particular, can also be done using selections, you'll often find that it's more intuitive to paint the area you want to modify using one of these tools.

Figure 11.3 The Dodge tool lightens a selected image area.

Figure 11.4 You don't need a laboratory to clone sheep.

■ **Paint Bucket:** Although paint bucket tools don't use brushes (they fill a selection), they still belong in the painting tools section of this chapter. In some ways, paint buckets operate like selection tools: they fill only adjacent pixels, using a specified tolerance setting. In most cases, though, you'll want to create a selection before applying paint because it's easy to "overflow" and color areas you don't want to fill. One variation on the paint bucket is the gradient tool, which lets you fill a selection with a continuously varying blend of colors you select.

Tip

All editing packages provide an eyedropper tool that can be used to pick the exact tone with which you want to paint. The eyedropper is an essential tool when working with grayscale and color images that may have 256 or more individual tones that are difficult to differentiate with the eye.

Other Effects

Most of the remaining tools found in an image editor enhance an image, change colors, or add textures or other effects. You can use these effects to enhance images in a variety of ways.

Text Tools

The text tools enable you to add text to scanned images using any of the fonts installed on your computer. You should be aware that once text has been converted to part of your bitmapped image, you can no longer edit it. Nor are you able to enlarge or reduce the text without risking the jaggies that afflict any pixel-based image. Fortunately, image editors generally enable you to keep text in a separate editable layer until you decide to render it as a bitmap. At that point, you can add colors, gradients, textures, and other effects to your bitmapped text.

Color and Brightness/Contrast Controls

As you learned in Chapter 10, "Optimizing Color," all image editors have controls for modifying the amount of particular colors in a picture. Assuming you're working with an RGB image, you can add or remove red, green, or blue, or any of the intermediate colors produced by combining those primaries. Color correction helps you produce a pleasing image or, if you like, one that has strange colors applied as a special effect.

Brightness/contrast controls enable you to modify the relative overall darkness or lightness of an image, or the brightness of certain tones. You can also adjust the number of different tones in an image for contrast. In a high-contrast image, all the shades of light and dark fall at the extremes of the range. In a low-contrast image, the tones are closer together.

Note

Using the controls provided in the HP Precision Scan Pro series of HP scanners, you can adjust the brightness and contrast (highlight and shadow) of the image during the scan. Because of the high-quality image processing in the scanner, and the fact that the scanner works with more data than is usually available in the image editor, you will get a much better result by adjusting in the scanner. These controls are only available in the higher-end scanners — but using scanners to complete this process is much better than doing it in Photoshop.

Filters

Filters are plug-in miniprograms that perform image processing on a selection in your image. Although the current widely used plug-in framework (or architecture) was established by Adobe for Photoshop, you'll find that virtually all image editors for both PCs and Macs are compatible and can use any third-party plug-ins, such as Kai's Power Tools, as well as the plug-ins furnished with the editor.

Filters perform some functions on an image, based on the rules built into the filter and the settings you choose when you apply it. For example, a simple "invert" filter looks at each pixel in an image and changes it to the opposite value, creating a negative image. Other filters may remove pixels entirely (say, to minimize dust spots), move them around (to warp an image), or increase the contrast between pixels (to improve apparent sharpness).

The exact filters found in image editors such as Adobe PhotoDeluxe and Photoshop, PaintShop Pro, Corel Photo-Paint, and Ulead PhotoImpact vary. Third-party filter vendors such as Alien Skin or Andromeda offer even more variations, finer controls, and brand-new effects. Even so, most filters for editing your scanned images fall into one of the following categories. Figure 11.5 shows some typical filter effects.

Figure 11.5 Typical filter effects, clockwise from upper left: Swirl, Diffuse Glow, Find Edges, and Water Color

- **Image enhancement filters.** These filters improve the appearance of your scanned image by sharpening, removing dust or scratches, or even blurring an image (to minimize unsightly grain).

- **Attenuating filters.** These filters act like a piece of glass, fabric, grainy photographic film, or other substance placed on top of your image to add a texture to an image or selection.

- **Pixelation filters.** These filters act like attenuating filters, adding a texture to images. However, they take into account the color, contrast, and other characteristics of the pixels underneath to give an image brushstrokes, pointillistic effects, or other arty transformations.

- **Distortion filters.** These filters move pictures around in your image to create ripples, waves, twirls, spheres, or other effects.

- **Rendering filters.** These filters create, or render, something new in your images: cloud effects, lens flares, wavering flames, drop shadows, or chrome surfaces.

- **Contrast altering filters.** These filters take advantage of the difference in contrast at the boundaries that separate two colors or tones in an image. They increase the brightness of the lighter color and darken the darker color, making the boundary or edge appear more distinct and sharper. You can use these filters to create outlines, embossing, and other interesting effects.

- **Miscellaneous filters.** Many filters don't fit into one of the previous categories. These filters let you explore fractal designs, tile portions of an image in kaleidoscopic ways, perform magic with text, or convert images into animations for the World Wide Web.

Selecting an Image Editor

The process of choosing an image editor to work in tandem with a scanner has changed dramatically over the years. Originally, scanners were furnished only with a stand-alone scanning application, and you were free to use any image editor you liked and could afford. Later, scanners came equipped with a dedicated image editor customized to scan images directly with that vendor's own image-grabber. Most users stuck with that editor for as long as they owned the scanner.

Eventually, the TWAIN interface between scanners and editing software was developed, and all scanners for Windows-based machines were shipped with a TWAIN driver, which had a lot in common with the stand-alone scanning applications of the past. TWAIN drivers can often be used by themselves or from within an image editor like Photoshop. Scanner vendors often supplied a "lite" version of Photoshop or another editor for free with the scanner — you could upgrade to the full version by paying a modest fee. Additional software, such as optical character recognition (OCR) applications and document management tools (such as the PageKeeper software furnished with the newest HP scanners) was also included.

Today, it's not uncommon to unpack the scanner box and find only disks to install the scanner itself and the driver software. Sometimes you're even on your own when it comes to selecting which image editor you'll use. Because good image editors vary in price from hundreds of dollars (for Photoshop) to less than $100, you'll want to make a wise choice. Even if you already own an image editor or one was furnished with your scanner, it's often a good idea to trade up to a new package that has the exact features you need. This section examines some of the most popular products for the Macintosh and PC.

Full-Featured Image Editors

These professional tools come with all the bells and whistles — but not necessarily prices to match. Even though these products can be considered full-featured, all of them lack a few key capabilities so you'll want to look at your needs closely before choosing one. Adobe Photoshop, for example, still does not create graphics for the World Wide Web in an easy manner. Ulead PhotoImpact works only with RGB images. Corel Painter is strongest at adding natural media effects to scanned images or creating paintings from scratch.

Adobe Photoshop

The latest version of Photoshop is full of surprises, ranging from some cool enhancements for which Web developers have been yearning to a whole raft of must-have features that Adobe has long chosen to leave out of its flagship image editor. If you need multiple levels of undo, more control over type, automated tools for creating beveled buttons or drop shadows, and faster ways to select complex shapes, Photoshop delivers the goods. Creating Web graphics has become easier since Adobe folded the features of its stand-alone product, ImageReady, into Photoshop.

Photoshop will appeal to several groups of users. If you make your living as a graphics professional, you must become adept at Photoshop. There is no alternative to this worldwide standard — Photoshop skills should be on the resume of anyone doing serious image editing.

However, even if you're self-employed and can use any image editor, Photoshop may be your first choice. Anyone who needs a great deal of control over color corrections will find Photoshop the best tool for the job. Photoshop can do just about anything to an image, but other image editors have automated some tasks, made them easier to perform, or provide extra options.

With versions 5.0 and later, Photoshop joined the rest of the industry with improved support for multiple levels of undo/redo. A History palette records the state of an image through the 20 most recent editing changes. Photoshop workers who constantly save multiple versions of a project-in-progress will love this feature. However, the History palette won't replace taking periodic snapshots (saved versions of an image): If the changes are coming fast and furious, you'll find that 20 steps aren't enough. If you close Photoshop, however, the History list is discarded. The program also includes a cool History Brush tool, which makes it easy to "paint" an earlier version of an image onto alterations in the History palette.

Anyone who creates lots of graphical type will appreciate Photoshop's more powerful Type tool, which offers capabilities that, in the past, required using Extensis's PhotoText add-on. Now, Photoshop can incorporate text with complete freedom to flow text, format character by character, and adjust size, kerning, or tracking. Four separate type tools are available from a single fly-out Toolbox: two each for creating type in horizontal and vertical orientations onto layers or as selections in the current layer. You may return and change the text at any time until the type layer is "rendered" or flattened, so a simple typo won't require painful hours to fix.

Although you'll still want third-party add-ons such as Alien Skin's Eye Candy or Ulead's Web.Plugins for the most flexibility in creating buttons and similar objects, Photoshop's Layer Effects menu has five dialog boxes for creating drop shadows, glows, bevels, and embossing effects. Because the special effects are created on layers of their own, you can hide them at any time if you want to compare or contrast different looks. Adobe's rivals also don't have the following feature: If you change the shape of an object, the effects edit themselves to match the layer to which they're attached. Photoshop's drop shadow effect is shown in Figure 11.6.

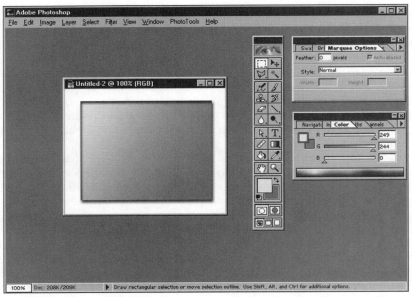

Figure 11.6 Automatic drop shadows are only one of Photoshop's new features.

Adobe has cleaned up Photoshop's interface significantly, combining similar tools and relocating some menu items to more logical positions. Other useful tools include the "magnetic" selection lasso, which clings to the edges of any object with sufficiently high contrast with its background; an Eyedropper that can create a color from up to four user-defined samples; and a Ruler tool that shows the length and angle of a line drawn with it. If you need to separate complex objects from a background, the Extract command can help you delineate the edges of portions of your subject matter using a paintbrush.

Available in Windows, Mac OS, and UNIX versions, the program operates identically on all platforms (with a few minor exceptions).

Warning

Photoshop has the most tools but, as is often the case with this type of full-featured product, expect to spend some time learning how to use it. Working through the tutorials is a good idea, especially to learn the new Web graphics-oriented tools.

PhotoImpact

With PhotoImpact, Ulead Systems has stopped chasing Adobe Photoshop and now is making a run at the real graphics growth segment: Web developers. This image editor and its suite of utilities escorts you from brewing attractive backgrounds and buttons through optimizing JPEGs to an FTP Web publishing tool. Whether you need flaming text or a Web-based slide show, this program has an answer.

The latest version has an even stronger list of Web-oriented features, ranging from a Java Rollover Assistant for creating interactive buttons, to "image slicing," which lets you cut up images and optimize each part for best display on the Web.

PhotoImpact can easily create image maps from selections, collect all the images on your site (or referenced by a URL) into a browsable album, and add sophisticated frame transition effects to turn your video files into eye-catching animated GIFs. Despite its low cost, Ulead's pixel-pusher is geared for high-volume Web production environments.

PhotoImpact consists of an image editor with most of its Web tools built in, as well as a selection of stand-alone utilities such as PhotoImpact Album and GIF Animator. The image editor is an impressive piece of work on its own, combining some of the natural-media features in Corel Painter with Adobe Photoshop's image optimization capabilities. Some features, such as the filter plug-ins — which offer you a choice of nine variation previews on a theme using the selected plug-in, or a pair of side-by-side before and after looks — are the easiest and fastest I've ever used.

The editor's automation tools make processing a large number of images a breeze. For example, this edition allows you to record macros (like Photoshop's Actions) for recycling repetitive tasks, such as reducing a full-color image to a browser-safe palette of 216 hues or adding edge or frame effects. Batch processing can apply one of these user-editable procedures to a whole folder of files consecutively. You may also walk through the macro one step at a time when an image requires some specially tailored attention. Automated tools such as the Post-Processing Wizard help correct images grabbed from a scanner or digital camera. An improved version of Ulead's SmartSaver makes it easy to preview before/after images in GIF, JPEG, and PNG formats to select palette, compression ratio, and transparency options.

Even advanced users will need time to absorb PhotoImpact's rich Web feature set (most of which are available from an integrated Web menu). For example, the Button Designer can create push buttons from any shape; allows the specification of light source angle and elevation, bevel size, and smoothness; and controls whether the button should appear raised or depressed on your page. The Frame & Shadow Designer offers five different styles (such as 2D, 3D, or photographic edges), as well as drop shadows with full control over offset and transparency of the shadow. PhotoImpact's Buttonizer is shown in Figure 11.7.

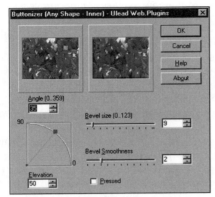

Figure 11.7 PhotoImpact's Buttonizer is a valuable tool for creating Web page buttons.

A smooth-working Background Designer pops up with a dozen low-contrast palettes, a dozen and a half customizable textures, and user-editable gradient ramps for those times when you need to blend a specific set of colors into your background. You may also create seamlessly tiling background patterns from any rectangular selection. Artistic texture and particle filter options create effects such as rain, snow, or bubbles.

To create an image map, just outline the rectangular, oval, or irregular polygon shape you want to use to define a region in the map; then select the Image Map Tag menu item and select either client-side, NCSA, or CERN image map formats. An integrated HTML Assistant generates the code required to display the current image (or any other image from your hard drive) on your Web page using parameters selected from tabbed dialog boxes. Both tools produce error-free tag strings, which you can copy to the Clipboard and paste into your HTML editor.

The separate GIF Animator program is a miniature video-editing studio, with cool touches such as peeling-page, clock-sweep, and other transitions in addition to the traditional wipes and slides between "scenes." Move frames around to your heart's content, and then preview the minimovie within the utility or your favorite browser before exporting to standard animated GIF format. The program also accommodates QuickTime, FLI/FLC, and AVI files to recycle existing video clips and animations.

Ulead has given its venerable Album application an Internet-friendly twist, allowing cataloguing and managing local images as well as those stored remotely through a "URL-aware" filing scheme. Users with full-time Internet connections can even create Web slide shows that page through images on multiple sites. Anyone who has tried to maintain hundreds of different albums with earlier versions of this product will appreciate the ability to grab albums from a scrollable toolbar at the side of the application window. Another toolbar can be outfitted with your favorite software (from Microsoft Word to your fax utility) so you can drag and drop images between OLE-compliant applications.

Paint Shop Pro

Paint Shop Pro wasn't called the Photoshop of shareware for nothing. However, it's long since outgrown its shareware origins and is now dressed up as a slick commercial package you can buy off the shelf in most computer stores, or download from the Jasc Software Web site (http://www.jasc.com). The latest version lets you design animations with Animation Shop 2, included free. You'll also find layers, multiple levels of Undo (which Photoshop lacked until Version 5), and compatibility with almost dozens of different file formats, including Adobe's native PSD.

Professional artists will appreciate the program's support for pressure-sensitive tablets and the sophisticated color-optimization capabilities. If you're in a hurry to grab your Web graphics and run, Paint Shop has TWAIN support for popular scanners and digital cameras. Plenty of support is also available from Jasc, third-party books, and dozens of Web sites with Paint Shop tips and tutorials. Whether you are an individual user or choose software for a large organization and need an economical way to provide designers with a powerful image editing program, Paint Shop Pro has the credentials.

Corel Photo-Paint

With the introduction in late 1998 of Corel Photo-Paint for the Macintosh and in 2000 a version for Linux, Corel joined an exclusive club of high-end image editors (including Photoshop and Painter) available for both Windows and Mac machines, and is one of two available for both Windows and Linux (the other being GIMP (the GNU Image Manipulation Program). Figure 11.8 shows Corel Photo-Paint in its Macintosh incarnation.

Using a system of menus and dialog box roll-ups similar to Corel Draw, Photo-Paint is notable chiefly for its (relatively) smooth integration with other applications in the Corel suite, plus some interesting image-processing filters. These filters include most of the effects in Photoshop, plus seven different artistic filters such as Smoked Glass, Terrazzo, and Paint Alchemy, a natural-media brush add-on.

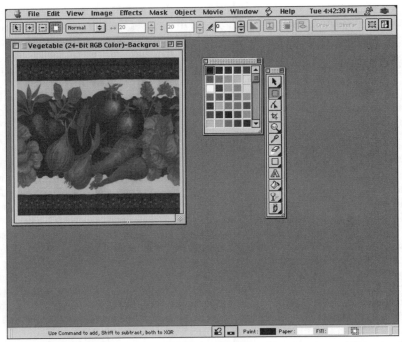

Figure 11.8 Photo-Paint is available in Windows, Macintosh, and Linux versions.

Corel Painter

Why does Corel need a second image editing program? That's simple: There's nothing quite like Corel Painter (née Fractal Design Painter and then MetaCreations Painter), which has always marched down its own path, specializing in an incredible selection of natural-media tools — from paint brushes to pencils, crayons, chalks, charcoals, and imaginative canvases or textured papers. All these tools are customizable in an infinite number of ways, using an often bewildering selection of dozens of toolbars, palettes, and dialog boxes.

Painter was created as a way to give traditional artists the tools they needed to "paint" images much as they did in the real world. However, other users soon discovered that Painter could perform amazing transformations of scanned images and was a powerful way to turn a mundane picture into a prize winner. Today, serious graphics professionals often own both Photoshop and Painter. If you must choose one, examine the capabilities of each before making your selection. While Painter matches much of Photoshop's functionality (it is now compatible with Photoshop 5's layers feature), there are some things, such as color correction, in which Photoshop is superior. However, Photoshop can't touch Painter's natural-media and Web-oriented tools.

The latest version of Painter has a built-in facility for creating seamless tiled backgrounds for Web pages, more flexible text creation features, and the capability to "slice" large images into smaller modules that are faster to download. Once an image has been sliced, Painter creates the Web page instructions needed to reconstruct it in the visitor's browser after all the pieces have been downloaded. Painter also includes "Web-safe" tools that use only colors that can be displayed easily by all browsers, regardless of the color depth set on their video cards. Figure 11.9 displays some of Painter's capabilities.

Figure 11.9 Corel Painter has a broad range of natural-media tools.

Other Tools

Simplified image editors make it easy for neophytes to correct their images with a minimum of fuss. This section concentrates on more traditional image editing applications, and includes a description of the must-have image editing add-on, Kai's Power Tools.

Adobe PhotoDeluxe

If "Photoshop guru" is not in your job description, PhotoDeluxe is the Adobe product you can use for fast, simplified image processing of scanned images. Its paint-by-numbers tabbed instruction sheets are as easy to follow as a wizard and lead you through every step in the most common image-tweaking processes.

You can also work on your own using large icon-festooned buttons that lead you through resizing, trimming, distorting, and other functions. Choose Touch Up photo, for example, and a tab appears with Size/Orientation, Quality, and Red

Eye buttons. Behind each of these buttons is a series of tabbed steps you follow in order to complete the operation. The Transform Photo tab has procedures for distorting, adding motion blur, creating interesting text, building collages, or using one of the included special effects filters.

Beginners will love the simple operation until the hand-holding reaches frustrating levels. You cannot, for example, exit a process without clicking on the Done button. Even so, even imaging tyros will quickly learn how to improve photos destined for Web pages, and perhaps even build a few buttons, arrows, or other page artifacts using PhotoDeluxe's surprisingly ample toolkits. When you're ready to fly solo, you'll find facilities such as layers, precision cursors, scratch disks, and even a full panoply of traditional menus with more than a passing resemblance to their Photoshop counterparts. In fact, if you click one of PhotoDeluxe's giant buttons or oddly placed menu choices, a Photoshop-style dialog box is likely to appear.

Saving options are limited (actually, you must Export images to convert them to a Web-compatible JPG and interlaced or transparent GIF format). JPG files, for example, can be stored only in Low, Medium, High, or Maximum quality formats (which are inversely proportionate to the amount of compression each produces).

Veterans of image editing will find PhotoDeluxe slows them down, but if you want an easy entry into creating simple Web graphics or retouching scanned photos, digital camera shots, or pictures on photo CDs, this program is a painless way to get started.

Note

PhotoDeluxe comes in various flavors, such as PhotoDeluxe Home edition and PhotoDeluxe Business edition. Automated tasks and templates are tailored for the home or business, respectively, in the different versions. For instance, PhotoDeluxe Home edition includes automated tasks to make cards, decorations, and so forth. PhotoDeluxe Business edition focuses on business graphics.

Microsoft Picture-It!

Microsoft Picture-It! (exclamation point is Microsoft's, not mine) is a bargain image editor that beginners can use to get comfortable with modifying scanned pictures before moving on to more fully featured products. Available as a standalone application, Picture-It! is also part of the Microsoft Works Deluxe Suite.

This easy-to-use program (shown in Figure 11.10) automates many fix-up tasks, such as removing red-eye effects (caused by reflection of a flash off the subject's retina), removal of dust and scratches, or erasing distracting objects using cloning tools. You can revamp old photos with new looks using painting, distorting, and other capabilities. Built-in wizards lead you through most tasks, including capturing photos from scanners.

You can crop, rotate, zoom, or flip your images, and combine several photos into a collage. Refine the brightness/contrast and color balance, remove wrinkles, or rotate your images. Picture-It! has many more capabilities than you'd expect from an application that is inexpensive and easy to use. If you're just beginning to edit images, you may want to start here.

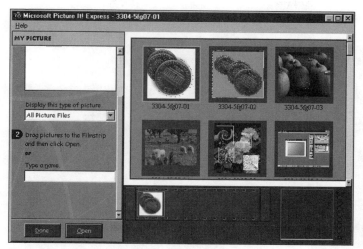

Figure 11.10 Microsoft Picture-It! simplifies correcting a scanned image.

Kai's Power Tools

Now you can choose from three versions of the most successful third-party Photoshop add-in package: the latest Kai's Power Tools 6, or Kai's Power Tools 5, each of which offers a rich selection of new image-twisting tools with little, if any, overlap with Version 3 (the software skipped Version 4), which is still available. If none of these pixel movers can transmogrify your image in ways that will wow your friends and colleagues, it can't be done.

KPT 6 includes 10 plug-ins, from KPT Goo (for finger-painting your images), through KPT Gel (for realistic 3D painting of textures), and KPT LensFlare (for generating your own glows), and KPT SceneBuilder (for generating complete 3D scenes). All-different KPT 5 includes a wonderful selection of imaginative filters, such as Blurrr, which adds spiral, zoom, and weave blurs as well as other effects to your repertoire. Noize adds clouds, nebulae, and other interesting textures. There's a radical warping filter, several options for playing with fractal designs, and the Orb-It tool, which has more options and hundreds more effects than you can achieve with KPT 3's Spheroid Designer. The ShapeShifter filter is a must for anyone who needs to create beveled images with realistic 3D textures. As with previous versions of KPT, this update includes a vast number of preset effects you can apply, and provisions to save your own custom settings for reuse. If none of these have what you need, the previous KPT 3 is included on the KPT 5 and KPT 6 CD. Figure 11.11 shows an example tool found in the KPT 5 toolkit.

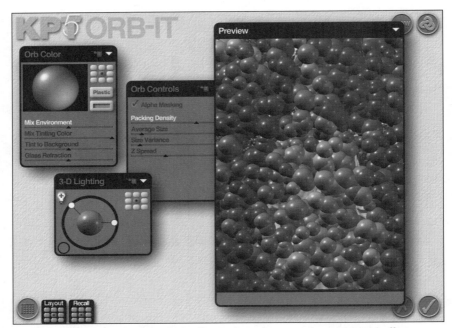

Figure 11.11 Kai's Power Tools 5 offers a broad range of new special effects.

KPT 3 includes modules that intelligently sharpen and blur images, suck images into wild vortexes, or add an infinite variety of textures and shapes. If you're looking for interesting buttons, KPT 3 has a Spheroid designer that enables you to position several lights, adjust the spherocity and transparency of an image, and liven things up with bump maps.

There's also a gradient designer for creating blends that will look good even at GIF's 256 colors or sensational as JPGs, and a texture explorer that can come in handy for building unique backgrounds for your pages. While the Version 3 interface isn't as slick as the upgrade in Version 5, it retains the old, quirky Kai flair and adds larger previews, controls and parameters for previously single-step filters such as Vortex Tiling, and easier-to-navigate dialog boxes for filters that had only difficult-to-remember keyboard options. There's even Help available, along with new Planar Tiling, Twirl, and Video Feedback effects. Older tools such as Gradient Designer and Texture Explorer have refinements such as hue, saturation, brightness, contrast, and blur tweaking.

Look to Kai's Power Tools when you want otherworldly images that will add a unique touch to your graphics. Both KPT 3 and KPT 5 have tools that can turn even the most mundane image into something special. The KPT Fractal Designer, for example, produces effects like those shown in Figure 11.12.

Figure 11.12 Create great fractal effects with KPT 3.

Moving On

This concludes the technoid portion of our program. You learned about different image editing options in this chapter, including Adobe Photoshop and other high-end editors as well as simplified image editors and add-on tools such as Kai's Power Tools. In Part II, you'll move right into creating imaginative projects using the scanning techniques described in the first part of the book.

 # Scanner Projects

Getting Started with Scanner Projects

IN THIS CHAPTER
- Creating name and picture ID tags
- Cataloguing images
- Keeping your images safe

Scanners reveal a world of possibilities. This chapter begins with a simple project to get you on the path to creativity. Then we will talk about how to organize yourself for the parade of information, images, ideas, and projects that will be at your disposal. Half the fun is learning how to use your scanner; the other half is making the actual projects.

Of course, the first thing you will want to do is simply scan something and print it out. Try it! Then come back here and check out a few simple projects, such as making a doorknob hanger or a name tag for a party.

Next, get your images and materials arranged. Imagine that you need to track down a particular family snapshot — where would you look? This problem is intensified with computer images because formats and archive techniques affect where and how you find the picture you want. How do you cope with all these variables?

The answers are in this chapter. Read on.

Name and Picture ID Tags

Been to a reunion lately? Inevitably, they scan your high school picture out of the yearbook and pop it onto a name tag, button, or other form of identification. This project shows you how to accomplish this simple task. Starting with a black-and-white photo, you can turn the scanned image into a name tag with text that can be used for reunions, company meetings, or other events where there are lots of newcomers. Scan in a photograph of each person, clearing out the background (if necessary), add their name and a short one-line title or description, and then arrange them to print on name tags. Trim and slide the name tag into a plastic holder and away you go!

Look for prescored name tag kits at your local office supply dealer. These come with several name tags laid out on one 8½×11-inch sheet of firm index-weight paper. You may also be able to find kits with the plastic covers included in the package. If not, look for the plastic covers in an office supply store. They generally come in packs of 50 to 100 with the pin-on sections already attached. If you can't find any of these, you can make your own. After you have printed a page of name cards, trim them into individual pieces. Take them to your local copy shop and have them laminated. Check the minimum size for laminating. Buy small pin-backs and attach each one with tape or glue to the back of each name tag.

You will need to scan in the pictures and edit them as necessary. These techniques are described in the project instructions that follow.

MATERIALS

Photographs of people

Image editing software

Draw program or page layout program

Tag board or name tag layout paper

Scissors or utility knife

Plastic covers for name tags

Preparing the Photographic Images

1. Scan the first picture at a resolution appropriate for final printing on high-quality paper.

Cross-Reference

See Chapter 4, "Resolution, Interpolation, and Sharp Images," and Chapter 10, "Optimizing Color," for more information on the technical aspects of scanning.

2. Use your software tools to erase all of the background and any objects that obscure the face. If the photograph color seems flat or dull, spice it up using the contrast and brightness controls on your scanner. See Figure 12.1 for an example.

   If your image is fuzzy, try the Sharpen filter of your image editing software (if available).

Figure 12.1 Using software tools to clean up the image

3. Resize the image so it will fit your name tag. Prescored name tags are generally 3½ by 2¼ inches, so size your image to fit an approximately 1¾ × 2-inch window. Save this image in the format and at the resolution best suited to your printer specifications.

4. Save this image and name it with the person's last name.

5. Continue to scan and save one photograph per person, naming each file with the appropriate person's name.

Positioning Your Images

6. Calculate how many pages you will need. If you can place eight name tags on one page, divide the total number of photos you need by eight. You will need this number of pages to accommodate all of your pictures.

7. Open a blank page in your draw or page layout software. Make sure that your paper or canvas size is set to 8½ by 11 inches. Your page will be laid out in this way: two images wide and four images high. See Figure 12.2 for page layouts for both four-up and eight-up masters.

Figure 12.2 Page layouts

8. Save this blank page, calling it "Page 1." Using your Save As command, save it again, calling it "Page 2." Continue this process until you have as many pages saved as you calculated you needed in Step 6.

9. Open the blank "Page 1" and the first photograph. Copy and paste the photo in the upper-left corner. Check the positioning against your actual name tag paper output.

Tip

To check positioning, print a sample of your image at a low resolution. Place it on top of a piece of your cardstock or name tag paper and hold both up to the light. Take accurate measurements to reposition your image in the correct spot. Better to double-check than to waste your special paper and additional ink.

10. Open the next photo. Copy and paste it in the upper-right corner, referring back to Figure 12.2. Continue to open the remaining images and position them accurately.

Adding the Text

11. Type the name of the first person and a one-line description or title. In our example, we used the office the person held, but you can also use a description that recalls the person's "best remembered for" deeds. We positioned the "62" numerals first, then placed the person's name over them in dark blue text. If you like, move the text so that a bit of the person's picture overlaps the text. This approach connects the picture and the text visually. Figure 12.3 shows our final layout.

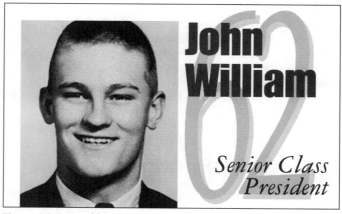

Figure 12.3 Final layout

Tip

Experiment with all those great fonts you may have on your computer. Because letters need to be legible from about four feet away, use type sizes over 18 points.

12. Remember to save often! Complete the name tags for this page and move on to the next.

Tip

You could also lay out one page with the first eight images on it, save it as "Page 1," save it again as "Page 2" using your Save As command, replace the images one by one, and then save again. Decide which method suits your style of working.

Printing and Assembling Your Name Tags

13. Print the first page on your highest-quality paper and at the highest resolution your printer supports. If your paper is scored for name tags, fold along the score lines before tearing. If you are using your own cardstock, mark your trim lines in the margins of each page and use a utility knife to trim the images.

14. Slide each name tag into its protective plastic holder. You are ready to hand these out!

Tip

For additional fun, find colored stickers or small metal ornaments to stick on your name tags. How about the self-stick small embroidered flowers and other motifs you can find in a fabric shop? Try apples for the teachers and stars for the football team.

Creativity

Here are some other ways you can use this technique. Try putting two pictures together — "then and now" or spouse with alumnus. When you scan your pictures, experiment with some of the special effects to alter the background or the apparel of the person. Select an area and reverse the colors of the person's garments. If your photos are really old and in black and white, use your image editing software to "colorize" them. Start working on the clothing to test your special effects. Then try your hand at editing facial features or hair color.

Managing All Those Images

Now that you've tried a simple project, you've probably noticed that scanning can be an addictive habit. Every time you scan something, you want to keep it forever, just in case! Here we offer some guidelines on when and why to keep, throw away, save, catalog, and index your images.

The first set of questions revolves around what to keep and what to toss. Then you need to get creative about storage — both hard copy and electronic. We discuss managing huge files, keeping backups, and other considerations. We also give you a practical way to keep track of everything. We include a couple of quick projects that not only exercise your scanner skills, but also give you a nice finished product to show off your newly acquired knowledge.

Start early with good habits and your computer will thank you!

Decisions, Decisions

You could fill up all the hard drives on the planet if you kept every scan you made. Luckily, most scanning software has a "preview" mode to cut out some of the initial work involved in getting a good scan. Take advantage of this capability and learn how to use your scanner software to make the best scan the first time.

Cross-Reference

See Chapter 4, "Resolution, Interpolation, and Sharp Images," for more information on the technical aspects of scanning.

Once you have what seems to be a reasonably clear image, save it. Create a file-naming convention that works well for you. Your computer will keep track of the file extension or type and the creation and modification dates, so all you need is a few words to remind you of the image. Remember that your file manager lists filenames alphabetically — use this to your advantage. Our recommendation is to start the filename with the largest or most significant description of the image. For example, if you are scanning family pictures, use the last name of the family as the first word, and then the person's first name, and then a word that describes the setting. In this manner, your computer naturally groups the photos together. See Figure 12.4 for an example of an organized naming scheme.

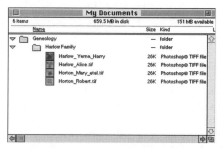

Figure 12.4 A naming scheme for your files

Version Madness

As you work, you create variations of your original image. Save these with successive numbers in the title. If you called the original image "Canada Mountains01", you would call the second version in which made changes "Canada Mountains02". Remember to call the second image "02" instead of "01."

The next step is organizing where your images are stored. This is important for two reasons: finding them again and archiving for security and backup. Create a folder called "My Documents" and save everything in this main folder. You can then break it down into subfolders if you have separate projects. When you create a new image in some software, the default "Save to" location may be the folder in which the application resides. Take the extra second or two to locate the storage spot you really want. Refer to Figure 12.5 for an example of folder organization.

The big issue is when to toss things. The same standards apply here as apply to your closet, painful as that may seem. If you haven't used it in a year, there is no point in keeping it in the most active part of your hard drive. Archive it off to auxiliary storage and consider compressing it to save even more room. Once a year, go through these old archives and erase anything that you can either easily replicate (from an original source such as a photograph) or have no more need for.

The temptations abound to save the scans of every really cool texture you make. You will soon find that the image you need for a particular project is always a little different from what you've got, so off you go again to make a new scan. Save only the most brilliant and the hardest to re-create images.

Another tip: make sure you group together all of the scans that are used in a composite image. For example, if you have scanned five photos for a family tree and have used Adobe Illustrator (prior to Release 7) to lay out the page, make a separate folder for the family tree and the five photos. Illustrator software doesn't actually keep a copy of each of those family photos in the layout. It simply has a placeholder that tells the computer to look for each photo wherever you told your computer you had stored the image. Put all of these images into one folder and you will save time and aggravation when using this type of software.

Cross-Reference

See the upcoming section entitled "The Family Attic — Keeping It Safe" for more information on keeping family heirlooms.

If you have all your images in one folder, backup is simple. Most backup software enables you to select which specific file it copies so you can tell it to back up only the "My Documents" file. Some software also lets you set parameters on when to back up your work. If your images are crucial, back up daily. If the data is easily replaced, backing up weekly should suffice.

Size Matters

The following is an exercise to demonstrate sizing considerations graphically. Scan a photograph at multiple resolutions and save these to your hard drive. After viewing them, print out the different options and keep them for inclusion in your Scanner Control Book described later in this chapter. Compare the quality of the image with the size of the file. You will soon begin to see where your natural trade-off point is, since larger files take more storage and open slower than smaller files. Have some fun with this by selecting a picture that you like and can play around with.

Scanner Resolution Sample Sheets

In this exercise, you will create several sample sheets — scanning an image and manipulating its size and print characteristics. Save, print, and study the results closely.

1. Select a photograph that has some significant detail — a landscape is a good choice. Scan it at five different resolutions: 10 dpi, 50 dpi, 100 dpi, 150 dpi, and 200 dpi.

2. Open each picture to see how it looks onscreen. With all five images open, compare the clarity of the image and your ability to discern subtle color changes and small details, such as tree limbs or other fine characteristics. Remember to compare all of the images at the same size relative to each other.

3. Print a copy of each picture. Remember to print all five images at the same size relative to each other. You may want to include some text explanation. Note the scan resolution. Make a note of your observations about which image looked best on your screen. (See Figure 12-5 for an example.) For your files you may want to add the title of the saved image so you can refer back to it as necessary.

4. Keep these sheets — we will include them in the upcoming "Scanner Control Book" section.

The 10-dpi scanned image can actually be used for fun effects. See the project "Scan an Autumn Leaf and Make a Work of Art" in Chapter 15 for more ideas. While you're at it, take the time to test some of the image editing software filters and features — see your software reference manual for information. IDG Books Worldwide publishes several books on these topics.

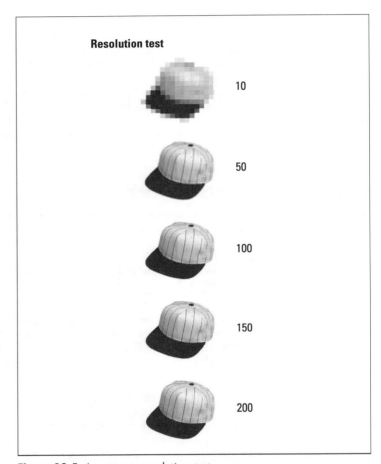

Figure 12.5 A scanner resolution test

Now, Where Did I See That Great Picture of Paris?

When you buy software programs, they frequently include copyright-free images that have already been scanned. Most of these are fairly generic and reside on the CD-ROM that comes with the program. Additionally, there are other sources of clip art images that you can use for special projects.

Cross-Reference

See the appendix, "Resource Kit," for additional sources of digital images and image editing tools.

The trick is in remembering what you have out there. Readers and image library products are often included on these CD-ROMs, and you can use them to preview the contents. When you go looking for an image, though, it is inconvenient to swap CD-ROMs in and out. You may also wind up with several types of image readers open on your desktop. Our solution to this problem: print "thumbnails" of the images.

Thumbnail Image Sheets

In this project, you open several software image libraries and begin to build thumbnail layouts for later reference. This process may seem time-consuming, but it saves future time and frustration.

1. Open your image editing program. Title the entire page with the name of the CD-ROM from which these images are taken.

2. Open an image library on your CD-ROM.

3. Begin by opening the first image. Copy and paste it onto a blank page in your image editing program. Resize the image so that the horizontal dimension is 2 inches. The vertical dimension will vary, depending on whether your image is a rectangle or a square.

4. Add text to describe the image title, the file size, and the file format.

5. Fill the page by continuing to cut and paste images and by adding descriptive information. (See our example in Figure 12.6.) About eight images per page are sufficient.

6. Print each page and see the following "Command Central" section for ideas on how to combine these scans into a complete Scanner Control Book.

Figure 12.6 Adding images to the page

Cataloguing Your Own Collection

Images you scan yourself also need to be catalogued in a similar manner. Many image editing programs will have small preview windows that you can use to pick out the exact image you want, but with some forethought, you can make this cumbersome process a little easier. Begin by using the software's own built-in cataloguing help. See Figure 12.7 for a screenshot of the Photoshop information page. You can use this page to store specifics about the image.

You need to catalog the following characteristics:

- Format
- File size
- Name
- Date
- Description and copyright information

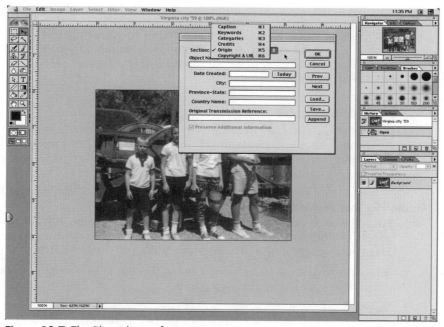

Figure 12.7 The Photoshop information page

See the preceding project, "Thumbnail Image Sheets." Follow these instructions to prepare printouts of all of your own images.

Command Central

Protecting your own images is important. If you are using these scans for personal use, the issue is of less significance but should still be understood. If you plan to make professional use of the scans, you will need to consider two major topics:

- Watermarking or other forms of digital protection
- Copyrighting your image

For more information on copyrighting, turn to either the U.S. Copyright site at `http://lcweb.loc.gov/copyright/`. A Stanford University site, `http://fairuse.stanford.edu/`, also has good information. *Digital watermarking* is the process of electronically encoding information in a file so that it displays the equivalent of a "watermark" as seen in traditional papermaking processes. It is indelible and unique. This means that your creation is protected to a certain degree: No one can use the file without gaining authorization. A great digital watermarking site is located at `http://www.zdwebopedia.com/TERM/d/digital_watermark.html` and would be a good starting point.

Scanner Control Book

In this project, you will make a cool binder that you can use as a reference tool for your scanner. First you create the information you want to keep; you then assemble a multisectioned reference work that shows off your skills and keeps you in control.

Gathering Your Materials

1. From the preceding thumbnail project, gather your hard copy image sheets — both the ones you scanned and the ones from other sources. Make sure everything is printed on your highest quality paper.

2. Add your resolution exercise examples. Make sure these examples are printed on your highest quality paper.

3. Make a color swatch reference by creating 2-inch square grids of each major color in your image editing software palette. (See Figure 12.8 for our sample.) Add text and the RGB or CMYK formulas. Print these on your highest resolution paper.

4. Test several versions of an image with various color correction techniques applied. Add text to remind yourself of what steps you took and what filters or other special effects you applied to the image.

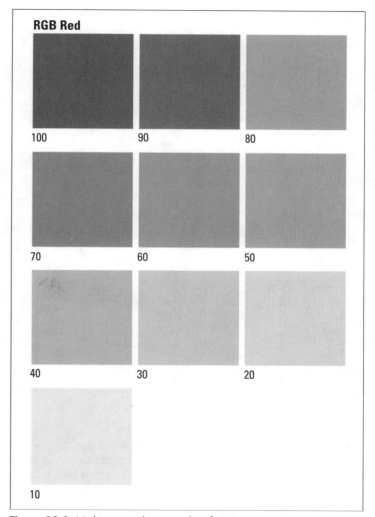

Figure 12.8 Making a color swatch reference

Making It All into One Binder

Now you can assemble all these materials into one three-ring binder. If you bought a binder with a see-through plastic insert cover, make a collage of your images or use one big image. You can also cut a strip to insert in the spine. Use dividers to separate the sections and top-loading page inserts to keep your work clean and neat. You can have fun with this process by decorating, using wild fonts, and adjusting your images with the color correction tools. This is a great place to try some new special effects — things for which you may never have another use.

1. Make a cover, back, and spine page for your binder. See Figure 12.9 for our examples.

Figure 12.9 The Cover, back, and spine for our binder

2. Print these pages on your highest-quality paper and cut the spine section using a paper cutter, scissors, or a utility knife. For a 2-inch-thick binder, the dimensions of the spine piece are 1¾ inches by 11 inches.

3. Slide these pieces into your binder cover.

4. Prepare the tab sections: Scanner Info, Resolution, Color Swatches, Samples, and so forth. Select the topics that best describe the materials you want to keep.

5. Load the sheets, two to a protector. Sort these protectors and file them under the proper tab in your binder.

6. As you gain more expertise and see examples or articles that you want to keep, add these to your binder. As you add technology or change or upgrade your equipment, be sure to experiment with your new configuration and add these examples to your binder. With this sort of reference you can be more efficient when starting new projects.

Creativity

Make each page a work of art by exercising your library of images, your image editing software, and your scanner. Check out the appendix for great reference works and sources for additional information.

The Family Attic — Keeping It Safe

Every family has a wealth of treasures that the whole clan would like to savor, be they photographs, wedding gowns, christening garments, or wedding rings. This section deals with ways to preserve an image of your heirloom so that you can store the original safely and use the digital image in all sorts of ways.

Over the past few years, there has been a lot of interest about how to protect family heirlooms. Unfortunately, the chemicals utilized in the manufacture of many of the products we use to store photos and treasured items are quite harmful to your treasures. The biggest culprit is acid. Many types of acids have been used in the manufacture of photo albums, papers, boxes, and other storage devices. Now is the time to sort through your possessions and give them the archival care that they require.

What Is "Acid-Free"?

Acid-free products have been manufactured so that the balance of chemicals in the products is as close to pH-neutral as possible. High school chemistry teaches us that acid and alkaline are the two ends of the spectrum. Salt is an alkaline substance. It has been used as a preservative over the centuries, but in high concentrations, it can be very corrosive. (Think of the New England winters during which salt is used to melt ice — the salt also pits the bottom of vehicles that slog through the salted slush.) Acid is also a corrosive, and the products that you use for crafting (papers, inks, and glues) are more likely to be too acid than too alkaline. As a result, archival products are called "acid-free" as opposed to "pH-neutral."

Why Should I Care?

Over time, the acids in a box that holds your family photographs will eat away at the paper of the photographs themselves. Also, if you have stored your treasured soccer jersey or your first baseball cap from Little League in an old corrugated cardboard box, some day your heirloom will fall to pieces, decimated by the contact with the acids in corrugated paper. You can prolong the life of these mementos by storing them in acid-free containers.

What Scanners Can Do to Help Solve This Problem

Scanners can't change how or why or where you store your stuff. Scanners can, however, document what you have. Since you are now keeping digital copies, you will always have the pictures of your ancestors, that trip to Paris, or a scrap of the lace from your mother's wedding dress.

If you choose to store your mementos in a safe fashion, document your heritage digitally and move the originals to safe, archival-quality storage containers. Seal them up and continue to use your computer archives for everyday projects. See the preceding section on how to store your images in order to ensure you can find them again.

Tip

Be careful when scanning your heirlooms. Trying to flatten an old album or book against your scanner's glass can damage the spine or binding. When positioning a photograph or document on the scanner, it's easy to crimp or fold the edges. Your scanner can go a long way toward preserving your heritage, but be sure to handle fragile items with care.

Making Storage Safe

Consider these ideas for maintaining a safe storage environment. The first enemy is moisture. Keep your original photographs and materials out of damp basements. Attics may be less humid, so investigate your attic as a permanent storage archive spot. But always keep in mind that drastic weather changes from season to season may hurt your prized possessions, so thoroughly investigate any place you decide to store things. Place your objects in sturdy archival-quality boxes, which are available from a variety of sources.

The second enemy is air. Acid in the air will be absorbed by your precious mementos — and then the damage begins. Keep all of your original materials in airtight storage. Place a layer of archival tissue paper between each item. This strategy minimizes any contamination that the back of one image may cause to the front of another work.

The third enemy is light. Photographic images will fade over time if exposed to daylight. This is why museums keep their prints and their negatives out of direct sunlight. Plan to do the same for your work.

Inkjet printer inks will also fade with time. Black inks, because they are dyes rather than pigments, will last longest. If you want to permanently display a creation in strong daylight sun, think about making several versions and replacing the original every eighteen months or so.

Balancing safe storage with the desire to use your treasures is really a win-win situation. Digital scans are so good that you don't lose any quality when you substitute a scan for the original photo in a project. Scanning means that you can even improve on the original in many ways, such as removing "red eye" from your pictures. As you can see from this book, a technique such as removing red eye is just the beginning of what you can do with your pictures. Experiment with your work to clean, change and enhance your images.

Moving On

Read on in subsequent chapters and start trying out new techniques that really open up your world. There are projects for the home, the office, special occasions and for making your Web site look better. The scanner is an essential tool to creating the rich visual imagery that sells your product or communicates your idea. The digital revolution has come to our families as well as the workplace. We all integrate ourselves into the global economy — either as a consumer of goods made in Asia or as a business person whose company trades with Europe or Africa. Make your messages and offerings stand out by using digital technology to create an intensely personal reflection of you. Have fun!

CHAPTER 13

Projects for the Office

IN THIS CHAPTER
- Making personal logos
- Creating fancy notepads
- Enhancing plain binders
- Taking advantage of screen backgrounds
- Improving fax cover sheets
- Designing decals

We have some great uses for a scanner at work. This chapter is separated into two sections: projects for your office or company, and projects to help you sell or communicate your message to the outside world. Scanners can put some humanity into the often dull medium of business communications. Get ready to use your equipment in new ways that enhance your daily tasks.

Logos with the Personal Touch

If you want a business image that stands out, you can make a logo using your scanner and an image of your product or building. Include anything relevant to your company. Your own photograph, if you are a one-person organization, would be ideal. Your catchy product, with great packaging, can also be included. Visual puns could also be useful. Every business has some unique angle that could be exploited. For example, a travel agent could use a small collage of worldwide scenes to set the stage properly. Think about the image you want your customers to remember you by.

With the advent of inexpensive scanners, you'll see more and more photographic images used as logos. A strong visual reference is much more meaningful than a generic abstract design in telling the world about your services. Make sure that your logo tells a story and doesn't limit you. Try several approaches and ask others for input.

Of course, you should use this sort of advertising judiciously for electronic delivery. People receive many press releases with attached art and will delete them unread if it takes too long to download the files or if they are unsolicited. Make sure that your efforts have news value and are irresistible to open.

MATERIALS

Image editing software

Page layout software

Photos or other graphic images

Image Gathering

Because this is a trial-and-error process, start with at least five or six images. Scan them in and then play around until you find something that suits you. You may hit the right image on the first try, or you may want to test out several ideas before you make a final selection for your logo.

Take the time to make up several logo styles and show them to business associates as well as family and friends. Everyone has different tastes, so accept all opinions and solicit information about what your logo means to others. Look out for legibility and typos. Then decide how you will use the logo. Have a creative ball with this project.

Warning

Check how long the files take to download. You don't want to waste your clients' time if you are sending the information via e-mail.

1. Make a rough sketch of your layout. This enables you to position elements in the most attractive layout.

2. Scan in several images. Edit them to enhance the clarity and color. Resize them to match your paper's dimensions. Save them in the file format and at the resolution that best match your final output resolution and page layout software requirements.

Cross-Reference

See Chapter 4, "Resolution, Interpolation, and Sharp Images," and Chapter 10, "Optimizing Color," for more information on the technical aspects of scanning.

Testing Out Potential Layouts

3. Open your page layout software to a new page. Insert the first of your scanned images. Position it as indicated on your rough draft.

4. Add type to convey the necessary information. Remember to include crucial information: name, address, telephone numbers, and the name of the business. Also remember to double-check carefully for correct spelling, accurate phone numbers, and correct Web addresses.

5. Style the text to suit your scanned image. Save this and print a test page.

6. Repeat this process until you have several potential layouts. Consider where the eye is drawn in each one.

And the Winner Is . . .

7. Select your final design and print it on plain, high-quality letterhead paper. Looks good! You can print several sheets of letterhead at a time, or use this as a template for each letter. Check your software owner's manual for more information. See Figure 13.1 for an example of a logo we created.

Figure 13.1 The final logo design

Creativity

Now let's make envelopes, mailing labels, and business cards! You can buy business cards on prescored sheets that are "laser cut;" when you separate them, the edge is clean and smooth. Eventually, when your business gets larger, consider having your letterhead printed professionally, which saves time and money in the long run. Check with your local copy center for ways to turn your artwork into a complete package: letterhead, envelopes, and cards.

You can also create personal stationery in the same way. Take a picture of your home and use it with your name and address printed below in an interesting font. Make a statement by capturing a picture of a work of art you made in a college class, or include a scan of yourself wearing your favorite sports team shirt or cap. Anything goes when creating your own logo. Look in the back of computer magazines for companies that offer funky fonts. Browse the Web for copyright-free pictures and download one, adding a scanned image of your own. Put this combined photograph together with a line from your favorite hero or movie and you have an eye-catching image to use on any of your printed materials.

Notepads of Distinction

As we get started with new equipment, we often create lots of trial printouts. Here is a way to recycle paper into a fun and useful item for your office, a gift for clients, or a special treat for friends. Any paper with one clean, blank side can be used. About 50 sheets of plain bond make a ¼-inch pad. If you divide your page, you will have additional pads. Message pads for the office can range in size, but remember to leave lots of space for taking notes. Grocery lists or "to-do" lists can fit sideways, three to a page. Scorepads for games such as bridge or phone message pads may look better in quarter-page format.

Aleene's Tacky Glue is the best known "padding" glue but Elmer's white glue or yellow carpenter's glue works quite well. If you don't have C-clamps, you can use a brick, a heavy weight, or a heavy can from your pantry. Remember that heavier is better: the tighter the packs are held together during the gluing process, the less the paper will warp as it absorbs moisture during the gluing stage.

For this example, we will use the logo we created in the previous project.

MATERIALS

Drawing program or layout software

Scrap paper

Glue

2 C-clamps

Wide rubber bands

Paper cutter

Cardboard for backing

The logo you created in the previous project

Disposable sponge paintbrush, 1 inch wide

Creating Your Notepad Layout

What size pad do you want? With an 8½ × 11-inch sheet divided into four pieces, your pad would be 4¼ by 5½ inches. This is the easiest size pad to make, so the following instructions will refer to these dimensions. The goal of this project is to create a give-away advertising piece for a small business, with all the information customers need to get in touch with you when the need arises.

1. Open your graphics program and draw guidelines as illustrated in Figure 13.2.

2. These guidelines will enable you to place your graphics properly. They will also serve as cutting lines in the assembly phase. Use light-colored lines so that they will be nearly invisible on the final product, or just place a very small dot at the center of the page as a guide.

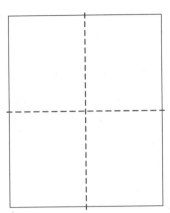

Figure 13.2 Drawing guidelines for your notepad

3. Either use a pre-existing logo, as we did, or scan a new piece of art.

4. If you are using a new scan, adjust the color balance, feather the edge, or add a creative "edge" treatment, and fix any other flaws or inconsistencies in the picture. Save this image at a resolution and in a format that is most appropriate for your equipment.

5. Copy and paste the logo or new art into your notepad layout. Position the art.

6. Add the desired text, making sure the fonts you use are compatible with the style of your logo. Experiment here to find the optimal arrangement. Check the positioning against your actual pad size.

Tip

To check positioning, print a sample of your image at low resolution. Place it on top of a piece of paper and hold both up to the light. Take accurate measurements to reposition your image in the correct spot. Better to double-check than to waste paper and additional ink.

7. Add straight horizontal lines that start and stop about ⅜ of an inch from each side. The lines should be about ⅜ of an inch apart — a comfortable writing space — and stop within your printer's margins. Use your program's "align" capability to distribute them evenly, or just use the rulers and guidelines to line them up.

8. Select all of the picture, text, and ruled line elements and group them. Copy and paste them three times, aligning them in the remaining three quadrants. Again, check your positioning. We now have a complete image for the four-up layout of the notepad. See our example in Figure 13.3.

9. Save this image in the format most appropriate for your own system.

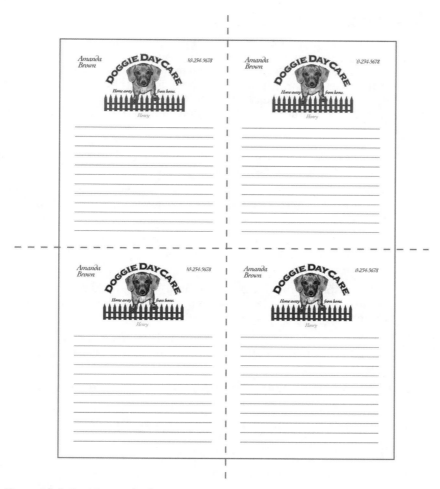

Figure 13.3 Positioning the logo

Printing Your Notepad

1. Print 50 sheets on the selected paper. If you are using recycled paper that has already been used on one side, make sure that you follow your printer directions to place the paper in the loading tray correctly.

2. Allow the pages to completely absorb the ink by setting them aside to dry for about an hour.

3. Cut to size, using your guidelines and a paper trimmer. You may also use a utility knife and a padded surface.

Assembling and Gluing Your Notepad

Because glue always involves some amount of mess, first prepare your work area. Locate a workbench or a table where you will be able to leave your work-in-progress for several hours. You will be clamping your notepad stacks to the edge of the table, so use a surface that will accommodate about a 3-inch stack of material plus the thickness of the table. Protect the surface and the edge with either newspaper or some other scrap paper. Remember to put lots of newspaper on the floor.

1. Trim scrap cardboard sheets to fit your notepad dimensions. You will need one cardboard backing piece per notepad.

2. Arrange your cut paper sheets into notepads about ¼ inch thick, which will generally run to about 50 pages. Place a cardboard backing sheet under each stack.

3. Stack the notepads in piles. You can stack as many as eight pads into a pile about 2 inches thick in one operation. You can use thick rubber bands to keep these stacks in place.

4. With the spines (the edges to be bound) aligned and extending slightly off the edge of the table, arrange your 2-inch-thick stack in a position where it can be clamped to the work surface.

5. Put a few pieces of stiff cardboard or a piece of scrap wood on top, aligned with the spine edge. Clamp this to your table with your C-clamps.

6. Using your disposable paintbrush, spread an even, moderately thick layer of glue over the spine.

7. Allow to dry thoroughly, according to the glue manufacturer's directions. Carpenter's glue needs just one coat, but Elmer's white glue or Aleene's Tacky Glue will require a second layer.

8. Wait several hours for the stack to dry, and then use a thin knife to separate the pads from each other.

Creativity

If you have leftover colored paper, make your pad out of alternating colored sheets. Some craft stores or rubber stamping and scrapbooking stores have die cuts. The machines cut your paper into creative shapes — simple objects such as a star or a house. Look for a die cut that has one straight edge and cut all your paper in this image; then bind on the straight edge.

You can also use this technique to create special notepads for work groups in the office. Take coworkers' photographs, scan them in, and use the photos, instead of names, at the top of the pad. Rule the pad off with the necessary lines and you have an extremely nice gift for your officemates.

These also make great holiday gifts. Take photos of your company's holiday decorations and make personalized notepads for clients. How about making these notepads for a new product offering? You can make each pad with a different view of a new product. The possibilities are endless, and it is a fun project for any skill level.

Photo E-mails for a Meaningful Message

The following project enables you to see how scanned images can enhance even boring old e-mails. Depending on your e-mail software, you can spice up a message with a continuous header that always appears in your message, or you can add an ad hoc creation, one note at a time. We will also tell you about attaching graphic images to an e-mail and give you advice on formats and file sizing for attachments. Make sure that the image you plan to send is fairly small. You don't want this process to take so long to download that the recipient gets tired of waiting. Test it out first by sending a sample to yourself to judge the timing.

MATERIALS

Image editing software

E-mail program

Follow the directions for your particular software vendor. Make sure that you test this out because cross-platform and even cross-network incompatibilities often occur.

Scan Your Image

1. Scan your image in your image editing software. Select an image that will show up fairly well in a small space. Clean up the scan and size it to be about 1-inch square. Save this scan in the format and at the resolution most appropriate to your equipment. A resolution of 72 dpi is adequate for most onscreen viewing.

2. Review the software with which you intend to send and receive e-mails for such functions as "Paste Special" and "Attach." Select from the following options the method that is best suited to your environment.

Cut and Paste an Image into a Message

Select the application method based on the type of software installed on your computer:

- **Lotus Notes:** In the source application, select the image you want to transfer. Select Copy or Cut. Shift to the spot where you want to insert the image in Lotus Notes and use the Paste Special command.

- **Netscape Navigator:** In the source application, select the image you want to transfer. Select Copy or Cut. In the Netscape New Message window, use Insert Image to place the graphic into the body of the message.

- **ClarisWorks e-mail:** Open the original application in which the image was created, open ClarisWorks e-mail, and cut (or copy) and paste the image into the message.

- **Microsoft Internet Explorer:** To copy information from a Web page into a document:

    1. Select the information you want to copy. To copy the contents of an entire page, click the Edit menu, and then click Select All.

    2. On the Edit menu, click Copy.

    3. Open the document in which you want the information to appear, and then click the location where you want to place it.

    4. On the Edit menu in that document, click Paste.

Attaching a File to a Document

You can attach a copy of a file to an e-mail message. This will allow you to preserve the formatting of a document. The key is to ensure that the person to whom you are sending the message has a compatible setup. If you are working under deadline pressure, make sure to test early in the cycle. There are so many little quirks to making two systems talk to each other that only by thorough testing can you ensure the results you want.

Warning

In our experience, sending large files (anything over about 1.5MB) is sometimes difficult. If you have a large graphic, use a direct modem-to-modem connection or an FTP (File Transfer Protocol) transfer between yourself and the recipient. Check your communications software and test a file transfer.

In most e-mail applications, you will follow these general directions to attach a file:

1. With the document in edit mode, click at the spot you want the attached file to appear.
2. Choose File ➪ Attach.

Tip

Your e-mail software (Lotus Notes, ClarisWorks e-mail) may also show an icon for attaching a file — generally an icon that looks like a paper clip.

3. Either select the file's drive and directory and then select the file, or enter the path and name of the file in the File Name box.
4. Click Create (or Open on the Macintosh).

Note

To prevent your software from compressing the file, deselect Compress. If you are sending a graphic image to a Macintosh and you are on an IBM-compatible machine, non-compression is necessary because the two platforms use different compression techniques. Remember, this means that it will take longer to transmit the file.

Creating E-mail Stationery

Making a "Stationery" template enables you to put together a standard format that you can use for all your e-mails. Use this to reinforce your company's identity. Make up a graphic image so that recipients will always see your logo and even a brief message, such as your company slogan. This section uses the logo we created in the previous project.

The following directions are for Lotus Notes, but your software may differ. To complete this project, follow the instructions, making sure that your application supports this function:

1. Create a message whose format and recipient list you want to use again.
2. Choose Actions ➪ Save As Stationery.
3. Type a name for the stationery message, and click OK.

Notes saves the message as stationery in the Drafts folder. To create a message using this stationery, open the Drafts folder, highlight the stationery, and click Use Stationery.

Setting an E-mail Banner in Lotus Notes

When you create stationery, you can choose a form that you can customize with your own header and footer text or picture.

1. Choose Actions ➪ Mail Tools ➪ Create Stationery.

2. Choose Personal Stationery, and click OK.

3. In the first field (above the From field), enter your text or a picture at the top of the stationery.

4. Complete information in the address fields and the Subject field.

5. In the field below the Subject field, type the body of the stationery.

6. In the last field on the form, enter text in any format or the picture you want at the bottom of the stationery.

Note

You can change any delivery options by clicking Delivery Options.

7. Click Close.

8. When Notes asks if you want to save the stationery, click Yes.

9. Type a name for the stationery, and click OK.

Creativity

You may want each employee at your company to make their own banner with their photograph in the header. This may be the time to buy a digital camera and keep it on hand. See Chapter 12, "Getting Started with Scanner Projects," for another use of employee photos: making ID badges. Chapter 14, "Advanced Projects for the Office," includes an employee recognition project called "The Employee Wall of Fame" that also uses employee photographs.

Remember that adding a logo will substantially increase the size of your file. A simple 5K file may inflate to 500K — a possible concern for the person downloading the file, especially when efficiency is an important consideration.

This technique is great for all sorts of messages. Even personal e-mail can be dressed up. Try putting pictures of the dog in your banner. Then you could use the famous line, "When you're on the Internet, no one knows you're a dog." If you have a family e-mail account, consider putting in a picture from last year's holiday photo as the header. Then you could send your holiday letters by e-mail! Instant communication and Seasons Greetings!

Turn Your Plain Binder into a Work of Art

The plain white binders covered in plastic that you can get at any office supply store are a work of art waiting to happen. You can quickly personalize these binders and give them some real class. Consider letting the spine do the talking with a graphic that calls attention to the binder and explains its function. Office policy doesn't have to be boring.

Three-ring binders covered in plastic can be used for business or home purposes. Think about using them for recipes, family photos, and so forth. By using your computer and some imagination, you can dress up these bland binders.

Simply buy a binder that has a set of plastic pockets on the front, back, and spine. You can find these binders at any stationery store — usually in white or black but you can also find colored binders. We are using a 1½-inch-thick white binder for this project. We want to create a company history binder, and our theme is photos from the 1930s. We want to use this binder to keep track of old press clippings and sales materials from a company started in 1933 by an uncle in Iowa. Create your own theme based on the purpose of the binder and your available materials.

MATERIALS

Image editing software

Page layout software

Photographs and other scannable images

Three-ring binder with plastic display pockets on front, back, and spine

High-resolution paper

Pinking or edging scissors (optional)

Utility knife or rotary cutter and self-healing mat

Straightedge or ruler

Making the Images

We use three images for this project, one each for the front, back, and spine. The style of this project is an old-fashioned forties look. Sepia works best for this project because it gives you a beautiful, rich appearance. See the Creativity section for more ideas and styles.

1. Scan in your images.

Cross-Reference

See Chapter 4, "Resolution, Interpolation, and Sharp Images," and Chapter 10, "Optimizing Color," for more information on the technical aspects of scanning.

2. Edit the images to enhance the clarity and color. Clean up any scratches using the clone tool (if your software supports this function) and the pencil and pen tools. Because sepia photographs use a limited range of colors, it is easy to improve clarity and color.

3. Resize the images to match your paper's dimensions. Make the front and back images about 3 inches wide by 4 inches high. Save each in a separate file in the format and at the resolution that best match your final output resolution.

Set Up a Layout

The layout is important in creating the appeal of the binder: arrange the elements so that they have the formal feeling of something old-fashioned.

4. In a page layout program, set two guidelines — one that divides the page horizontally and one that divides the page vertically.

5. Draw a 7½ × 10-inch box and center it on your guidelines. Fill this box with a sepia-toned color — using your ink dropper tool to select the right tone from one of your photographs. This box will leave half-inch borders on all sides of the paper. When your page is completed, the effect will be reminiscent of the white borders found on old photographs.

6. Insert your photograph in the center of this page. See Figure 13.4 for our example.

7. Type in a title using the text tool. Change the type color to a sepia-toned brown and change to an old-fashioned font, such as New York, Garamond, or Baskerville. Or try a font that has a handwritten look. Type in the pertinent information: purpose of the binder, information about the cover photo, and creation date. We added another copy block below this with the company name reversed out of a brick-red color. Don't forget to save.

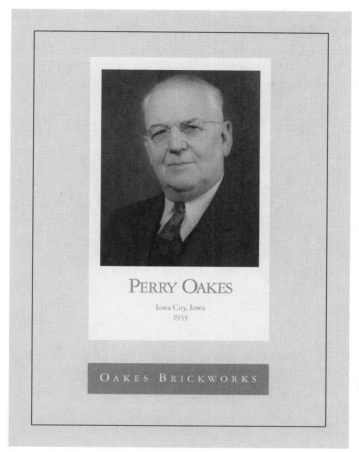

Figure 13.4 Inserting the photograph

Repeat for the Back and the Spine

8. Make a layout for the back of the binder, following the preceding steps. Save this.

9. For the spine, use the image you saved in the earlier step and size it to fit the spine area: 1⅜-inch wide.

10. Tint the picture so that the text, when placed on top of or next to the image, will stand out.

11. While using the same typestyle as in Step 7, type in the title of the binder and position the text below the photo in your document.

12. Save this. See our example in Figure 13.5.

Figure 13.5 The spine

Finishing Up

13. Print all three pages.

14. Use paper-edging scissors to pink the edges of the front and back covers, which gives the image a deckled edge just like the old Polaroid pictures.

15. Cut the spine page to size and insert all three pieces into the plastic covers on the binder.

Creativity

Perhaps your office keeps anthologies of articles that relate to the company or business. If there's some sort of library where these documents are kept, decorative binders may be used to signify what each binder contains — what articles, from what years — and make the library shelves more attractive.

There are so many ways you can personalize a binder. Here are some ideas for home or office:

Binder Color

Red — Use primary colors in your layouts and use a look reminiscent of the sixties. Mod typestyles and color photographs in bright colors would look great. This approach would work well in an office with a crisp, modern décor such as an architectural firm.

Black — Make an austere arrangement with a black-and-white photo. In some programs such as Photoshop, you can use filters to turn grayscale images into stark silhouettes. Use Helvetica or other bold, sans-serif fonts for the text information. Law firms could make great use of this look.

White — Try making a softly colored press clippings album by using pastel colors and flowery photographs. Hospitals and other organizations in the non-profit sector may want to present a softer face to their company communications.

Themes

You could create a collage of faces for an "our company is one big family" album. Scan in color photos and crop everything but the actual face. You could make a bold visual image based on eyes. Scan in photos of people's eyes, blow them up to a standard size of 1 inch long and then line them up in a grid pattern. Use this for company benefits information or other human-interest communications.

For the home, create a Recipes Book by scanning photos of food. Try all brand-named objects, all vegetables, or all fruits. Size them using your software so the objects are proportional to one another. Overlap them into a crazy-quilt layout.

To avoid having the objects float alone on the page, a simple rule of thumb is to select two objects and then place them in relationship to one another. Anchor them by aligning them with the text, using them in multiples to create a border all the way around your page, or blowing them up and using them as a background underneath text.

Desktop Wallpaper That's Really Something

Although you can leave your background pattern at the neutral setting that comes standard with Macintosh or Windows, it is really fun and a great office-spirit builder to personalize your machine to express your company's philosophy. Think of the great marketing possibilities and open your eyes to a new opportunity.

Now that you own a scanner, there is no need to buy expensive software to do the job. Start using your favorite photographs, and then branch out and develop your digital editing skills to create terrific textures for backgrounds. Just remember that making wallpaper scenes takes memory and uses disk space. Delete any graphics that you do not intend to use. In Chapter 18, "Projects for the Web," we show you how to create interesting textures from your scans. Another idea for using background wallpaper as part of your sales presentation is presented in Chapter 14, "Advanced Projects for the Office."

For this simple activity, scan some photographs in, place them in the right file, and select using your control panel. That's all there is to it!

MATERIALS

Image editing software

Photographs

Such Simple Efforts, Such Great Results

This is so simple and provides such satisfying results; you've got to try it! The first time we tried this project, we were amazed that it really worked! The only trick is to understand how the image is placed on the screen. The picture will be "tiled" if you have an image that is not sized to your screen. If your image matches the onscreen dimensions and you check the "centered" box in your display properties control panel, your image will fill the entire screen.

Remember that each monitor may have different dimensions so what works on your laptop's 12-inch screen will not fill the desktop 17-inch monitor you use at work. So check this out on your own machine and see what you can make happen. We have seen where a person rotates images from a client's most recent commercials. We have prepared intriguing textures that blend seamlessly as they are tiled across the screen. A friend uses a congratulations note from the vice president of sales to remind herself to succeed.

Here we will simply scan in a photo that will tile over the face of the screen. Remember that an image that is larger horizontally than vertically is best suited to the rectangular nature of your display. Play around with size versus resolution to optimize your picture. These wallpaper files take up lots of space so delete old files that you know you will never use.

Scan and Edit for Best Viewing

1. Scan in an image. Adjust the photo to achieve the effect you want. Resize or crop it to your monitor's dimensions. See Figure 13.6 for a few examples of photographs that would make good candidates for wallpaper.

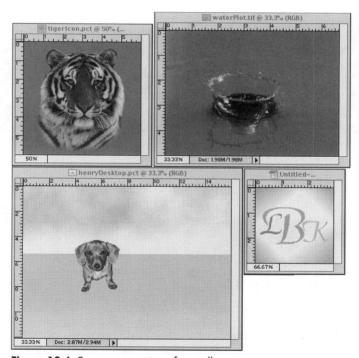

Figure 13.6 Some suggestions for wallpaper

2. Save the image in the file format and at the resolution that best match your monitor's requirements.

3. Place this in the correct file for your equipment. On Windows machines, put your image in the Windows/Systems folder with an extension of .bmp. See Figure 13.7 for placement of the file in your directory.

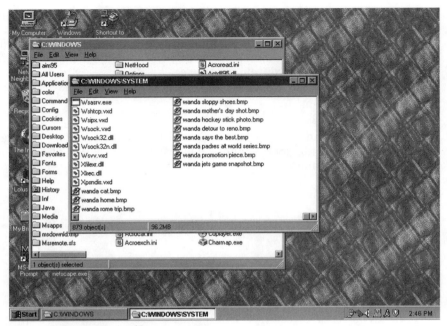

Figure 13.7 Saving the file

4. Select the Display icon in the Control Panel and select the Background tab.

5. In the right-hand section entitled "Wallpaper," select the Browse button and navigate through the files to find your newly created wallpaper. Select OK. It is as simple as that!

Macintosh Wallpaper

For Mac users, the following instructions apply:

1. With your image editing software and your scanner, create the image you want for a desktop pattern. Save as a PICT file.

2. Open the Apple menu and choose Control Panels.

3. Click Desktop Patterns.

4. Then select the image and choose Copy from the Edit menu.

5. Click anywhere in the Desktop Patterns control panel to make it active. Then choose Paste from the Edit menu.

6. To change your desktop pattern to the one you created, click Set Desktop Pattern (at the bottom of the Desktop Pattern window).

7. Newer operating systems have you choose Appearances in the Control Panel and navigate to the desktop.

Tip

You can also change the utility pattern, which is the pattern used as a background on some of the windows such as Find File, Calculator, and Jigsaw Puzzle. To change the utility pattern, press the Option key. The Set Desktop Pattern button changes to the Set Utility Pattern. To set the Utility pattern, click the button while holding down the Option key. Click the Close box to close the panel.

Creativity

Wallpaper can be fun. Consider sending all your employees a new wallpaper image each month. You could create an image that has the "employees of the month" awards on it. Or put information about your new product into a wallpaper file for everyone to have on their desktop. Stick to images that don't detract from the necessary desktop icons.

Fax Cover Sheet Dress-Ups

Fax cover sheets are essential, and here is how to take your company logo or other material and repurpose it to make a nice, legible fax cover sheet. You already made a personal logo in an earlier section of this chapter; now it is time to consider the fax machine. Remember that fax machines are fairly low resolution, meaning that pictures start to lose their fine details. In this project, we show you how to work with this handicap and turn it to your advantage to make an interesting graphic image to send along with your fax. We also give you some helpful hints for faster transmission and increased legibility.

MATERIALS

Image editing software

Page layout software

Company logo or other graphic image to scan in

An Ounce of Planning . . .

This project is relatively simple, but it gives you a big bang for your buck. The key to making your own fax cover sheets is to find or create an image that scans well. Before you complete your work, test by faxing your new cover sheet and checking the quality of the image across the phone lines. The following are some guidelines for finding the right image:

■ Grayscale images do not fax well and may not work well with your fax software. Some fax software cannot accommodate grayscale images, even though they seem to show up in your fax software's editing windows.

■ Color images need to be converted to black and white before you can transmit them.

■ Fine lines, small text, and other details may be obscured. Send a copy to your own or another fax machine nearby to look at the output.

■ Vertical lines slow transmission speed. Keep vertical ruling to a minimum.

■ Leave a big white space for messages.

■ Because some machines detect the end of the page differently, keep your image within a 7-inch length. This way, the receiving machine won't turn your fax into two pages.

Preparing the Page

1. Before you begin, make a mock-up of how you want your page to be laid out. Decide on the size of the final image.

2. Check the documentation for your particular brand of fax software. The user's manual will tell you which fields it will automatically place on your page. Most commonly, this will be:

   • Name of the sender

   • Your fax number

   • Date

   • Number of pages

   • Recipient

   • Recipient's fax number

3. Plan to add a field with the following message: "If you have received this message in error, all information is confidential. Call us immediately at 555-555-5555."

4. Figure out how the pages are counted. Does your software include the cover page in the number of pages sent? If so, plan to say this on your cover page.

5. Include your company name, department, and a message you want all recipients to see, such as "The West's Best Garden Landscapers" or "1999 Award Winning Photographers."

How to Make an Image for Your Page

6. Scan in your image — either your company's logo, a picture, or a hand-drawn image. Resize your image to the correct proportions for your layout. Convert to black and white using your image editing software controls. Save this image in the format required by your fax software and at a resolution of around 72 dpi.

Cross-Reference

See Chapter 4, "Resolution, Interpolation, and Sharp Images," and Chapter 10, "Optimizing Color," for more information on the technical aspects of scanning.

7. Send this image, just as it is, to a fax machine and compare the quality of the output to your original image. If you are satisfied, proceed. If not, rescan the image or edit the image until you have a clear, legible scan. This may still not ensure how it comes across once it is embedded in your page template, but it's a good start.

8. Open your page layout software and set up a new page. Because the main focal point on a page is the upper-left corner, insert your scanned image into this area. The necessary information will take up the upper-right corner.

Adding Text

9. Using your text tool, place all of the necessary fields. Save this. We recommend naming this cover sheet with your company initials or abbreviated name. When your fax software presents the list of choices to you, it will be easy to distinguish yours. For example, call your cover sheet "ABC Co. cover."

10. Below these fields, draw a horizontal line to divide the send and receive information from the message. Using your text tool, place the word "Memo" below this horizontal line. See our layout example in Figure 13.8 for placement and style.

11. Save. Now test it again by sending it to a fax machine and checking the hard copy output. Adjust as necessary.

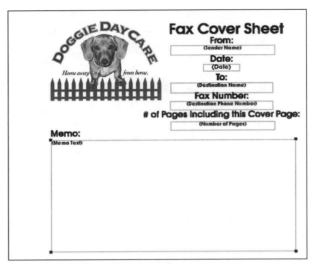

Figure 13.8 Placing text on the cover sheet

Creativity

You may want to set up several fax cover sheets: one for you personally and one for your business. Because there are some occasions that don't warrant a funny fax cover page, make sure you have at least one option that is straightforward and businesslike.

Also try some creative effects in your image editing software. Try scanning in a picture of yourself and changing it to monochrome and a fairly low resolution.

The image becomes black and white and a nice silhouette effect is achieved. Many software products have "filters" that can be applied to an image. If you have such filters, try the "posterize" filter on an image. This filter flattens out the picture, transforming it into a graphic image.

Window Decals for Fun and Profit

In this project, we will show you how to make decals in bulk, print a gang of them, and include them in a cute cover card for a mailing to prospects or clients. The scanned image can come from your product line or your most current annual report cover, or provide another nice reminder of your business. These decals can be made in two different forms: the plastic film that sticks to windows, or the clear, self-adhesive type that can be peeled off and stuck to any surface. What would you like to use them for? If yours is a consumer-oriented business, consider the plastic film — it also sticks to refrigerators. For business-to-business sales, the self-adhesive style might be better — associates can stick them onto Rolodex cards, attach them to your folder in their office, or use them in other ways to keep track of you.

You will need to plan your sizing beforehand. Do you want your decal to be the size of a business card? These could get lost in the shuffle. Maybe a card about the size of an index card would be more noticeable. And for a really important look, try making a piece that is a quarter of a sheet of 8½×11-inch paper. Then you could use a sheet of paper folded in half as the mailer. Remember that your printer has non-printable areas for the tractor device. Factor that into any page layout you create.

MATERIALS

Self adhesive overlay paper or window decals

Index-weight paper

Utility knife

Straightedge or ruler

Image editing software

Page layout software

Tape

Think It Through Before You Start

Plan your work first. You are actually creating two pieces: the decal and the mailer for the decal. They need to work together, so make some mock-ups first to ensure that the pieces work together. We decided on a 3×4-inch decal. That size will fit nicely into our mailer, which is half of an 8½×11-inch sheet of paper. We've decided to give a "face to put with a name" for all the clients who call our pet care service. So, the service representative's photo was scanned in and used along with the telephone numbers. This makes a complete mailer — very personal and very eye catching. People will love to stick this decal on their filing cabinet or refrigerator at home for quick reference. Consider how you can best use this idea for your own business.

Laying Out Your Page

1. Scan in your photograph. Resize your image so that it corresponds to the final size you will use in your layout — not more than 1½ inches wide and 2 inches high.

Tip

Select a photograph taken in a softer light that shows the person smiling. Avoid photos in which the person is squinting or the picture is blurry. Because the images will be fairly small, go for clarity. Digital cameras can make this task easy — you see the image before you print it. Take the picture, view it on the screen, and okay it or snap another! Very simple.

2. Use your editing tools to remove distracting background elements. Adjust the color and fix any imperfections in your scan. Save it at the best resolution and in the format most compatible with your page layout software.

Cross-Reference

See Chapter 4, "Resolution, Interpolation, and Sharp Images," and Chapter 10, "Optimizing Color," for more information on the technical aspects of scanning.

3. Open your page layout program and orient your page in horizontal or landscape position. Draw a box that is 3 inches wide by 4 inches high.

4. Place or insert your scanned images within the box, resizing as necessary.

5. Create your design and message. We had phone numbers and logos to display as well as the person's name. For a more casual approach, try display fonts — you can buy them from mail order sources. (See the appendix, "Resource Kit.") See Figure 13.9 for our finished example.

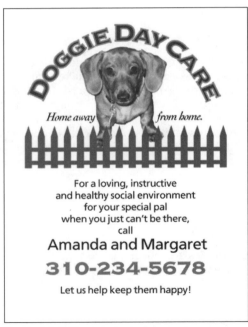

Figure 13.9 Placing the image and text

6. When you have completed the styling, copy all of the elements and paste them into the upper-right corner of your page, within the printing margins. Now you will have two pieces that are exactly the same. Continue this until you have four identical images on your page (see Figure 13.10).

Figure 13.10 Copying the image

Printing Your Decals

7. Print the necessary number of pages. Let them rest to keep the ink from smearing. This is very important when working with plastic films. Handle them carefully.

8. Cut these pieces out, using a utility blade or a rotary cutter and self-healing mat.

Tip

Scissors will work, but they never make as perfect a cut as you can achieve with a straightedge and blade.

Making Your Mailer

You will have two surfaces to use to add some message to your mailer. Remember to keep one surface clear for addressing and postage.

   9. Open up a new legal-size page in your page layout software and orient your page horizontally or in landscape mode.

   10. Set guidelines that divide the page in half lengthwise. You will make two mailers per 14×8½-inch sheet. The mailer has three panels. The short panel folds in, providing protection for the decal. The measurements are shown in Figure 13.11. You will be printing on both sides. Call this first page "Inside" and lay out a message on the top half of the page. Save this document.

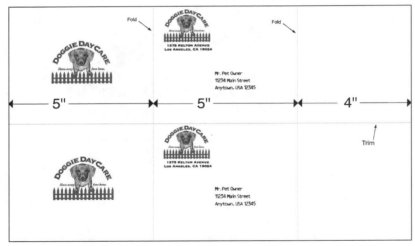

Figure 13.11 Laying out the mailer

   11. Open the document you have just saved, and use "Save As" to save a new document called "outside."

   12. Adjust the guidelines to mirror the first document, as shown, and place graphics for the outer portion. See Figure 13.12 for our example. We used our logo.

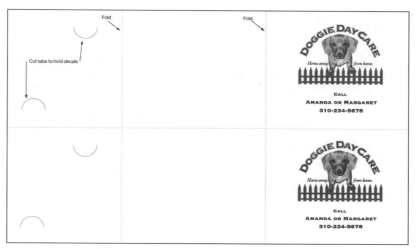

Figure 13.12 Completing the outside of the mailer

13. Lay out the area for the recipient's address information. Place a return address and a prepaid postage bulk mailing permit, if appropriate.

Print and Assemble Your Mailer

14. Print your mailers on index weight paper. Reload and print the reverse side, checking to make sure that it is printing correctly.

15. Using scissors or a utility knife, cut the two tabs to hold your decal inside the folder. Refer to Figure 13.12 for placement.

16. Score and fold the mailer. Slide a decal into the two slits. Use a sticker to close it. Turn the mailer over and address it with either handwritten addresses or mailing labels. Just wait until you hear the responses to this one!

Creativity

Have fun with this idea. You can make an ongoing series of mailings along these lines: every month select a photograph or other object that represents that season. Mail a new decal with that and a catchy phrase about how your company suits this seasonal need. Constant reinforcement of your message is important.

If your mailing list is long, consider having the mailers and assembly done by an outside fulfillment service or your local copy shop. They can print, cut, and fold for a reasonable fee. They will also do inserts. Take an example to them and discuss the logistics. Many of them will accept computer-generated input on removable media such as a Zip drive or floppy disk.

Moving On

Your scanner opens up a world of new business opportunities. Think about each of the projects in this chapter and brainstorm variations on the theme. You want to personalize every communication that you have with each client, customer, or prospect. How can a scanner help you to do that? This chapter and the next should start your company thinking about marketing itself. Don't overlook the chapters for the home and children — they may also lead you to an interesting and clever idea to get your point across. We all can use more ideas for selling ourselves and our products, so keep on reading!

Advanced Projects for the Office

Business today is competitive, and customers are looking for companies that provide extra value. What better way to demonstrate your company's merits than with well-targeted marketing and business communications? Remember that personalization is the key. Your scanner gives you the ultimate capability to personalize.

Scanned images can make even the most mundane topics more interesting and visually arresting. Clip art started to move us away from a black-and-white page, but most clip art is generic by its very nature. With only an additional step or two, the scanner gives you the capability to build your own art library.

Now that you have tried out your scanner on some of the simpler ideas, why not venture a little farther? The following projects require a few more tools and materials and may take a little more time, but they are surely worth the effort.

Build up a customized clip-art library for your company. Take photographs of special occasions and learn to edit them for focus and clarity. Look for the funny shots, dramatic shots, and moments that best convey what you want to communicate about your company. Whenever an interesting event occurs, grab that camera.

Once you have a nice bundle of images, use them to showcase your employees as well as dazzle customers and prospects. You can project a more polished and professional image by visualizing the message you want to convey and using your own scanned images to reinforce that message.

For example, if your company wants to promote its "human" face, make sure you have pictures of all your employees and use them liberally. If your company is launching a new product or a new line with distinctive packaging, incorporate the packaging's color scheme and design elements into your projects. For companies whose product is their service, you could collect images of happy customers and, with their permission, include these snippets of real life into your marketing plans. The possibilities are endless.

Personalizing the Icons on Your Desktop

The office doesn't have to be such a serious place. If you have to work at a computer all day, it might be nice to see photographs of people you like looking back at you.

It is fun to buy software or search the Web to find eye-catching icons. But it is even more fun to make them yourself. You can get crazy, or you can simply add some marketing spin to the desktop. Decide what you want to do. The icons that come with your computer can be changed into any sort of picture. This project is fairly easy and very light on materials, but you have to search out some good images to use for this purpose — they have to be clear at a fairly low resolution and in a fairly small space. Hand-drawn images as well as photographs and other source materials are good starts. If you have a distinct marketing flair, you could use your product packaging or a recent ad and edit it to fit.

MATERIALS

Image editing software

Photographs, drawings, or other materials to scan

Instructions for Windows Users

Start by testing many sources of images. Scan items, and then bring them up in your image editing software and test out several techniques. You first want to see how the image will look at a small size. Most icons are only ½ inch high. Resize your image and test for legibility. Test it at 72 dpi, which is the screen resolution most commonly found in the marketplace.

1. Create a folder called "Icons" and put it in a convenient directory.

 Cross-Reference

See the section "Managing All Those Images" in Chapter 12 for information on storing files.

2. Scan your image at around 72 dpi. The simpler the image, the better. Clean up the scan and save it as a bitmap file. (These files have an extension of .bmp in Windows directories.)

3. Using Windows Explorer, open the file you want to make into an icon. Select the file by clicking it once — it will be highlighted. Select File ⇨ Rename, and change the .*bmp* to .*ico*. Windows alerts you that if you change the file extension, the file may become unusable. When it asks if you still want to continue, click Yes.

4. The operating system automatically adjusts this file to suit the icon requirements.

5. Click Start ⇨ Settings ⇨ Control Panel.

6. Double-click the Display icon, and then click the Effects tab. A representation of the desktop icons is shown. Click once on the icon you want to change and then click the Change Icon button. You will be shown a bunch of stock images.

7. Click the Browse button to search through your directories.

8. Maneuver to the correct file folder and double-click the image you want to substitute — you're done.

9. Place a check in the Use Large Icons box on the Effects menu and your icon images will be shown slightly bigger, which may help with more complex images.

Tip

Did you know that you could also rename the icons? To change "My Computer" to "The Pit" or "Our Company's Information," right-click the My Computer icon and then click the Rename button. Type in your text and that's it!

Instructions for Macintosh Users

Programs such as Zonkers help you to change icons, buttons, and so forth. They come with all sorts of preset choices and can be useful and fun. Zonkers was created by Nova Development (http://www.novadevcorp.com/) and it can be purchased at online sources such as Codemicro (http://www.codemicro.com/ctsrch/content1n16n16.html). You can also create your own icon and allow Zonkers to place it and help with the mechanics of making the change. Generally, these programs rely on ResEdit, which is the Macintosh operating system resource editor. This editor enables you to edit functions that are not commonly accessible to end users. You can obtain ResEdit from several sources; check the Mac sites on the Web for more information. An easy source for downloading ResEdit is http://asu.info.apple.com/swupdates.nsf/62c10253abd2be98862566bb005fbe67/6b1e991512582243862566b2005f263c?OpenDocument.

Here we show you how to make simple changes to icons, without even needing to use ResEdit. So start thinking about ways to update your desktop. Here we go!

1. Scan your image, adjust the color balance, and clean up the scan so it's as crisp as possible. The resolution should be about 72 dpi.

2. Size the image to 1 inch in either direction. Save this in the format most convenient for your image editing software. See Figure 14.1 for a scan we used to make a nice, clear icon.

Figure 14.1 Choosing a scan for your icon

Cross-Reference

See Chapter 4, "Resolution, Interpolation, and Sharp Images," for more information on scanning resolution. See the appendix, "Resource Kit," for additional sources of digital images and image editing tools.

3. With the image still open, select the entire image and select Copy.

4. Go back to your desktop and click on the icon you want to change. Click only once; if you double-click it, the document or folder will open.

5. Select File ⇨ Get Info. You should see the icon you want to change in the upper-left corner of the information box. Click once on the icon. A small box will appear around the icon.

6. Choose Paste from the Edit menu.

Tip

If you download files and documents, you may notice that the icons often look like blank pages. You can change these blank pages to attractive icons with this technique as well.

7. That does it! When you close up the box, your new icon will appear. Have fun.

Replacing One Icon with Another

Now that you have a good scanned image, it is simple to place it on other icons. You can copy the image from one icon to the others. The only difference is that you start out by clicking the icon you would like to use, instead of selecting and copying a graphic image. You could change a whole bunch of icons in one session.

1. Select File ⇨ Get Info. You should see the icon you want in the upper-left corner of the Info box.

2. Click once on the icon. A small box appears around the icon. See Figure 14.2 for an example.

Figure 14.2 Replacing an icon

3. Choose Copy from the Edit menu.

4. Locate the document icon that you want to change and click once.

5. Choose File ⇨ Get Info.

6. Click once on the document or disk icon. A box appears around the icon.

7. Choose Paste from the Edit menu.

8. You're done! When you close the box, your new icon will appear.

Tip

If you ever turn on your Mac and find that all your custom icons are gone and replaced by plain boxes, rebuild your desktop. They will reappear.

Creativity

Once you start this project, you can have a world of fun. Think about giving everyone in your company an icon based on the company logo. That scan you made of the new packaging for your hot-selling product could be used for the company documents. Perhaps for special occasions you could send out holiday buttons — a ghost for Halloween or a Christmas tree in December. Think about making a button out of your best friend — every time you go to use it, you click her face!

The Employee Web Site

One of the great ideas to come from the development of the Internet is the creative use of dynamic graphical representations of your company. This project is for an internal Web site, called an *intranet*, but you could create something similar for your external site. In that case, make sure that you consider privacy issues — many people will not want their photograph or name used in such a way. But this project is fun for an internal network, especially if your company changes rapidly or is growing quickly. People love to see the names behind the faces, and you can add snapshots of company events, the building, products, awards, and other interesting items.

In our company, we built the site with a wall texture behind it and added faces to it based on the employees' date of hire. People love to see who started when. Take snapshots of everyone, get their names and dates of hire, and combine the information with a scanned background made from a photograph of a brick wall. You can write the HTML yourself or use a simple Web-authoring tool. This is a quick project and one that continues to reap benefits over time.

Creating Icons

Develop a couple of simple icons to dress up your page. Use them to provide directional buttons or to help move around the site. We show a couple of examples of very simple, adaptable images in Figure 14.3.

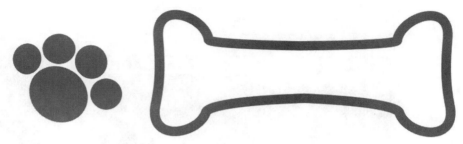

Figure 14.3 Choosing images for the page

Gathering Your Snapshots

1. Take photographs of each employee in your company or division. As you take the shots, stand the same distance from each person so that their faces are the same size. Use a standard background with a fairly neutral color for all the shots and keep the lighting consistent. Focus on capturing the head, with open eyes and smiles on all the faces. Take at least two shots of each person to minimize having to retake shots.

2. Scan the photos. In your image editing software, correct the color and remove or soften any distracting background elements. Save each photo with the person's name and put all of these images into one folder.

 Cross-Reference

See Chapter 4, "Resolution, Interpolation, and Sharp Images," for more information on scanning resolution.

3. Take a photograph of a brick wall or other suitable background.

4. Scan the brick photo and, in your image editing software, adjust the contrast, balance, and clarity of the image. Set the image size and save this to the same folder as your photograph scans.

5. Using a Web-authoring software program or HTML, design the page as shown in Figures 14.4 and 14.5.

6. Place each employee photo on the page, and add text to indicate the names and dates of hire.

7. If you want to provide more information on the individual employees, create a linked page with more details.

8. As new employees come on board, continue to take pictures, scan them, and add them to the Web page.

Figure 14.4 Designing the page

Figure 14.5 Adding to the page

Creativity

If you really want to get fancy, take snapshots of people in their offices or cubes and add these. With more detailed photos, it is very important to make good, clean scans and to adjust the resulting image for clarity. Your image editing software will allow you to erase distracting sections, change color schemes and replace objects as needed. You can also scan photographs of awards and trophies and put them into a special section. Use the scan as a header or a background for the write-up on an award. You could have a monthly employee recognition program, which includes the photo of the employee and a photo of the trophy or plaque that was bestowed on that person. For an external site, consider a similar idea: publish your successes with graphic representations of the awards and kudos you have garnered.

Framing and Matting Photographs Like a Pro

A scanner can put lots of those photographs you have had forever into circulation. Part of the process of using these remembrances is to frame and mat them in appropriate ways. Of course, you can slip down to the local drugstore and find a cheap metal frame for a few bucks, but you can also use the power of your scanner to create your own frames and mats. This section has two projects: making a frame covered with patterned paper that you create using your scanner, and using an interesting matting technique.

You can create a wonderful gift for an employee or client by personalizing the frame to suit the contents of a photo. Don't miss this opportunity to customize one more item that comes out of your company.

If you are going to use a regular photograph, have it professionally printed in the correct size. Here we use a photo with an image area of 4 by 6 inches, and a ¼-inch white border around it.

MATERIALS

Image editing software

Photograph

Fabrics or other texture sources

Bristol board

Glue stick or spray mount

White glue or household cement

Utility knife

Photo-quality paper

Marbled paper or fabric

Acrylic or gouache paint and paintbrush

Ruler or straightedge

Thin sheet of acrylic (optional)

Instructions

Notice what colors are dominant in the photo and what tones are most appropriate for the theme you want to convey. For example, how do both of these elements look with the background in the photo? Find some common ground. Our project uses a family photo so there are plenty of colors from which to choose. We decided to pick a strong teal blue and green theme that allowed us to complement the entire group and still have a standout piece.

Next, we made some marbled paper. Look for examples at your local art stores. Fabrics also make great sources for scanning patterns. If this is a commercial project, make sure that the pattern is copyright-free or that you obtain the artist's permission to use his or her work.

Scanning Your Fabric or Paper

1. Scan your samples. Because this process requires experimentation, make several test files initially. Test the resolution settings to get the optimum trade-off between dpi and storage considerations.

2. Save these scans in the format best suited to your image editing software.

3. In your image editing software, open your scan and set the image size to the largest area that your hardware will print.

4. Go wild! Try filters or try adjusting the color settings. Keep at it until you get nice, rich, all-over design. Save this, naming it something like "Frame all-over pattern." Figure 14.6 shows our example.

Adding a Text Message

Now you will resave the page and add some information to it. This information could be the date of the event or the name of your company. Don't cram too much onto the frame — add just enough information to intrigue the viewer. The text should be in a fairly large type size — around 60 points, depending on the font you use.

5. Using your text tool, add a caption.

6. Place the text 1½ inches from the bottom margin. The text should be no longer than 6 inches and be centered between the left and right paper edges.

Figure 14.6 Starting with a pattern

7. Enhance the look of the text by making the letters white and then setting the opacity value to around 40 percent. This will give you a translucent effect that incorporates the marbled paper texture.

8. Save this, calling it something like "Frame texture and text."

Printing Time

You will print two copies of the allover texture and one copy with the text. This will provide enough paper to cover the entire frame. In case of mistakes, you may want to print a couple of extra sheets. Keep your work surface clean as you use the glue, which can cause the printer ink to run.

1. Print two copies of the allover texture on your best paper. These copies will be used to cover the back of the frame.

2. On your best paper, print the marbled paper with the message. Do not use cardstock or heavier-weight papers — they do not crease and fold as cleanly. You might want to use self-adhesive paper. It is a little trickier to handle, but the results are nice!

Assembling the Frame

This may look like a lot of steps, but the process is simple: Cut cardboard to create a back, a front and an easel. Cut up your paper printouts to size, glue them to the board, and then assemble the pieces together. In Steps 12 and 13, we use two pieces glued together because the thinner weight Bristol board is easier to obtain, cut, and handle than thicker board. If you have access to the materials and tools, you can select a board that is ¼ inch thick.

3. Cut four pieces of Bristol board: three 7½×10-inch pieces and one 3×6-inch piece.

4. Using a utility knife, cut out an area 4 by 6 inches at the exact center of two pieces. (See Figure 14.7.)

5. Glue the two pieces of Bristol board with center holes together and let dry.

6. Using a matte acrylic paint or gouache, mix a color that dominates your paper. Use this color to paint the inner edge of all four corners on the inside of the frame so that when the paper is cut and turned under, none of the Bristol board will show.

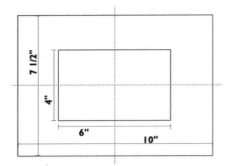

Figure 14.7 Laying out the Bristol board

7. Position your paper on top of this frame and ensure that your image completely covers the frame. If it does not, trim your boards to fit. Coat the Bristol board with spray mount or a glue stick, and place the paper on it, making sure to align everything squarely.

8. Using a utility knife and a ruler, cut a small box out of the center of the marbled paper, leaving a 1-inch flap to fold under. Cut diagonally into the four corners.

9. Using spray mount or a glue stick, glue the flaps and turn them under neatly, making sure that no Bristol board is showing on any of the four edges on the reverse side (see Figure 14.8).

Figure 14.8 Turning the corners under

10. Trim the outer four corners on the diagonal. Glue the paper, and then fold under each of the four sides, making sure that the corners are covered properly. Let dry.

11. Cover the third piece of board (the back) the same way.

12. For the easel, cut a 5×8-inch piece of the printed paper and cover one side of the easel stand. Trim the corners diagonally. Glue and fold the edges under. Let it dry.

13. Cut a 2¾ by 5¾-inch piece of printed paper. Apply this to the unfinished side of the easel stand, covering the folded-under edges. Let this dry.

14. Score the easel on a horizontal line, 1 inch from the top, folding it slightly (see Figure 14.9).

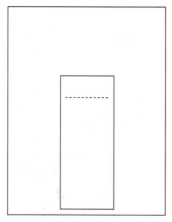

Figure 14.9 Scoring the easel

Finishing Touches

15. Glue the easel to the back panel. See Figure 14.9 for positioning — the easel needs to stop half an inch higher than the bottom edge of the frame so that it will lean properly. Let it dry thoroughly.

16. Turn the front of the frame on its face to prepare to glue it to the back. Using fairly thick glue, such as all-purpose glue, household cement, or a glue gun, make a thick line of glue around both sides and the bottom edge, about ½ inch in from the edge. Let it get slightly tacky before attaching the back panel.

17. Let the assembly dry overnight. Slip your photograph into the slot on the unglued side. You can also include a thin sheet of acetate to protect the image — use the sheets that are sold for making transparencies or get a sheet from your local art supply shop.

Creativity

By building the frame up with an extra layer of cardboard that is the same thickness as your glass or acrylic sheet — typically ⅜ inch — you can make the frame thick enough to accommodate glass or acrylic. Here is how to calculate it:

If your photo window area is to be 4 by 6 inches, then make this extra layer the same outside dimensions with a 4¼ × 6¼-inch window. Glue the outside frame sections to this additional section and then cover the whole thing with your marbled paper. Proceed as above, but before gluing the back to the front, insert the glass or acrylic, cut to size, in this holder. Be careful if you use glass — if it breaks, the frame cannot be opened without damage.

Another way to decorate and personalize a frame is to use the person's name. Decide on the dimensions of your finished frame and divide that into equal units. Then fill each unit with a letter. Graphically, it looks more interesting if the letters run down one side of the frame and the characters are all capital letters. For example, with the name "Kelsey," you could have a frame that is 6 inches high and create a letter block that is 1 inch high. All sorts of decorative capital letters could be sized to fit. This kind of personalization is what computers are all about!

Making a Mat

When you put a frame together, a mat makes a wonderful focusing device and improves the appearance. The mat forms the bridge between the image and the frame and ties them together visually. The mat also serves as a protective barrier between the glass and your photo. Without this barrier, a photograph can stick to the glass and be ruined permanently. Mats are bevel cut at a 45-degree angle. If you want a professional look, it is essential to use special mat-cutting knives. Matting photos with white Bristol board is a fairly conservative method.

If you would like to jazz up your mat a bit, try this project and surround your photograph with a fast and easy punch of color.

MATERIALS

Bristol board

Rubber cement or spray adhesive

High-quality paper

Frame and glass or acrylic

Photograph

Mat-cutting knife or utility knife

Straightedge

Right-angle tool

Museum mounting tape or adhesive tape

Instructions

1. In your image editing software, scan a texture or image that contains the colors you want. Use this as the basis for a pattern that can be used as a mat.

2. Clean up the image and save it at a resolution and in a format that are most compatible with your configuration.

3. Test out some filters that come with your software. Turn your scan into a pattern, using colors and textures to create new designs. Some of the most common filters are gradient designers, noise, wind, and mirroring effects. See Figure 14.10 for some examples.

Figure 14.10 Sample patterns

4. Save the new pattern. If it does not cover the full page, either change the size of the image or add more texture. Use cut-and-paste techniques, clone tools, or selection tools to place pieces of the image into new areas. Save.

5. Print this image on your best quality paper. This can also be printed on self-adhesive paper.

Mat Cutting Time

6. Measure your photograph. Your window will be ⅛ inch smaller than the photograph so the mat will hide the edge of the photo.

7. Measure the inside dimensions of your frame. The mat dimensions will be ⅛ inch smaller than these dimensions.

8. Using a utility knife, cut the outside dimensions of the board. Remember to place a scrap piece of board on your cutting surface so you don't cut into your surface.

9. Measure and mark the window dimensions on the back of the board. To position the window measurements, subtract the window measurements from the overall board size and divide by 2. See Figure 14.11.

Gluing the Paper

In this step, you will glue the textured paper on the mat board. Keep your work surface clean. We often use an old copy of the yellow pages. We use a sheet, tear it off, and have a nice, firm, new surface. Remember to spray the adhesive in a well-ventilated area.

10. Using spray adhesive, cover the front of the mat lightly.

11. Position your textured paper on the board and put aside to dry thoroughly.

Bevel Edge Cutter

12. If you are using a bevel mat cutter, set the blade cutter 1/16 of an inch deeper than the mat board thickness. Because you will be working from the back of the mat, angle the blade outward when you are cutting the mat.

13. Set the cutter so that the blade meets the board at one of the corners. Align your straightedge with the cutter.

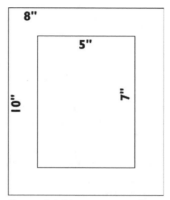

Figure 14.11 Laying out the window dimensions

14. Lift the cutter up carefully and measure the gap between where your straightedge will rest and where your pencil line is drawn. Mark this gap on the other sides of your window.

15. Position the cutter back against the straightedge. Holding the straightedge with firm, downward pressure, cut from pencil mark to pencil mark, over-cutting by $\frac{1}{16}$ of an inch.

16. Cut one side, turn the mat, and cut the next until you complete all four sides.

Assembly

17. Pop out the window and make sure you have a clean cut.

18. Slide your mat into the frame next to the glass.

19. Position your photograph and attach it with the tape in two spots. Attach a scrap piece of board as a backing board and seal the edges with mounting tape or adhesive tape.

20. You've done a professional job!

Creativity

The mat can be a collage of other photographs, objects, or anything else that catches your eye. Be on the lookout for materials from which you can get a good scan. Did you eat lunch from a tin can today? Scan in that nice metal ribbing and use that on a project. What does the bottom of your shoe look like? It might be a beautiful starting point. Rocks and minerals are also great resources. Anything that has variations in color or texture is a candidate so keep your eyes peeled.

Personalizing Diplomas and Certificates

Corporate life is filled with events and occasions that cry out to be noticed in some way. Business is based on achievement so diplomas and certificates are a natural part of motivating employees and customers. Think about using such documents as awards for employees. Loyal customers also love to receive these and will frequently display them on their walls — thus offering more exposure for your company. All of your business partners, people you buy from and sell to, should have a certificate of endorsement from you, shouldn't they? And don't forget gift certificates for clients, employees, and even for the loyal spouses of hard-working employees who have put in lots of overtime on special projects.

You can buy preprinted certificates and diplomas. But why go to that expense when you can create personalized ones on your own? All it takes is a few minutes and some imagination. Your scanner gives you the chance to make an impact. And if you send these out after a ceremony, you can add photographs from the event itself.

MATERIALS

Page layout software

Image editing software

Images you wish to incorporate

Good quality paper or cardstock

Gold seals (optional)

Red grosgrain ribbon, ¾ inch wide — 6 inches per certificate (optional)

What's the Occasion?

Is it a class that participants have successfully passed? Is it participation in a charity drive? Aim your certificate at the crowd. An event is even more special when a certificate goes home with each participant. We will show you a certificate that is never going to be mistaken for a generic, fill-in-the-blanks model. Use your company colors to make the picture complete.

Scanning Your Background

1. Scan your background element. We found a hand-made paper in one of the organization's colors. Size it to 9 inches wide by 6½ inches high. Since we don't have to worry about proportions with the texture, we made it exactly the size we needed by just changing the image size. Save it in a format and at a resolution optimal for your equipment and page layout software (see Figure 14.12).

Figure 14.12 Creating a background

Cross-Reference

See Chapter 4, "Resolution, Interpolation, and Sharp Images," and Chapter 10, "Optimizing Color," for more information on resolution and file formats.

2. Open your page layout software to a new document and set the page orientation to horizontal or landscape. Insert the scanned image and center it on the page.

Creating a Decorative Name

3. For each person receiving this certificate, we need to turn his or her name into a piece of art. You can accomplish this by creating each name in calligraphy. Scan these names in as line art. Or, you can use a decorative font. Either method produces a very attractive piece. You could also use initials, creating a very decorative piece of art — worthy of framing (see Figure 14.13).

Figure 14.13 Preparing the participants' names

4. Import the scanned name into your page. Center it visually on the page — every name will be a little different.

5. Under the name, type the message of the certificate. Ours was to honor a group of people who usually go unnoticed on a daily basis. The copy can be personalized for each person — noting what he or she, in particular, has done — thus making a much more personal and meaningful piece (see Figure 14.14).

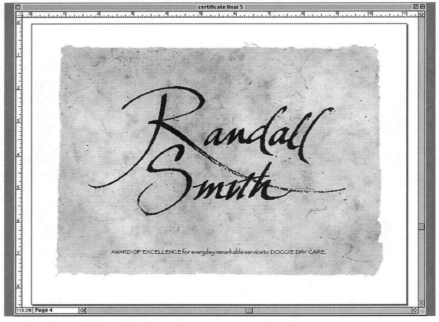

Figure 14.14 Adding the message

Create a beautiful montage of heirloom family photos that will delight your family for generations.
See Chapter 15 for this project.

Customized binder covers can help you organize your office space. Find the instructions for this project in Chapter 12.

Use a panoramic photo to design decorative book covers that will spruce up any shelf. The instructions for this project are in Chapter 16.

Make every holiday even more unique and special with your own brand of homemade greeting cards. Find instructions for this project in Chapter 15.

There is always someone at the office whose work deserves recognition. With this project in Chapter 14, you can create awards certificates for that deserving person.

A custom-made clock can be the perfect decoration to spice up a dull office atmosphere. See Chapter 14 for this project.

Learn inexpensive ways to create an array of promotional items for your business. See Chapter 14 for details.

Are you looking for just the right wallpaper border for that room in your house? Go to Chapter 15 to learn how to make customized borders.

Make favorite photos even more special by learning how to make decorative frames and mats. Instructions for these projects are in Chapter 14.

Give your doorknobs a personality all their own — or just send a message to your family members with the doorknob hanger project found in Chapter 16.

A couch or bed can become a photographic showplace when you learn how to create pillows with any image. Find the details for this project in Chapter 15.

Scanned art is the best way to create new holiday decorations every year. See Chapter 17 for the details of this project.

Thanksgiving is just one of the holidays for which coordinated tablecloths, napkins, and place cards are a great decorating idea. See Chapter 17 for this project.

This project in Chapter 14 can help coworkers learn more about each other on an employee intranet.

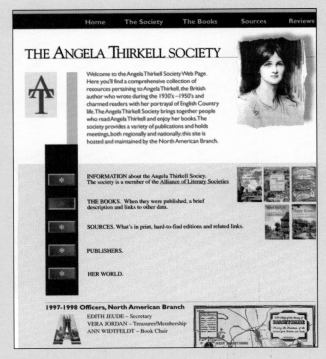

In Chapter 18 you learn how scanned art can greatly enhance your Web site.

Printing and Assembling Your Certificate

6. Print your piece on the selected paper stock.

7. *Optional:* Cut a 6-inch length of ribbon and fold it in half. Place this on a good spot on your diploma and cover the folded end with a big gold seal. It is now ready to deliver!

Creativity

There are all sorts of styles of certificates. Try making an old-fashioned, classic model using Gothic typestyles. Get an embossed look by making two sets of type: one black and one gray. Position the gray text behind the black and slightly offset, so it forms a shadow. The results are very classy.

You can also use these certificates to reward people with extra services. Think about making one for your parents: a "One Night Out" promise to baby-sit a younger sibling. Or give them out to your soccer team — a reward for everyone! Figure out what achievement each player should receive — "Team Player," "Dirtiest Socks," and other categories.

Low-Budget/High-Impact Self-Promotion Ideas

We all could do more to promote our businesses and ourselves. However, this process takes time and is easily put off in the rush of day-to-day events. Here are some clever ideas that you can quickly carry out to let people know you exist. These versatile pieces can be used for a variety of purposes.

Because it's tough to be creative on demand, count on your scanner to help you out. Think of it as a creation crank. Put an image down on the glass and crank out lots of uses for it. If you have tried some of the earlier projects, you may now have an image library of scanned objects from which to choose. We will take those images and make quick, eye-catching marketing pieces that you can use in many ways.

This section consists of three projects: a logo mosaic wallpaper, a small calendar, and a personalized wall clock. Let's get started.

Project 1: Partnership Selling

Here is a great idea for a marketing presentation: Change your wallpaper to the logo of the company to which you are presenting. Then, whenever the background shows, your prospective customer sees his or her own business card or logo. It is a subtle way of telling them that you pay attention to the details. We've seen this work!

As we discussed in Chapter 13, "Projects for the Office," you can create customized wallpaper in about five minutes. In this project we'll create a very small image that will be *tiled*, meaning that it will be repeated to fill the whole surface of your monitor. It will look like a mosaic!

Even though each monitor has different dimensions, the tiling effect is managed by the operating system so there is no need to worry about sizing. Remember that a horizontal image is best suited to the rectangular nature of your display. Play around with size versus resolution to optimize your picture.

MATERIALS

Client logo

Image editing software

Windows Wallpaper

You need a clean copy of the client's logo from a business card or a brochure. You will scan just the logo and save the image in a format that your computer can recognize as a wallpaper pattern. Then it is simply a matter of a few extra steps and you are on your way!

1. Scan your client's logo. Size it to be around 4 inches square, depending on the size and complexity of the logo. See Figure 14.15 for our artwork.

Cross-Reference

See Chapter 4, "Resolution, Interpolation, and Sharp Images," and Chapter 10, "Optimizing Color," for more information on resolution and file formats.

2. Save the image in the file format and at the resolution that best matches your monitor's requirements.

Figure 14.15 A sample logo

3. Place the image in the correct folder for your equipment. On Windows machines, put your image in the Windows\Systems folder with an extension of .bmp. See Figure 14.16 for the placement of the file in your directory. On our system, we placed the file in C:\Windows\Systems.

Figure 14.16 Saving the file

4. Now open your Display Properties window and select the Wallpaper tab. Select Browse and find your newly created wallpaper. Select OK. It's as simple as that!

Macintosh Wallpaper

For Mac users, the following instructions apply:

1. Open the Apple menu and choose Control Panels.

2. Double-click the Desktop Patterns control panel.

3. With your scanner and image editing software, create the image you want for a desktop pattern.

4. Select the image and choose Copy from the Edit menu.

5. Click anywhere in the Desktop Patterns control panel to make it active, and then choose Paste from the Edit menu.

6. To change your desktop pattern to the one you created, click Set Desktop Pattern (at the bottom of the Desktop Pattern window).

Tip

You can also change the utility pattern, which is the pattern used as a background on some of the windows, such as Find File, Calculator, and Jigsaw Puzzle. To change the utility pattern, press the Option key. The Set Desktop Pattern button changes to the Set Utility Pattern. To set the utility pattern, click the button while holding down the Option key. Click the Close box to close the panel.

Creativity

Make this project a stunner by including the team from your company mixed in with the team from your client's company. Talk about relationship selling — this really shows it. If your client has a rectangular product or product packaging, scan in the front and edit it to size. You could tile the background with anywhere from ten or fifteen images to hundreds! If you make the images very small, the package can become a wild graphic pattern.

Project 2: Teeny Calendar

Companies love to give out calendars because it is a gift that keeps on giving. By passing out small calendars, you can capture people's attention repeatedly. One organization we know has done handy, pocket-sized calendars for years. You can, too. They are simple and can be created and produced in whatever quantity your budget can stand. Consider making only a handful if your company has a small, select client roster. Farm out the printing work if you are going to distribute them to hundreds of people. Remember that a subtle image on each page is much better than simply splashing the company logo on the front cover. So, gather up some images, including seasonal ones, and get to work promoting!

MATERIALS

Image editing software

A variety of images from your company, including some seasonal themes

Cardstock

High-quality paper that can be printed on both sides

Stapler

Paper cutter

Empty ballpoint pen

Bone folder

Instructions

You will need twelve distinct images, one for each month. Additionally, use at least one image on the front cover and maybe one or two more on the inside covers or on the back of your calendar. Consider providing a list of your products and services on the inside front cover. You could put some handy industry information on the inside back cover, sized to fit. For example, if you are in the food service business, provide a weights and measurements table. We are using a pet care company logo, so we include a list of favorite dog breeds.

Image Gathering

1. Find twelve images for the month pages plus images for the cover, back cover, and inside cover.

2. Scan and save the images in the format and at resolutions optimized to your hardware and software configuration.

Cross-Reference

See Chapter 4, "Resolution, Interpolation, and Sharp Images," and Chapter 10, "Optimizing Color," for more information on resolution and file formats.

3. Open your page layout software and set up guidelines as shown in Figure 14.17. We will be making a calendar with final dimensions of 7 inches by 3 inches — great for slipping into a pocket or folder. Remember to center each image on the 8½×11-inch page. This is crucial when you print on the second side. All art must be centered. Save this as your Master page.

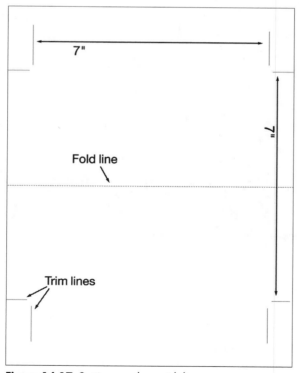

Figure 14.17 Setting up the guidelines

4. Open the Master page and do a Save As, saving the new file with the file-name "Cover." Set up your cover — front and back. On the front, we used a scanned element from our company logo. On the back, we placed contact information: the company address and phone numbers (see Figure 14.18). Save this page.

5. Open the Master page again and do a Save As, saving the new file with the filename "Back Cover." Set up your inside cover. Save this layout.

Figure 14.18 Including an image and contact information

Putting in the Dates

Before you lay out your monthly pages, you will need to gather several pieces of information. Will the upcoming year be a leap year? What holidays are essential to include for your client base? Find a calendar for the coming year for reference.

You will be printing on both sides of the paper so some planning and testing is required. Using scrap paper, make a mock-up of your calendar. Fold it, and then write which pieces of text will appear on each page of the mock-up. Write in "Cover," "Inside Cover," "January," "February," and so forth. Take this apart and use the pages as a guide to your layouts. Note that each page has two months oriented in the same direction. The folding process puts them in proper order. The pairing of the months is crucial, if a little bit confusing. Refer to your hand-written mock-up: December and January pair up together, as do February and November, October and March, August and May, June and July, and, finally, April and September. See our mock-up in Figure 14.19 for a representation of this.

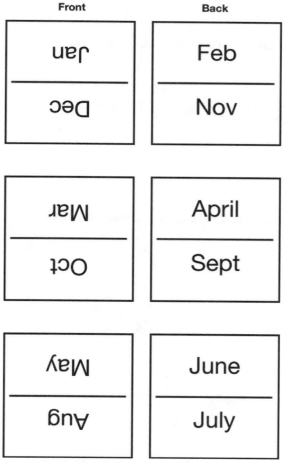

Figure 14.19 Making a mock-up

Make some test printouts, using draft mode, and test how the paper must be loaded in order to print properly.

Setting up the Master Month

6. Open your page layout software to a new page. Use guidelines to position the elements.

7. Create a grid of boxes for the days of the month. Refer to Figure 14.20 for positioning.

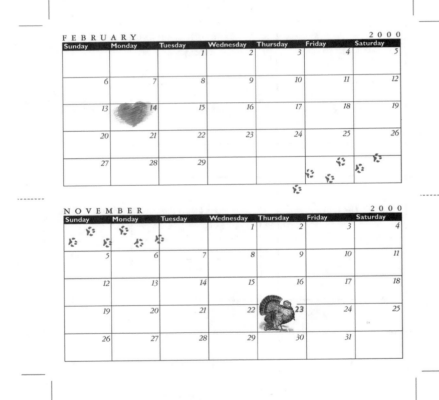

Figure 14.20 Positioning the days of the month

8. Using your text tool, type individual numbers and position them, one to a box, in the correct boxes for that month.

9. Using your text tool, type the days of the week and position them at the top of the calendar layout, centering them over each column of days. Type the month; position and style the text. Group all of these elements. Now you are ready to create a page with two months on it.

Creating Twelve Months

10. Open a Master page. Set guidelines for the margins. Copy and paste your master month, and position it on the top half of the page. Do the same on the bottom half. This can be saved as the "Month Master" page.

11. Referring to Figure 14.20, begin to create the months. Open the "Month Master" page, and do a Save As, saving as "Dec-Jan." Change the month name. Adjust the days so they read correctly for that month. Type in any appropriate holidays or special events.

12. Insert one of your twelve scanned images.

13. Position the image in an empty box. Resize it to fit.

14. Using your text tool, add a caption to the image that you inserted onto the calendar. Have fun with this part — include a favorite quote or a funny line relating to the image.

15. Set up the second month layout the same way (see Figure 14.21).

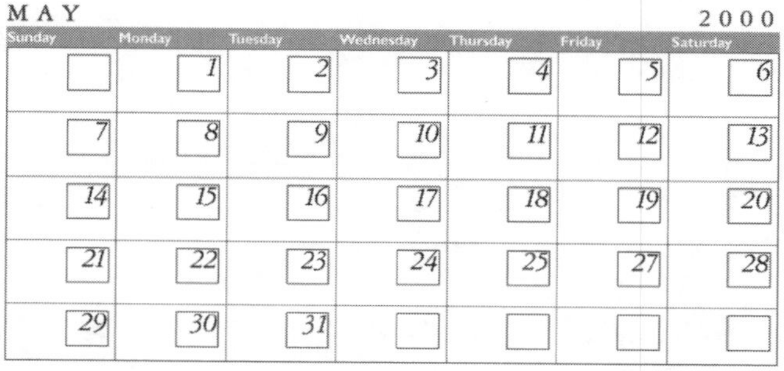

Figure 14.21 Setting up the second month

16. Repeat this process with each month, making sure that you have the proper number of days per month. Remember the old ditty, "Thirty days hath . . . " Make sure that each month starts on the correct day of the week. Save each page separately.

Printing the Pages

17. Print three sets of calendar pages: the August/May pair, the October/March pair, and the December/January pair. Print as many copies as you plan to make calendars, plus about 10 percent extra for mistakes and spoilage.

18. Carefully reload the paper tray, making sure that you are printing with the proper orientation.

19. Test this step first on one sheet to ensure that you will print properly.

20. Print all the sheets. This time, print the June/July pair upside down on the back of the August/May pair, the April/September pair upside down on the back of the October/March pair, and the February/November pair upside down on the back of the December/January pair.

21. Print your outside covers on cardstock, one per calendar.

22. Again, replace these sheets in the printer and run a test print to ensure proper paper loading. Print the second page: the inside cover.

Assembly Line

23. Using a paper cutter, trim the calendar sheets and covers to size.

24. Using a straightedge and a scoring tool, score each cover along the halfway guideline. Fold gently in half and, using a bone folder, make a firm, crisp, straight fold.

25. Assemble sets of calendar pages (see Figure 14.22) and fold these in half along the guideline.

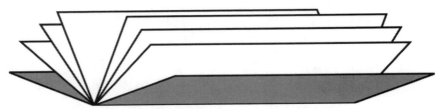

Figure 14.22 Assembling the calendar

26. Staple the sections together along the fold line.

27. Now pass these out to grateful clients and friends. They'll be looking forward to them next year so be prepared!

Creativity

You have twelve months to show off — but use the space wisely. Does your product or service lend itself to a month-by-month depiction of its use? Is it a seasonal product that your clients must be reminded to order early? Can you imagine featuring a different group of employees each month? Or a month-by-month product review? Here's an idea: On each successive page, show your product in different stages of the building process. Start with a photo of the raw components, then show it being assembled in the next month, and follow the process all the way through to shipment.

Project 3: Wall Clock

Nothing could be simpler than to pick up one of those inexpensive but nice-looking clocks at a hardware or household supply store and turn it into a never-forgotten reminder. These clocks are the molded plastic models — they have a simple battery-powered quartz movement and come in basic colors such as black and white. They cost about ten dollars each and are easy to disassemble for this project. Some of the clocks are quite large, but you need one with a face about 7 inches in diameter, so that an 8½×11-inch sheet of paper will cover its face. All you need is some nice artwork to make this a killer project. Got any ideas? How about hand-drawn numbers for the face, with your logo used as the center point? For this example, we used hand-drawn images and colored them with markers. You might think about making a representation out of your company's products and use one for each number. Create the numerals by first drawing an outline of the numeral. Then fill it with scanned images. Each number could be a different product or a different color.

> MATERIALS
>
> Image editing software
>
> Photographs and other items to scan
>
> A plain clock
>
> Batteries for the clock
>
> Utility knife
>
> Circle cutting template or a plate the size of the clock face

Instructions

We drew funky numbers, using a colorful scheme. Every number has a different look, but we used the same typeface. Play around with this. You can make each number from a different font, or cut the numbers out of images.

Doing the Numbers

1. Scan an image for each of the twelve numerals. Save them in the same format, resolution, and size.

2. Scan one company logo or other identifying piece of art. Again, save this image in the format and resolution to match your other scans.

3. Open your page layout software. Insert the first numeral indicator and position it as shown in Figure 14.23.

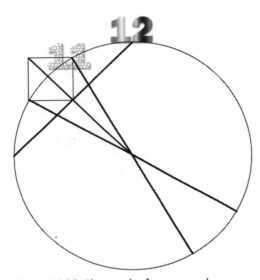

Figure 14.23 Placing the first numeral

4. Continue to insert the number designs, placing them accurately around the face.

Tip

Clock numbers are 30 degrees apart. There are two ways to space the hours accurately on your clock face: You can bisect each quarter circle and put hour marks where horizontal and vertical lines intersect the circle's edge, or you can draw a line from the center out and rotate that line in 30-degree increments. Refer to Figure 14.23.

5. Insert your company logo or other finishing artwork (see Figure 14.24).

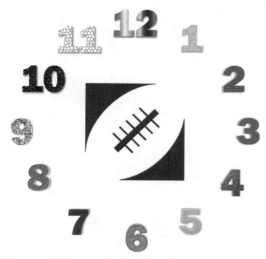

Figure 14.24 Inserting the logo

Printing, Gluing, and Cutting

6. Print this image on your highest quality paper at your printer's highest resolution.

7. Using a circular cutter or a utility knife and a template, cut out the circle. Cut a small hole at the center to accommodate the clock hands.

8. Use spray adhesive or rubber cement to glue the new clock face to the clock face. See Figure 14.25 for our example. Let this dry thoroughly.

Little Assembly Required

9. Replace all the parts and you have a new eye-catching decoration for any room.

Creativity

Use these clocks for promotions, awards, or gifts in the holiday season. Use bold graphics for a more modern look, or use your scanned images as a guide.

Are any of your scanned pictures funny? Use a crazy display font, and type a huge message on the clock face that can be read from across the room. Try 72-point type for this effect.

Figure 14.25 Attaching the clock face

A Five-Minute Magnet

These magnets are great giveaways for customers and are also a great money-generating advertising approach. Your business can pass these out in many ways, depending on your budget. Have some magnets available in your reception area, or mail them along with your company newsletter. If your business sells strictly to other businesses, these magnets will wind up on file cabinets and overhead lateral file drawers. If you sell to consumers, the home refrigerator will be the display site. As you plan your design, make sure to maximize your impact on the recipient.

This quick project requires almost no materials. Just scan a photo, add some text, and print! The magnets come with self-adhesive backings, so cut your image to size and position it on the sticky side of the magnet. These magnets are fun to give as gifts and are inexpensive when bought in packages of 100.

MATERIALS

Business card-sized self-adhesive magnets

Paper

Scissors or utility knife

Straightedge or ruler

What Works for You?

The basic steps are to scan your art, lay it out on a page with your business contact information, and then make duplicate images to fill up a page. Print, cut them out, and apply to the magnets. The trickiest party is making a nice, compact image with easy-to-read text and a clean layout. What will your graphic be? It could be a product picture, a scene that is a pun on the name of your company, or a photograph of you or your founder. Remember that the recipient will have this magnet on a cubicle wall or refrigerator, so make the most impact with a dramatic image.

Creating Your Image

1. Scan your image. Resize the image so that it corresponds with the final size you will use in your layout — not more than 2 inches by 3½ inches (see Figure 14.26). We are using our company logo for this project.

2. If background elements are a distraction, use your editing tools to remove them. Adjust the color and fix any imperfections in your scan. Save it at the best resolution and in the format most compatible with your page layout software.

Cross-Reference

See Chapter 4, "Resolution, Interpolation, and Sharp Images," and Chapter 10, "Optimizing Color," for more information on resolution and color adjustments.

3. Open your page layout program and draw a box that is 3½ inches wide by 2 inches high. Fill this box with a color that coordinates with your scanned image.

4. Place or insert your scanned image within the box, resizing as necessary.

5. Create your design and message. We used a font that matches our logo.

Figure 14.26 Resizing the scanned image

Laying Out the Page

6. When you have completed the styling, copy all of the elements and paste them into the second box on your page. Now you will have two pieces that are exactly alike. Continue this until you have ten images, all the same, on your page (Figure 14.27 shows a blank layout of the ten image areas).

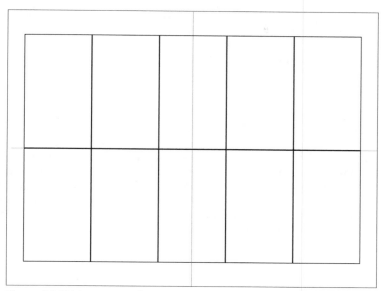

Figure 14.27 Laying out the images

Printing and Assembling

7. Print the necessary number of pages. Let them rest to keep the ink from smearing and to allow the paper to flatten out.

8. Cut out these pieces, using a utility knife or a rotary cutter and self-healing mat.

9. Take one of the two pieces, remove the self-adhesive backing, and carefully position the printed square of paper on the magnet. Smooth it out neatly.

10. To complete the process, continue to stick the rectangles of paper onto the self-adhesive magnets.

Now pop one of these magnets onto a metal surface and check out their irresistibility. You've got to look. . . .

Creativity

You can buy two types of self-adhesive magnets: business card-sized pieces or larger magnetic material in a 5 × 8-inch sheet. There is also a printable magnetic sheet — designed for ink jet printers. It is thinner than the others are, but it is neat to print directly on the magnet. These great materials enable you to make interesting projects for a variety of uses. Make reminders of reorder points for your product, or list all of the common part numbers or reference information on these larger sheets. Personally, you could have fun with this as well. Think about digitizing your Hawaiian vacation pictures and putting them on full-sized sheets. What a reminder!

Moving On

In the next chapter, we start having fun with projects for the home. We begin with ideas that are one step up on the complexity scale — meant to be completed fairly quickly with a minimum of extra tools and materials. This doesn't mean the projects aren't loads of fun. We pack a lot of creativity into some pretty straightforward ideas. Try some of these for gifts and to show off the tons of family photos that you probably already have.

Projects for the Home

In this chapter, we explore some interesting possibilities for home projects. All of these projects are relatively simple, require a minimum of tools, and are relatively low on the complexity scale. Any one of these could be completed in a few hours, if not less than an hour. Part of the charm of using a scanner is that it provides instant access to a world of pictures and colorful patterns and textures. We all have tons of family, vacation and travel, and personal photographs; this chapter is a way to start pulling them out of that shoebox and getting them into circulation.

Quick and clever greeting cards can be made for the price of a sheet of paper. Use card-making kits, such as the beautiful HP Printable Expressions, or make your own. We also show you how to compose greeting card poetry and imagery. You can use these messages in your own cards or insert them into the card-making software program of your choice.

We show you how to make a photo-collage pillow and an unexpected commemorative object, wallpaper borders made up of images of your own choosing — the perfect accent for a special room! And, finally, for the extra-added touches — fabric leaves that can be used in any way that your imagination can think of.

Quick and Clever Greeting Cards

Personalized greeting cards made on a computer are increasing in popularity. Have you received one yet? Most of them use images from greeting card software packages and may be printed on plain old bond paper. A new offering from Hewlett-Packard called Printable Expressions is now in computer stores, catalogs, and other retailers. The specialty packs, which feature such things as beautiful watercolor images, include a CD-ROM, the paper, and matching envelopes. Printable Expressions is a "point-and-click" package that produces professional and lovely results in a minimum of time. See Figure 15.1 for an example.

In this chapter, we also show you how to make your own cards. First, we will show you a simple starter idea that takes advantage of your scanner's capabilities. Try making cards with one of your kid's drawings and add backgrounds from old illustrations. You can also take photographs, edit them, and turn them into visual feasts. Now that you have an idea of how to proceed, let's make a card that reflects the real you.

MATERIALS

Image editing software

Page layout program

A selection of drawings, photographs, or other scannable material

A selection of papers

A selection of envelopes

Printer

Scissors or utility knife

Ruler

Glue stick

Bone folder or straightedge

Figure 15.1 Making greeting cards with printable expressions

Preparing and Positioning the Image and Message

First, select the type of card you want to make. Decide on the layout and draw a rough sketch of your final card. This project will make a card printed on a piece of 8½×11-inch paper folded into quarters. If you are going to make your own envelope, remember to size the card so that one piece of 8½×11-inch paper will enclose it.

1. Scan your picture at a resolution appropriate for your final output onto high-quality paper.

2. If the photograph color seems flat or dull, spice it up using the contrast and brightness controls on your scanner or in your image-editing software. If the image is fuzzy, check your software's "Sharpen" filters.

3. Resize and crop the image so it will fit your card. Save the image in the format best suited to your printer specifications.

4. In your page layout software, open up your photograph and copy and paste it on the bottom-right half of your blank page. See Figure 15.2 for an example.

5. Use your text tool to type your greeting. See the next project, "Greeting Card Poetry and Imagery," for ideas on words and expressions for your card.

6. Rotate the text upside down so that it will appear properly when the card is folded. Figure 15.2 shows a sample card layout.

Figure 15.2 Positioning your photo

Printing Your Card

Lots of prescored papers are on the market. Try these papers for rich-looking results. You can also use any firm, index-weight paper. Ensure the proper loading of your printer paper trays before you start. Read the package instructions and compare these instructions to your printer owner's manual.

7. Print as many cards as you need. If you are printing multiples, monitor the sheet feeding, as some heavier weight papers may be more likely to misfeed.

8. Let your cards rest for a few minutes to allow the paper to absorb the inks.

9. If your paper is scored for greeting cards, fold along the score lines. If not, measure carefully and, using a straightedge or a bone folder, fold neatly into quarters.

Making Envelopes

If you are making your own envelopes, use the template in Figure 15.3 as a model for your own. For other sizes, adjust your measurements. If you are using purchased envelopes, skip Steps 10 through 16 and simply print directly on your envelopes.

10. In your image editing software, open your scanned picture. Find an interesting section in the image and crop a small piece, ½ inch wide by 1 inch tall. Save this, calling it "envelope image," in the format and at the resolution best suited to your setup.

11. Open a new layout in your page layout software. Insert "envelope image" in the upper-left corner, ¼ inch from the top and left edges. See Figure 15.4 for our example.

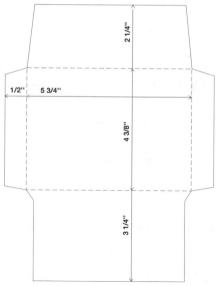

Figure 15.3 A template for making your own envelopes

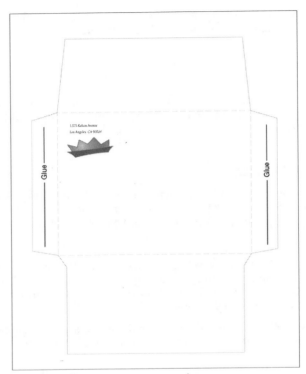

Figure 15.4 Laying out your envelope

Tip

To check positioning, print a sample of your image at low resolution. Hold it on top of a piece of your envelope paper and hold both up to the light. Take accurate measurements to reposition your image in the correct spot.

12. Using your text tool, type in the return address information. Position up against the scanned image. Save this as "envelope return address."

13. Print enough envelope sheets plus one or two extras to cover all of your cards.

Tip

Consider printing each envelope using a different font. This will give you the opportunity to try out all of those great fonts on your computer.

14. Using the template in Figure 15.3 as a model, cut out the requisite number of envelopes.

15. Fold along the dotted line, using a bone folder or a straightedge.

16. Apply glue to the spaces indicated in Figure 15.4 and press down on the flaps. Allow to dry thoroughly.

The Final Step

You are ready to sign and send. Slide each card into its envelope and your card is ready to mail!

Creativity

The possibilities are endless. Make cards that reflect your own life. Make envelopes that show off your scanner. Big images can cover an envelope. Be sure to create a white space for the address information. Can you imagine a family photograph splashed all over the envelope for your holiday card? The relatives will love it.

Use this for work, too. Imagine getting out of the boring white convention. An envelope with an image of your product gracing the cover will be a big attention-getter.

Greeting Card Poetry and Imagery

You have learned how to make basic cards. Now let's focus on how to get your message across with poetry and images. First, consider that your card is a small, short book. You have a cover, an inner page, a facing page, and a back. Let's use all of these surfaces to create a work of art. The personalization that computers offer matches the trends toward personalization you see in other parts of your life. So let's take this to the next level and have some fun!

MATERIALS

Image editing software

Good quality paper

Photographic images, hand-drawn images

Bone folder or straightedge

We will make a template that you can use for a variety of cards for all occasions. So gather up some images and get ready for a creativity session.

Creating Your Logo

This logo will be placed on the back of each card — commercial cards have the name of the company, the bar code, and price back there. We will make a small, all-purpose logo to enhance the professional look of your cards. If you already have a logo, use it. For this card, the design elements will be a photograph of the card creator's home and a bit of poetry.

1. Scan the image and size it to fit: about 1-inch square. Save it in the format and at the resolution appropriate for your equipment.

2. In your page layout software, open a new document and place guidelines that mark the center point of your page. Also include lines that delineate the printable area of your page.

3. Save this, calling it "greeting card template." If your software allows you to make a true template, follow your user's manual for directions.

4. Insert your photograph. Place it in the lower-left quadrant of your layout. See Figure 15.5 for our layout.

Figure 15.5 Placing your photo in the lower-left quadrant

5. Using your text tool, type in a short rhyming couplet to express the nature of your creations. We use:

```
"Roses are red, violets are blue,
I made this card just for you."
```

6. Position this couplet just below your photo, centered and with the text styled to look balanced.

7. Save this. Now you have a ready-made shell for any occasion.

Using Your Template

8. When you need to make a quick card, just pop in the cover art, type the message, rotate the text upside down, and print your finished work.

Creativity

A rebus is always a great way to use images. Each word in the message is replaced by a picture that represents that word. We'll show you an example, and then you can build your own.

1. Collect three images: an eye, a heart, and an object in the shape of a "U." The "U" can be either a fancy font scanned from a book of clip art or a picture of a natural object that forms a "U." How about the "U" from a "No U Turn" sign? If you cannot locate anything, draw a "U" with markers and color it with a lively set of colors. Have fun looking for heart and eye images. Did you ever paint a picture with a heart in it? Or have you ever made a needlepoint or a workshop project in which you carved or sewed a heart? You can use photographs of people as a source of eye images for your rebus. Enlarge the eye area and crop it closely.

2. Scan these images in, resize them, and save them in the appropriate format for your setup.

   Assemble these images in your page layout software. Adjust the coloring, size, and spacing of the three objects.

Look around for old ditties, poems, and songs that you can parody. Here are some poems you might use or edit to your taste.

```
"A_B_C_D_E_F_G,
here's a card that's made by me."
```

```
"How do I love thee, let my computer count the ways . . ."
```

Add some cute images that go with your poem. Build a library of images you can use.

Cross-Reference

See Chapter 12, "Getting Started with Scanner Projects," for helpful hints on building your image library.

Family Genealogy with Scanned Materials

This is the hottest paper craft going! People are falling in love with old heirloom photos, and scanners can help you in two ways: show off your beautiful heritage and protect the original prints from the elements. Normally, when working on projects that you mean to last for generations, you would use only archival-quality materials. This means that the acid/alkali balance of the papers and inks is as neutral as possible, the glues will last and not harm your precious mementos, and the scrapbook pages or other materials will isolate each photograph from others so that the chemicals do not damage anything.

If you want to avoid all the issues surrounding potentially harmful acids and you don't want to cut into or otherwise damage fragile items, use your scanner to document all your treasures and then store the originals in acid-free storage. This approach also enables you to make multiples so all family members share the memories. You can pass this creation along to other branches of a family, and they can include their materials as well.

Here's how we'll do it. Each scrapbook page will contain two images and will make an 8½×11-inch page. Before you begin, select two photographs that relate to one another. Pick a recurring idea in both of the photos. Is a trip involved? Is it a party? Find two sepia-toned photos that would look good together and are oriented in the same direction. In our example, both photos have their longest edge along the bottom. Old Polaroid photos, as used in this example, were generally printed on paper with dimensions of 4½ by 3½ inches, so use that measurement as your starting point.

There are two approaches to this project — one for older photos and one for more modern photos. Look over your materials first and decide which approach is best for you.

MATERIALS

Photographs

Small mementos such as wedding rings, pearl necklaces, bits of fabric, and so forth

Card stock in colors and white

Glossy, photo-quality paper

Scissors, rotary cutter, and self healing mat or utility knife

Ruler

Rubber cement

Three-ring binder

Top-loading page protectors

Images to coordinate with your photographs

Draw program

Paint program or photo editing program

Decorative edging scissors

Raffia

Glitter and stickers or other embellishments

Arranging Your Photographs

1. Scan the pictures. This is a great way to learn about your scanner as you adjust for color balance and resolution decisions.

 Cross-Reference

See Chapter 4, "Resolution, Interpolation, and Sharp Images," and Chapter 10, "Optimizing Color," for more information on the technical aspects of scanning.

2. Save the photographs in a format and at a resolution appropriate for your software and hardware. Print the pictures at the highest resolution your printer supports and on glossy photo paper. Trim all four sides with decorative edging scissors that give a rippled effect like the edges of an old Polaroid.

3. If your photograph is a posed shot of a group, use the following suggestions to complement the formality. Draw a box that is ¼ inch larger than the dimensions of the photo. Copy and paste this box, arranging the boxes so that they are one above the other and centered between the top and side edges, as shown in Figure 15.6.

4. Around these boxes, draw three more boxes that encompass the two rectangles, as shown in Figure 15.6.

5. Scan an image that complements your photographs. In our example, we use figures from an old book that belonged to the relatives.

Figure 15.6 Placing boxes for your photos

6. Place two figures on each rectangle as shown in Figure 15.7. You will use these figures to create holders for the photos in a later step.

7. Draw a small rectangle and place it below the largest rectangles.

8. In this box, type the text for the pictures. Include the full names of everyone you can document, the date of the photo, the occasion for the picture, and where it was taken. If you have a story about the event, include that information as well.

Tip

Select a typestyle that coordinates with the photo — use serif styles for an old-world look, funky styles for those great '50s and '60s color photographs, or a hippie style for photos from the '70s. Keep the style in line with the type of event pictured.

Figure 15.7 Drawing additional rectangles and placing figures

Printing and Attaching Your Photographic Image

9. Print the image on cardstock-weight paper. Select a color to pick up tones in one of the photos. Buff or an almond color is great for sepia-toned photos.

10. Cut out the portion of the figure inside the rectangle and slip your photo into these tabs to hold the photo in place.

A more modern photograph deserves a more up-to-date approach. Try the following for more contemporary photographs and mementos. First, select your theme. Ours is a family picnic in which the brothers and sister of one family got together for a birthday party. Follow along using your own materials and images, and go as wild as you want.

Scanning and Cropping Your Photograph

1. Scan your original photograph.

Cross-Reference

See Chapter 4, "Resolution, Interpolation, and Sharp Images," and Chapter 10, "Optimizing Color," for more information on the technical aspects of scanning and for help with resolution and color balance.

2. Use your image editing software to clean up the photographs, removing "red eye" and editing out any stray objects.

3. To make the photo as visually interesting as possible, tightly crop the image, which means selecting only the central image. Cut any extraneous backgrounds. Isolate the image by erasing and feathering out anything you don't like about the background. Next, adjust the color balance to suit your theme.

Creative Editing

4. Decide how you want to embellish the photograph. We scanned a variety of images that meant something to the family members, including the image of an eight-ball fortune-teller, which was among our "remember when we were kids" games. We also scanned a piece of the Hawaiian shirt belonging to one of the brothers to use as a background.

5. Adjust the colors. Because the dominant color in the photograph is a teal blue-green, we shifted the color of some of the images.

6. Edit out items you don't want in the photograph. We removed objects that detracted from the overall appearance.

Note

Creative editing is simple to do with the "clone" tool in most image editing software. If your program does not support this function, use your lasso tool and grab a section of an adjacent area. Copy and paste this section into the area that you want to cover.

Arranging Your Composition

7. Arrange your picture elements, balancing image against image. See Figure 15.8 for our layout. After you add text, you will place the images.

8. Add text to mark the occasion. Make the text in a decorative typestyle that matches the mood of your page. For a sporty page, choose a sans serif design. For a more formal look, pick an old-fashioned typestyle.

Tip

Generally, you should avoid typing everything in capital letters, and it's best to combine no more than two typestyles on a page. Make the type fairly large and spell-check it carefully. Always include full names of all the participants in photos (nicknames may not be remembered after 50 years), the date, the location, and the occasion. Add some fun comments as well because these compositions are meant to be warm and loving.

Figure 15.8 Our collage layout

9. Crop your images by selecting their outlines or by drawing boxes or lassoing them. Feather the edges a bit if your software supports this function.

10. After you have completed the work, sharpen the image if necessary.

11. When you are happy with your composition, save the image in the format and at the resolution most appropriate for your hardware and software.

Adding Finishing Touches

12. Print the image on your glossy photo-quality paper at your highest resolution. Make sure you let the image dry — glossy papers are the most likely to smudge.

13. You can embellish the image with other items such as stickers and glitter. Punch holes in the image and tie on a piece of raffia. Dress it up with anything you can imagine.

14. Slip your embellished page into the top loading sleeve and put it into the binder.

Cross-Reference

See the project "Turn Your Plain Binder into a Work of Art" in Chapter 13 for binder cover ideas.

Creativity

Each page can be a work of art. Any daily event can be the subject for an heirloom book. Try grouping all the female members of one family together along with representations of activities in which they have been involved over the years. You can also document a child's life as he or she progresses from birth through school.

Creating a Custom Pillow

Create your own fabric for throw pillows. Your scanner is the key to opening a world of creativity with fabric. Scan images, make designs with the images, and then, using fabric sheets you make yourself, print your creation on cotton or other firmly woven fabrics. In later chapters, we cover two other methods of putting your image onto fabric. You can print on fabric sheets that can be bought from a variety of sources. These sheets are real fabric attached to a plastic film that allows it to glide through your printer's feeding mechanism. The other method involves ironing T-shirt transfers on fabric.

Printing on fabric is fun and easy. Once you get the hang of ironing the fabric on freezer paper, you will have a new world to explore! Watch what you can do!

We will make a small pillow, but you can use these techniques in lots of other ways — see the Creativity section for the possibilities.

MATERIALS

A selection of images

One yard of muslin or firmly woven cotton

Firm, heat-resistant ironing surface

Plastic-coated freezer paper

Fabric softener

Spray-on static removal product

Artist's fixative

Resealable plastic bag

Ruler

Rotary cutter and self-healing mat

Scissors

Thread to coordinate with photograph and fabric colors

Sewing machine

Batting — a piece approximately forty inches square

Pins or basting thread and needle

Fabrics in coordinating colors, for the backing and for the ruffle: ¼ yard of 45-inch-wide coordinating fabric (fabric A); and ½ yard of 45-inch-wide coordinating fabric (fabric B)

Iron

16-inch pillow form

Sewing machine

Scanning and Creating a New Image

You will scan several images — the images can be fabrics, designs, or photographs. Save each image at the same resolution and in the same format. The idea is to build a dense patterning of color and texture derived from several sources. By combining snippets of several scans, you create an entirely new look. Use this technique to tie together different color schemes and patterns in a room. As a result, your final pillow will make a unique statement.

1. Scan your images.

2. In your image editing program, open the first image. Make sure your page or canvas size is set to 7 by 7 inches. Resize this first image to cover the entire printable area of the page. Work first on your background image — an all-over pattern is good for the background.

3. Open your second image. Using either an eraser or a lasso tool, select an area to be removed. Delete this section. Continue to edit this second image until only the sections you want to remain are still visible. Using your selection tools (either drawing around the image or using what some software programs call the "magic wand"), pick out the image. Copy the image and paste it into the page with your first image. If your software allows you to use layers, this process can be simplified by putting the second image on a new layer and using your eraser and selection tools to edit out the unwanted parts of the image. The first image will show through.

4. Repeat this with all of the successive images. Your file may get rather large if you are using layers, but you will merge the layers in the last step.

5. Keep flipping between images until they form a pleasing combination. When you are satisfied with your design, save it. If you were using a layers function, merge the layers together, remembering to save both before and after you perform this operation. Figure 15.9 shows you this completed image.

Figure 15.9 The completed image

Preparing to Print on Fabric

You can print this graphic using fabric sheets you make yourself. The trick is to iron muslin to freezer paper, trim it carefully to size, and load it properly in your printer.

Read the instructions carefully and plan to test the fabric for the colorfastness of the inks in your particular printer, and for color fidelity because color changes from screen to printer. You will also need to check the layout for positioning of the image. When you are satisfied with the test, print the image on your fabric sheet, following the directions for your printer.

Muslin, either white or natural, is a good choice for this technique.

6. Cut a 10×13-inch square and rinse it under running water to get it wet. Pour ¼ cup of fabric softener and ¼ cup water into a resealable plastic bag. Place your fabric piece in the bag, seal it, and squish the fabric around in the solution. Leave it to soak for about 15 minutes.

7. Rinse under running water, let the excess water drain, and iron it flat.

8. Cut a piece of plastic-coated freezer paper that is 9½ by 12½ inches. On a firm, heat-resistant surface, position the freezer paper on top of the muslin. Heat your iron to a medium setting, with no steam. Iron the freezer paper onto the muslin.

9. Trim the fabric to standard paper dimensions: 8½ by 11 inches. Use a very sharp rotary cutter or utility knife.

10. Spray the right side of the fabric heavily with a static removal product and allow to dry completely before printing.

Print Time

11. When dry, feed the sheet into your printer just as you would a sheet of paper. Remember to check which side loads up.

12. After you have printed it, spray it gently with an artist's fixative. Spray lightly so that it doesn't become stiff. If you are only going to clean this item gently, you can skip this last step. But the fixative will allow you to wash the finished pillow cover.

13. Trim the image so that there is a ¼-inch margin on all four sides.

Piecing the Pillow Front

This simple assembly process involves cutting out fabric strips to piece around the edges of your central image. Then sew on a ruffle and a back, and stuff with a pillow form. That's it!

14. Using fabric A, cut out four strips that are 7½ inches long by 4½ inches wide.

15. Using fabric B, cut four squares that are 4½ by 4½ inches. These will complete the patchwork design for the pillow front.

16. In order to make the ruffle using fabric B, cut a strip that is 7 inches by 100 inches, piecing as necessary and pressing seams open.

17. Cut two rectangles of fabric A that are 16 inches by 10½ inches. These will form the pillow back.

18. Cut your computer-printed fabric to 7½ inches square, leaving a ¼-inch seam allowance around the central image.

19. Piece the front of the pillow by sewing a square of fabric B to a strip of fabric A, followed by a square of fabric B (see Figure 15.10).

20. For the center section, sew a strip of fabric A to the computer-printed fabric, followed by another strip of fabric A.

21. The bottom row is formed by sewing the last two squares of fabric B to the remaining strip of fabric A. Press all seams open as you work.

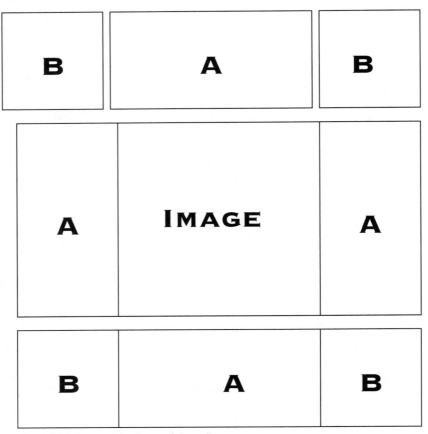

Figure 15.10 Piecing the front of the pillow

22. Assemble these rows into the pillow front. All seam allowances are ¼ inch.

23. Sew the first strip (two squares of fabric B and a strip of fabric A) to the strip with the computer-printed image on it, matching seams carefully and pressing seams open. Sew this to the last strip so that, when assembled, you have a 16-inch square piece. Make sure all your seams match perfectly.

Assembling the Pillow Back

24. For the back, take one piece of the backing fabric, turn under ¼ inch to the wrong side, turn under another ⅜ inch, and stitch this seam. Repeat this for the second backing piece.

25. Lay these pieces on your work surface, overlapping one side over the other and arranging them so that they form a perfect square, 16 inches by 16 inches. Using a basting stitch, sew a short line to anchor the two pieces to each other at the top and the bottom of the back.

Ruffle Time

26. To assemble the ruffle, sew the two short edges together. Press seams open. Fold the strip lengthwise in half and baste the two raw edges together, making sure the line of stitching is within the seam allowance (see Figure 15.11).

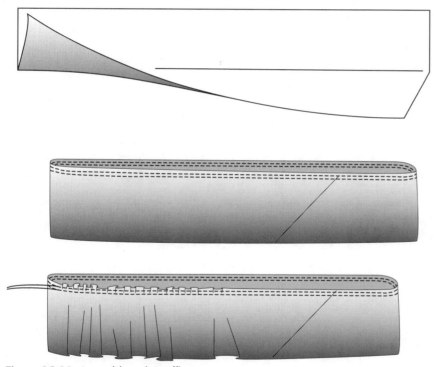

Figure 15.11 Assembling the ruffle

27. Run a gathering line of stitching down this same edge, within the seam allowance. Gather the ruffle and pin it to the right side of the pillow front, matching raw edges and basting or pinning. Arrange the gathers so that the ruffle fits the perimeter of the pillow, allowing slightly more gathers at the corners.

The Finale

28. Put the wrong sides of the pillow back and front together and baste or pin. Sew along all four outside edges, ½ inch from the edge. Make sure not to catch the ruffle in the seams. Trim corners and turn the pillow cover to the right side (see Figure 15.12).

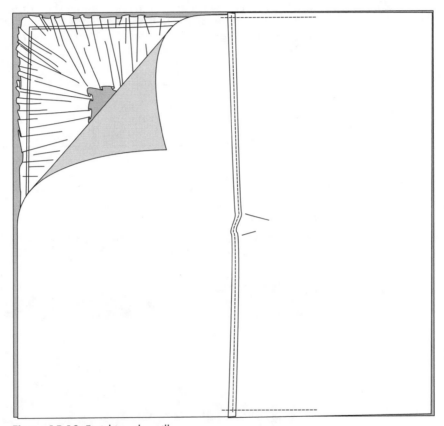

Figure 15.12 Finishing the pillow

29. Slide your pillow form into the pocket and put it in a place of honor! You now have a future heirloom. Display it with joy and pride.

Creativity

Use photographs of a child at several stages of development for a great look. You can also include text or other computer-drawn images. Select an image or create your own picture, using a draw or paint program on your computer. Maybe you have a child's drawing that is colorful and meaningful for you.

Try making a bag for your stockings or jewelry. Use the same techniques to create your fabric piece, and then combine it with other materials such as laces and satins for a luxurious effect. Try ironing silk onto the freezer paper — the resulting soft image will look nice with an abstract design.

Making Wallpaper Borders

Here is a very interesting technique for using scanner images to make unique wallpaper borders for a room. You may want to try this first on one wall or in a small room — a closet would be ideal. Pick a theme and then gather your resources to fit.

MATERIALS

Pictures of flowers

Scissors

Rubber cement or other decoupage glue

2-inch brush

Ruler

Utility knife

Polyurethane

Disposable brush for polyurethane

Selecting and Scanning the Images

Select your images. Here, we used a camera to capture gorgeous flowers from our garden. We then scanned the photos into the computer. Keep an eye out for colors that blend well together.

1. Gather up about 10 images and scan them. Clean up the images by correcting the color, removing unwanted parts, and isolating the central floral motif in each image. Save all the images at the same resolution and resize each motif so that they will all be approximately the same size when combined.

Cross-Reference

See Chapter 4, "Resolution, Interpolation, and Sharp Images," and Chapter 10, "Optimizing Color," for more information on the technical aspects of scanning.

2. In your image editing software or paint program, arrange a horizontal page that is 14 inches wide and 8½ inches high. This size makes best use of your paper and allows for the fewest number of pages. If your printer can use continuous form paper, make the image as long as your maximum banner. Generally, the maximum length that the hardware and software will accommodate, using continuous form paper, is about 5 feet long. Check your printer instructions and your editing software for more information.

Collaging Images Together

3. Open your first scan, and copy and paste it on this blank page. Open the second flower image and arrange it so that it slightly overlaps the first flower. Resize the second flower if the flowers are out of proportion to one another. See Figure 15.13 for positioning.

Figure 15.13 Positioning the first image

4. Continue to open flower images, and copy and paste them until you have a bouquet. Overlap the images to make them look like they have just been gathered up! When you have a composition that you like, copy that whole image and paste it in place next to the first one. Continue to do this until you have enough to fill the 13-inch page. We have sized it so that four bouquets fill the page, and have "split" the end bouquet so that the pieces will match up when one strip is put up next to a second one, making one complete bouquet. The border will be about 5 inches tall and will cover the width of your page, minus 1 inch for margins. Fill the upper border with flowers or color so that you have a fairly straight top edge; you will clean this up in the next step. The lower edge is meant to have an irregular shape, so do not fill this in evenly. Figure 15.14 gives you an example of the images pasted into one graphic.

Figure 15.14 Pasting the images into a bouquet

5. When you have created a border across your entire 13 inches, crop the image so that it has a straight top edge. Leave the natural bottom edge with its curves and gaps, as this will add charm to the border. Save this image in the format and at the resolution appropriate for your hardware and software.

6. This step is optional but can add interest to the border. Make several variations of the border, saving each one as a separate document. You might flip the whole border on its horizontal axis, and then replace some of the flowers with others. Change the color of some of the flowers using your selection tools. Make a copy of one of the flowers, resize it, and add it to another version.

How Many Prints Do You Need?

Calculate how much wall space you have. Measure the length of each wall, subtracting for doors or other openings that will not be covered. Remember that each border will be only 13 inches wide. Divide the perimeter measurement of your room by 12½ inches and add 15 percent to ensure some extra room for positioning, overlapping, and other changes. This approach will give you the number of pages you need.

Now Print Them

Plan on printing some extras of each image. If you have made variations on each pattern, print some of each variation and a few extra, just in case. You will find that, as you put up your border, you may want to cut out sections of one border to add variety and interest to the overall look.

7. Print, on plain bond paper, the number of sheets you calculated.

8. You might try printing on banner paper. With this media, you can print continuous strips. Be aware that there will be perforations in the paper and these can tear. Experiment to see if this works with your design.

Trimming and Pasting

Before you paste any of the sheets into place, plan their position. You may want to emphasize an area by adding cut-out motifs, or use your extra printouts to avoid a repetition. Lay out the borders on the floor around the room and check for positioning. When you are satisfied that the overall effect is balanced and pleasing, proceed.

9. Trim the top edge with a ruler and a utility knife, scissors, or a rotary cutter and self-healing mat. Using scissors, trim the lower edge and sides along the border.

10. Apply your glue or cement to the back of the first image and paste the image to the wall. Start at the least discernible corner of the room so that you get comfortable with the technique of positioning and arranging the pieces. Continue to paste all of the remaining images on the wall, overlapping slightly so that it is pleasing to the eye. In Figure 15.15 you can see how the pieces will match up at the seam.

Figure 15.15 Pasting the images to match at the seam

11. After you have completed the border, step back and check it from a distance. If something needs changing, reposition or add more motifs at this point.

Protective Touches

12. When you are satisfied with the results, let the border dry for about 12 hours. Examine the border and make sure all the ends are stuck down firmly.

13. The border must be sealed because the inks may run if splashed with liquids. Coat the entire border with spray fixative, polyurethane, or decoupage glue in a thin layer.

14. If you are using polyurethane, apply a thin coat using even brush strokes. Allow to dry according to the manufacturer's directions and then apply a second thin coat.

Creativity

Make a scroll with fancy text or family photos for around the top of a child's bedroom. Tint the polyurethane with a stain to add a depth of color to the entire border. Use images of old musical scores and old instruments for a romantic look. For a more subtle look, tone down all of the colors in the images or change a color. You can use this technique on a floor as well. Make sure that you seal floors very carefully, as they get much more wear and tear than walls.

Creating Art from Autumn Leaves

This is a simple but beautiful project that brings the outdoors indoors and creates a new electronic work based on the beauty of nature. These objects can be used for a variety of purposes, so make some extras.

MATERIALS

A leaf from a tree — oak, maple, or liquidambar are good choices

T-shirt transfer paper

½ yard of muslin fabric

Scissors

Florist tape

Thin wire

Fusible webbing

Iron

Ironing cloth

Scanning Mother Nature

Go out into the garden now. Find a beautiful leaf. Is there one that has already fallen? If so, use that leaf. If not, pick a leaf off a tree. Look for an unblemished leaf with a classic shape. This will be your scanned image. While you're at it, pick up a few more leaves and test them out as alternatives. You didn't know computers would make you commune with nature, did you?

1. Scan the leaf at a resolution of around 75 dpi. Resize it so that its longest dimension is about 5 inches. Save it in a format that you can use in your paint program.

2. Open the image in a paint program and change the "pixels per inch" setting. All software is different; Photoshop enables you to do this using the Image menu and the Image Size window. Select 10 pixels per inch. When you see the change in your image, it will certainly inspire you to use this technique on lots of projects. To achieve maximum differentiation in each pixel, sharpen the image with whatever tools your software offers. See Figure 15.16 for an example of the image after resizing and sharpening operations.

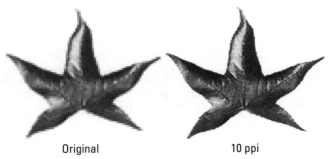

Original   10 ppi

Figure 15.16 The image after resizing and sharpening

3. You may need to make some additional changes to this image — use your pencil, brush, and spray paint tools to enhance the color variations and strengthen the leaf's structure. When you are satisfied with your image, save it at 10 pixels per inch and in whatever format is best for your software. Flip this image on its horizontal axis and save it again. This process creates the back of the leaf.

Printing on T-shirt Transfers

Before you print, review the instructions for both your printer and the transfer material. There may be special settings to optimize your results.

4. Print the image on the T-shirt transfer. Print one more, this time with the image flipped. Trim around your images to within ⅛ inch. Leave a small tab sticking up on each image so that you can pull off the paper backing after it has been transferred.

5. Prepare a firm ironing surface and preheat your iron. Remove any water from the iron and set the temperature gauge to the hottest setting. Make a test sample if this is the first time you have used this technique.

6. Arrange the muslin fabric on your surface, iron it smooth, and place the transfer paper on it, image side down. Make sure that you have a good ½-inch margin on all sides for your seam allowances. Iron the image onto the muslin. I have found that gently anchoring the image with short all-over pressure, and then returning to iron in gentle, circular motions works best. Follow the manufacturer's directions as to length of ironing time. Do not iron over your small tab for removal of the backing paper. When the image is completely fused into the fabric, pull the corner tab and remove the backing paper. Repeat this for the back of the leaf.

Trimming and Sandwiching Your Leaves

Once you have leaf images transferred to fabric, you will use fusible webbing to make a front and a back. You will insert the wire stem in the same operation.

7. Cut a piece of fusible webbing slightly smaller than the trimmed pieces.

8. Cut a piece of the wire about 12 inches long. Make a sandwich of the back of the leaf, the fusible webbing, the wire, and the front of the leaf. See Figure 15.17 for the layering.

9. Review the manufacturer's instructions for the fusible webbing. Use a damp press cloth and a hot iron. Hold the iron down on one spot for about 10 seconds, pick it up, and move it, with some overlap. Continue this method until you have fused the entire object. Let it cool.

10. Trim the leaf so that no white edges remain. Make sure you check both sides because any little shift in ironing will mean that the images are slightly off-kilter.

11. Cover the wire with florist tape. Trim the ends and bend the leaf into a natural shape. A handmade beauty!

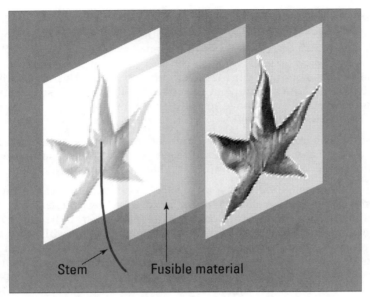

Stem   Fusible material

Figure 15.17 Layering the leaf with the fusible webbing and wire

Creativity

Bend the wire into a circle to make a beautiful napkin ring for a fall table. Change the color of each slightly so that you have a bouquet of colors. Make silk leaves in pastel colors for a bridal decoration. These leaves are strong, attractive, and can be packed flat and reshaped when needed, so make a bunch in advance and keep them for all sorts of occasions.

Moving On

In the next chapter we introduce you to some very fun and easy projects for kids. These projects are simpler, and are aimed at kids' interests. Even if you aren't a kid, you may want to look the projects over. The ideas are applicable to people of all ages: making books, book covers, and doorknob hangers are just a few of the projects we cover.

Projects for Kids

The projects in this chapter are geared toward things that children might enjoy. Trading cards and flip books are just two items your child will get a kick out of.

Door hangers are a perennial favorite for kids, and a good way to send a message! Another project in this chapter takes a favorite panoramic photo and turns it into a real scene-stealer on the bookshelf. This funny, attractive project takes advantage of the wide vista that panoramic cameras provide.

And writing a book is now within the realm of everyone's capability. Write your story, print it, and bind it. We show you a traditional Japanese folding book, which is so simple to make that even a novice can do it. In the appendix, we give you places to get more advanced information on this topic, including resources for buying kits to make books in the finest hand-bookbinding traditions, complete with all the tools. Check them out to discover what sort of author you can become.

You might find that your child would even like to assist you on these projects. It's a great opportunity to spark their creative side and you'll get a chance to spend some quality time together.

Doorknob Hanger

Here is a fun and easy way to send a non-verbal communication. If you have a door that closes, you have a potential spot to deliver a message.

This project is a good way to take a simple image and whip it into a nice, funny door accent. A quick photograph and blocks of color are all it takes to create an easy graphic image. First, you will scan in a photo or a picture that makes a statement. Then we show you how to combine the image with text and print, laminate, and trim the result. The whole process can be completed in less than 20 minutes. How's that for fast?

MATERIALS

Circle cutting device or circle template and utility knife

Image editing software

Good quality paper

Laminating material

Burnisher

Measuring and Planning Your Layout

To determine the dimensions of your hanger, measure the width of your doorknob. If it is significantly different than the standard of 2¼ inches, adjust the plans accordingly. Also, measure from the center of the doorknob to the edge of the door to ensure that when you shut the door, the hanger does not get stuck in the doorjamb.

1. In your drawing program, make a rectangle that measures 4½ inches wide by 8 inches tall. Do not use any outlining strokes; fill the rectangle with a deep purple.

2. Draw a circle that is 4½ inches in diameter using the oval (or "elliptical") tool while holding down the Shift key to "constrain" the shape to a perfect circle. Fill it with the same deep purple color, again with no outline.

3. Move the circle over the rectangle until the two forms make the shape shown in Figure 16.1.

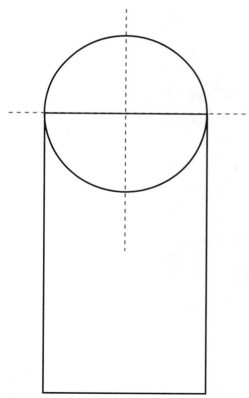

Figure 16.1 Laying out the doorknob hanger

4. Group the two objects (the rectangle and the circle) to link them. This will make them appear as one object.

5. Create the center hole for the doorknob by making a circle with a diameter of 2½ inches filled with white and no stroke. Center this smaller circle over the top circle of the grouped object (see Figure 16.2).

6. Using the text tool, type **Danger, Keep Out**, and apply a color. (We used the typeface Logger, which gives the appearance of trees being used to form letters.) Position the type below the circles (see Figure 16.3).

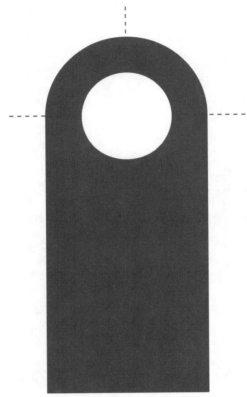

Figure 16.2 Creating the doorknob hole

Scanning Your Image

7. Select a picture or a photograph to include on this doorknob hanger. Scan it at the best resolution for your printer. Correct the scan brightness and contrast.

Figure 16.3 Typing the text

Cross-Reference

See Chapter 4, "Resolution, Interpolation, and Sharp Images," and Chapter 10, "Optimizing Color," for more information on the technical aspects of scanning.

8. Save your image in the format most compatible with your image editing software.

9. Copy and paste this image into your doorknob hanger layout.

10. Print the object on your best paper. Make sure you have the paper orientation set properly for the shape ("vertical" or "portrait").

Trimming and Laminating Your Image

Laminating paper is easy to use and puts a nice, durable surface over your creation. It adds body and allows the doorknob hanger to be wiped clean with a damp cloth, if necessary.

11. Trim the outside edges of the doorknob hanger to its finished size.

12. Cut two pieces of laminating plastic that are at least ¼ inch bigger than the paper containing your image.

13. Peel off the backing paper from one piece of the laminating plastic and carefully place the image face up on the adhesive side.

14. Peel the second piece of laminating plastic from its backing and carefully position it over the doorknob hanger (see Figure 16.4).

Figure 16.4 Laminating the image

15. Rub the pieces together firmly with a burnisher to make sure the laminating material adheres and to eliminate any air bubbles.

16. Tape the doorknob hanger to a padded surface or cutting mat.

17. Cut out the center circle — this is where the doorknob will slide through. To make perfectly round circles, use a circle cutter (see the appendix, "Resource Kit"). A circle cutter cuts circles and semi-circles up to about six inches in diameter. Otherwise, use a plastic template. If you don't have either a circle cutter or a plastic template, use a coffee mug. Position the mug and carefully cut around it. You may find it useful to have a utility knife (see the appendix, "Resource Kit") with a swivel blade that facilitates cutting curved lines.

18. Cut out the hanger, with its three straight edges and its domed top, leaving ¹⁄₁₆ inch of laminate beyond the paper to ensure a sealed edge.

Creativity

How about making a "Do Not Enter" or "No Parking" doorknob hanger? You can try other images as well. Print one with a messy picture on one side and a clean one on the other. Or scan a picture of your home to include on a "Welcome" hanger for houseguests. Make a happy birthday greeting with a photograph of the cake you baked for the special day.

How about making a treat for a family member? You could make a hanger that says, "No need to make your bed when the doorknob hanger says 'Surprise!'" Keep this on hand for special occasions and hang it on the inside of the door during the night. When the person wakes up, they see their treat!

There are lots of other ways to use this idea. Use a photo of your cat with "Tiger" printed below. You can even draw your own picture! Create a hanger that has a photo from a recent trip with "Memories" placed below. Hang it on a child's doorknob while they are asleep. This hanger is a nice way for a child to remember a special time when they wake up.

Book Covers with a Panoramic Photo

Have you ever made or bought decorative book covers for your books? With a little imagination, you can do the same thing on your computer. If you have a series of paperbacks, you can make each cover from one sheet of 8½×11-inch paper. Grab a bunch of novels and dress them up for your shelves or dorm room. Here's how.

You may have seen those great panoramic cameras — they take a wide, wide photograph. Take a picture of a beautiful scene, whether it is from a trip, your house, your dorm room, or a friend sitting in the backyard. Scan the photo and then lay it out in a page layout program. The trick is to divide up the photograph and make it into a series of images, each of which is saved individually. Then print them, one by one, and use each piece to cover a separate paperback book. When you finish them all, cover each book and line them up on a shelf; they form the entire scene along their spines! Neat trick!

MATERIALS

Image editing software

Draw program or layout software

Panoramic photograph of your choice

Plain bond paper

Bone folder or straightedge

Scissors/utility knife/rotary cutter and self-healing mat

12 paperback books

Making a Panorama

When lined up, the books' spines will create the entire vista from your photograph. Paperbacks are generally 4 inches wide by 7 inches tall and 1 inch thick. This is an ideal size for an 8½×11-inch piece of paper. The design you will create is for a group of 12 paperbacks. If your books are thicker or thinner than our dimensions, measure the spine width of your book and calculate based on this actual dimension. When you wrap your book in this cover, the scene will start to change so accurate measurements are necessary.

Creating Your Photographic Layout

What size is your picture? Most panoramic cameras produce an image that is about 10 inches wide by 3½ inches high. Select a photo with dimensions of this size or adjust the directions to match your picture. Scan in the photo and edit the image so it is crystal clear. Size it, calculating the number of books you have and the thickness of the books, and then prepare to print. It's as easy as that!

1. Scan in your photograph. Using your image editing software, adjust the color balance, feather the edge or add a creative "edge" treatment, and fix any other flaws or inconsistencies in the picture. Save this image at an appropriate resolution for your equipment. Name this image "Master Image." Remember to save your work in a format that also can be opened in your page layout program. With this step, the scene can be resized and positioned properly for the printing steps.

 Cross-Reference

See Chapter 4, "Resolution, Interpolation, and Sharp Images," and Chapter 10, "Optimizing Color," for more information on the technical aspects of scanning.

2. With your photo named "Master Image" open, save it again, and use the Save As command to name it "Image 1." Work on "Image 1" in the next step.

3. Make sure that your rulers are visible. Draw a guideline 4½ inches from the left edge of the photograph (see Figure 16.5).

4. Using your crop tool, drag from the upper-left corner of the image. Drag down to a point that includes the entire height of the photo but stops at your guideline, which is 4½ inches from the left edge. Refer to Figure 16.5 for a visual aid to cropping. Your cropping tool will form a "marquee" or border around your selection. When the marquee surrounds the exact section of the image that you want to keep, click inside this box. Now you will have only a portion of your photograph. Save this as "Image 1."

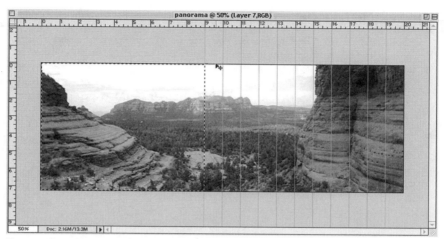

Figure 16.5 Cropping the image

Repeating the Process

In this section, you will build 12 slightly different images. Our measurements are in ½-inch increments, which in the final step will work out to be 1-inch measurements. Remember to adjust for differences in your book depth as you proceed.

5. Open your "Master Image" again. Select Save As and call it "Image 2." Move your existing guideline ½ inch to the right. Draw a second guideline ½ inch from the left edge.

6. Crop this image in between these guidelines (see Figure 16.5). Save Image 2.

7. Continue to reopen "Master Image" and move your guidelines to the right, ½ inch at a time. Crop within the guidelines and call each newly cropped photo "Image *X*." You will have 12 images when you are finished with this step.

Laying Out Your Book Covers

Here we open a page layout software program so that you can insert each of your images in a different page. This process enables you to position your picture element properly and save each as a completed page. When you have finished this step, you will have saved 25 documents. Storage space is always at a premium, so make sure to delete what you don't need when you are done.

Cross-Reference

See Chapter 12, "Getting Started with Scanner Projects," for helpful hints on managing all those images.

8. Open your page layout program and set the page orientation and your document setup to display a horizontal or "landscape" page area.

9. Draw guidelines as illustrated in Figure 16.6. These guidelines will enable you to place your photo properly.

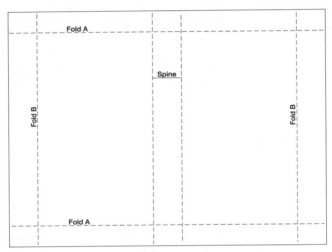

Figure 16.6 Drawing guidelines

10. Open "Image 1" and position it within the guidelines, resizing the photo to fill the space.

11. Save this as "Book 1." Repeat this process 11 times by following the next step.

12. Select Save As and call the document "Book 2." Delete the photo that appears. Open or insert "Image 2" in its place. Resize and position it within the guidelines. Save this as "Book 2." Continue until you have a page layout for each book cover photo.

Printing Your Book Covers

Next step, printing!

You will print each scene on your best paper. Plain bond is great, but you may also want to try some of the higher quality papers so that the photographic details really shine. You can also try printing on colored paper that enhances the look of the work. Remember to let the printed pages dry so they fold easier and don't smear.

13. Print each scene on a separate sheet of paper. Print at the highest resolution possible on your equipment.

14. Allow the pages to absorb the ink completely by setting them aside to dry for about an hour.

15. If necessary, cut to size, using your guidelines and a paper trimmer. You may also use a utility knife, a straightedge, and a padded surface.

Assembling and Folding Your Covers

Here comes the simple part: fold the paper and insert your book. Use a straightedge or a bone folder to get a firm, crisp edge. To check out how to fold the covers, see Figure 16.7.

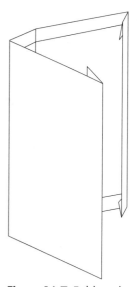

Figure 16.7 Folding the covers

16. With the image side facedown on your work surface, fold down ¾ inch on the top edge of the first book cover.

17. Fold along the bottom edge, ¾ of an inch from the edge, making sure that no white space appears. Check your book measurement. If it is more or less than 7 inches, adjust accordingly.

18. Fold in the left edge about 2 inches and slip this over the cover of the book. See Figure 16.7 for a visual display of this step.

19. Wrap the cover around the book and make a soft crease where the front edge of the book falls. Take the cover off, replace the soft crease with a sharp crease, and slide the cover back on the book.

20. Repeat this process for the rest of the 11 books in the series and align them on your shelf. Cool!

Creativity

Instead of using a photo, you may want to draw a scene and scan the drawing into your image editing software. Plan on a horizontal picture, and put most of the action in the center of the page so that it shows up on the spines of your books when they are exhibited on a shelf. If you want to place the book title and author's name on each spine, measure your cover very carefully, lining up the text with the absolute center of the image. Use text colors, sizes, and styles that allow sufficient contrast between your scene and the text for a legible result.

A Book with Personal Meaning

Of course you can make a book! It's as easy as A-B-C. The following project is a basic method for making a Japanese-style accordion book. When you have finished this project, check out the resources appendix for kits to build hardbound books and places to find out about taking this technique to the next level. We also give you lots of ideas and resources for completing this project. One book-binding kit in this section enables you to make a beautiful hand-bound book. We made one for a nephew's birthday and illustrated it with dinosaurs.

These books can be based on family photographs or other materials, so use your thinking cap.

In this project, we build a small book based on an adventure tale for young girls. The goal is to combine text and images into a carefree and delightful surprise. The accordion fold is an ancient technique that requires only simple materials and tools. Have fun, author!

MATERIALS

8½×14-inch paper

Scissors

Ribbon

Two pieces of cardboard

Bookbinding glue or other non-curling glue

Ruler

Bone folder or straightedge

Wallpaper or wrapping paper for the outside covers

Hand-drawn images and photographs

Fancy fonts

Image editing software

Page layout software

Planning Your Book

First gather and scan your materials and plan out your layout. We will be using small panels 2 inches wide by 3½ inches high. You can make two books from one sheet of 8½×14-inch paper. Each book will have six front panels, two covers, and four back panels. You can combine two strips by gluing them together to make a longer book, but eventually the book will become too thick and won't close nicely. Remember to take your printer margins into consideration if you adjust the measurements from our instructions.

After you print, cut, and fold the strips, you will attach the covers and add a bit of ribbon for tying them shut. Everyone loves these little jobs.

Setting Up Your Page Layout

1. In your page layout software, open up a new page with dimensions of 8½ by 14 inches and a horizontal or landscape orientation (see Figure 16.8).

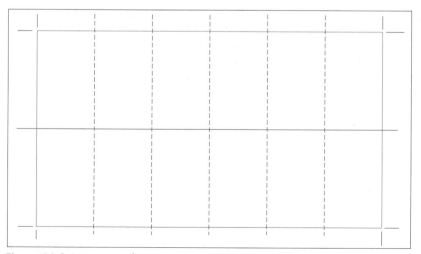

Figure 16.8 Laying out the page

2. Draw a box 12 inches wide and 7 inches high.

3. Draw a line that divides this box into two long rectangles each measuring 3½ by 12 inches (refer to Figure 16.8).

4. Using a light color and a dotted line, add vertical lines to your layout every 2 inches to create the separate panels (refer to Figure 16.8).

Writing and Positioning Your Story

Now you can get to the fun stuff. Use any materials that come to mind. If you don't have an image that works, try drawing it yourself and scanning it. Write your story in your word processing program. Make it funny, sad, or real. You can use real-life events or create a fantasy. Remember, these pages are fairly small, so be brief: A picture is worth a thousand words!

Use wild fonts if you have them. Choose the text color and type size to suit your efforts.

Cross-Reference

See Chapter 4, "Resolution, Interpolation, and Sharp Images," and Chapter 10, "Optimizing Color," for more information on the technical aspects of scanning.

5. Scan your images, photographs, and other materials, saving them at resolutions and in formats compatible with your equipment. Remember to size the scanned objects relative to each other and at the same resolution for proper layout appearance.

6. Add text as you go, using fun fonts, color, and styles that complement your story line.

7. Save these finished pages. Call the file "Book front."

8. Using your Save As command, save this page again, calling it "Book back."

9. Delete the earlier images and finish your story on the middle four panels (see Figure 16.9). The other two panels will be hidden by the cover pieces.

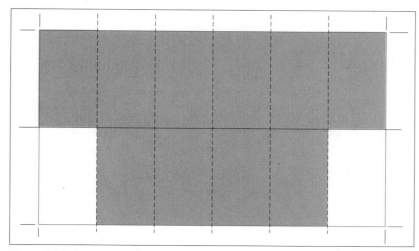

Figure 16.9 Positioning the story

Printing and Folding

In these steps, you will print your story on both sides of your paper — if your printer supports this function. Then you will cut out the strips and fold them. Almost done!

10. Print both pages on your best paper and at the highest resolution your printer supports. Run the first page through the printer, and then return the sheet to the printer and print the back.

11. Using a utility knife and a straightedge, cut the pieces of paper.

12. Fold the pieces accordion-style along the light markings you made in Step 4 (see Figure 16.10).

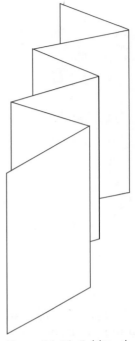

Figure 16.10 Folding the pieces

Assembling the Covers

Next, you create and print the cover designs, and cut and paste them onto the pieces of cardboard. Include a piece of ribbon, let them dry thoroughly, and tie the ribbon into a bow. The receiver will really appreciate this gift.

13. Scan a simple image for the front and back cover. Open your page layout software and insert this image into a rectangle ¼ inch larger in each dimension than your panel. In this example, the rectangle would be 2¼ by 3¾ inches. Add text, including the author's name and the title of the work.

14. Print the two rectangles on your best paper and at the highest resolution. Allow to sit for a few minutes to let the ink absorb.

15. Cut these two rectangles using a utility knife. Trim your piece of cardboard to 2⅛ by 3⅝ inches. Glue the covers to the cardboard, folding over the edges and securely gluing them to the back sides of each cover.

16. Glue the first page of the accordion-folded paper to the inside of the front cover, as in Figure 16.11.

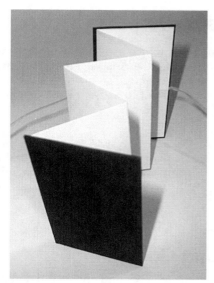

Figure 16.11 Gluing the paper to the front cover

17. Cut a 10-inch piece of ribbon and lay it down on the inside of the back cover. Glue the last page of the accordion-fold paper to the inside of the back cover, referring to Figure 16.11. The ribbon is sandwiched between the paper and the cover and is used to tie up the whole book for storage. Allow to dry thoroughly.

Creativity

This is only the beginning! You can make many other projects that teach you the art of bookbinding.

Tip

The following two books will be a great inspiration for projects like these: *Handmade Books* by Kathy Blake, Bullfinch Press, Little Brown and Company and *The Art and Craft of Paper* by Faith Shannon, Chronicle Books.

Here are some simple variations on this project. Print your pages on half-sheets of paper, assemble, and create covers of index-weight paper. Sew the book together along the spine using waxed linen cord. Experiment with different stitches and add embellishments such as trinkets, buttons, and charms to the binding. Scan patterned papers and use these pages as inside liners for your book. Your local copy shop will have alternative binding methods, including hardback styles. Now you can use the power of computers to help you write your text as well as publish your book in a beautiful and individual way.

Trading Cards for the Kids

This idea is aimed at kids but can be put to use in a variety of ways. You can make trading cards as "admission" tickets to a company party, or hand out cards with quick reference information to new clients. The main idea is to make the visual imagery so intriguing that people want to use and keep these clever little cards.

MATERIALS

Avery Dennison Laminated ID cards, Avery Dennison Self Laminating Tags, or card stock and Avery Dennison Self Adhesive Laminating Sheets

Utility knife

Ruler

Choosing and Scanning Good Images

Select at least two images. Examine these items and find a common color scheme. Is there a blue denim shirt or a white blouse in the photo? Key this characteristic to your second image. Finding a common thread will make the final image look more interesting and visually arresting. Now develop an idea for the card — a theme. If you're creating a trading card for a kid, think about either a slogan or a style that represents the child. Stretch your imagination beyond the usual. Try a soccer team affiliation, a cherished book character, or the child's favorite color.

If you are going to use these trading cards for kids, pick a good photograph of the child — a candid shot is more fun than a school portrait.

1. Scan the picture, cleaning it up as necessary.

2. This will be your main picture. Resize the image so that it is approximately 1¼ inches high. Save it in a resolution and in a format appropriate for your hardware and software.

3. Scan a photograph of a favorite pet or item, such as a soccer ball or a school logo. This secondary picture will be combined with the photo, so resize it to about ¾ inch high. Again, save it in the same resolution and format as your photograph.

Combining Images

4. In your paint program, open the photograph. Open the second image, and copy and paste it on top of the child's picture. Position the second image so the two images overlap in a pleasing way.

5. Add some text: the child's name and either the child's favorite slogan or some "statistics" on his or her best sports or classroom achievement (see Figure 16.12).

6. Position this image on your page. If you are using the Avery Dennison Laminated ID card kits, move the image to 1 inch below the top edge of your page and 4⅜ inches from the left edge of your page. If you are using the Avery Self Laminating tags, make sure your image is no larger than 3½ inches wide and 2 inches high. Place the image in the upper-left corner of your layout within the printable area on your page. If you are making your own cards with self-laminating sheets, you can size the image to suit yourself. Place it in the upper-left corner of your paper within the printable area of the page.

Alex Burden
Age: **6**   Team: **The Panthers**
Grade: **First**

Richmond West Side League

Figure 16.12 Adding text to the card

Printing Your Trading Cards

7. If you are using the ID Card kit, print your image on plain bond paper
   first. Hold the paper up to the light with a sheet of the Laminated ID
   cards behind it to check for orientation. Will it fit properly in the space?
   If not, adjust your image until it fits.

8. Load a sheet of the Laminated ID Cards in your printer and print your
   image. Follow packaged instructions for placing the lamination on
   the image.

9. If you are using the Self Laminating Tags, print your image on high-
   quality paper at your printer's highest resolution. Cut the image to size.

Assembling the Card

10. Peel off the tag backing and place your image on the tag. Press the lami-
    nating back over the image and seal.

11. If you are using the Self Adhesive Sheets, print the trading card on card
    stock. Remember to orient the paper properly. Let the printout sit for a
    few minutes to dry.

12. Trim the trading card to its finished size. You may want to leave about
    $\frac{1}{16}$ to $\frac{1}{8}$ inch of white margin to frame the image. If you want the image to
    bleed off the paper, allow the image to extend past the trim, being care-
    ful not to lose any important parts of your image. If you are making a
    two-sided card, paste the two sides together.

13. Get out your Self Adhesive Laminating Sheets. Cut two pieces of laminat-
    ing plastic at least $\frac{1}{2}$ inch bigger in length and width than your trading
    card. Peel off the backing paper from one piece of the laminating plastic.
    Carefully place the image face up on the adhesive side. Peel the second
    piece of laminating plastic from its backing and carefully position it over
    the trading card. Rub the pieces firmly to make sure the laminate
    adheres, and eliminate air bubbles as you smooth it out.

14. Trim all four sides of laminate to between $\frac{1}{8}$ and $\frac{1}{4}$ inch bigger than the
    trading card. Clean the edges of adhesive. Round off the corners to pro-
    tect them from splitting.

Creativity

We have walked you through one trading card, and you can now see the creative
possibilities! Look for images in photo albums, your drawings, and clip art. Here
are a few tips to follow when creating your cards:

■ Make the text large enough to fill the space and look nice. Make the letters
at least 20 points high.

- Add some decorative flourishes from a symbol font, Zapf Chancery font, or any number of clip art images or fonts you have on your system.

- Continue to experiment with the size of your images. Trading cards generally measure no more than 3 to 4 inches in width — use a credit card as a good sizing example.

- Produce several trading cards on one 8½ × 11-inch printout to conserve paper.

- Some software has a special feature that lets you align objects in relationship to each other automatically. Look in your software user's manual for instructions.

The Electronic Collage Factory

We love the look of image-on-image — the density of layers adds meaning to a picture. These techniques can be used in a variety of ways, as shown in the following Creativity section. We will walk you through the process of taking disparate scanned images and forming them into one beautiful image. Get ready to make something very personal. Here is a fun way to gather up all sorts of little pictures and turn them into a cohesive collection. This project can commemorate an event in a person's life or simply depict some of the fun things the person likes to do. The trick is to create an underlying grid to help organize the composition.

MATERIALS

A variety of found images, magazine clippings, and photographs that have personal meaning for you or the recipient

Glossy paper for output, if desired

Utility knife and blades

Rubber cement or spray adhesive

8½ × 11-inch piece of foam core board, ⅛ inch thick

A frame (optional)

Gathering Images

Gather up as many source images as possible. We found textures from fabrics and natural materials. We also included symbols from our school, play things, hand-drawn sketches, and cartoons. Additionally, we selected a border image from a copyright-free clip. Use text, photographs, and anything else that seems relevant.

1. Take the time to make good scans of all of your materials.

2. When you have completed all of your scans at the same resolution, start assembling the images. We recommend that you print each image on scratch paper for visual reference as you work.

Combining Images

3. Open a new document in your paint or photo editing software. Set the resolution and file type based on your final use of the image. For example, onscreen images for a Web site or a CD-ROM usually are set for a resolution of 72 dpi, but if you are going to print this collage, set your resolution based on the dpi of your printer.

4. Fill the page with a color and decide on a workable grid. An easy layout consists of 2-inch squares, which means your final composition will be 6 inches by 10 inches (see Figure 16.13).

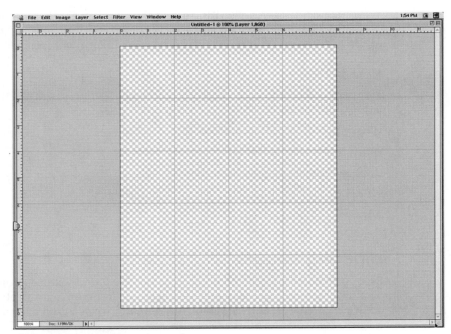

Figure 16.13 Laying out the grid

5. Look for the basic elements of design: line, shape, texture, value, form, space, and color. You may also have a particular theme such as "travel," or a new family pet to celebrate. Pick out two or three colors that relate to one another and at least two shapes that appear in several of the scans. For example, if you have old sepia-toned photographs, adjust your remaining images to reflect this color palette. If there are lots of vertical elements, such as people and upright lines, look for the repetition of these lines in other images. Reinforce these design elements when you combine them.

6. Using cut-and-paste techniques, combine your images on one electronic "page." Give yourself lots of room and don't let the images overlap just yet. Spread them out and look at them. Identify the shape you are seeking.

7. Begin to move the images into place, using your Save As command to get several varieties of images. Save each variation — this approach takes up disk space in the beginning, but you will delete these variations later.

8. Keeping to your grid, bring each individual piece into the collage and crop or trim it to the 2-inch grid. This will mean that some pieces are 2 inches by 2 inches while others are 2 inches by 4 inches, but they will all relate to one another. Fill the grid with the individual pieces until the surface is covered.

9. If your software allows you to create layers, your job is easier: simply put each image on a separate layer. You can then move them at will. Placing each image on a layer increases the file size dramatically, but in the final step you will merge all of these layers into one small file.

10. Arrange the text and any odd-shaped objects. If text is black, change it to a light color that allows it to be seen on the background. Or draw a box to place behind the text, using a fill color that is light enough to allow legibility. Group these two objects together so you can move them as one unit. Remember, the background colors must coordinate so the piece looks coherent (see Figure 16.14).

11. Another idea when adding text is to try all of your wild fonts. Take a character and make it huge — maybe 80 points. If the character has a negative space, such as the "o" in the middle of the "o," select an image and crop it so that it fills this shape.

12. Continue to fill and overlap items. Because this is a very personal work, overlapping items creates a sense of delight and surprise that lends more meaning to the projects.

Figure 16.14 Arranging the text and images

The Testing Process

13. Your approach will depend on your own style. If you are a methodical person, stay with a fairly firm horizontal and vertical grid. If you are a more spontaneous character, try placing images at random so they look as if they are exploding from the page. Keep your subject matter and overall tone in mind to produce harmony between all the elements.

14. Make sure to explore some of the special effects that come with your image editing software. Try blurring a section of your image. Another interesting technique is to convert the image from color to a duotone or a black-and-white image, and then "tinting" over it with brushes, spray paint, and pencils. Some software comes with special effects or filters such as "posterize," which flattens your selected image to look like a '60s psychedelic poster. Try it on a selected image and see what it can do. The key here is to experiment and save multiple versions of your work-in-progress. That way, you can return to an older image if something isn't working.

15. When the image begins to look "right" without looking bland, you are done. Check to see if your image looks good when you see it from a distance. Step away from your monitor and analyze it. The arrangement should keep your eye moving around the image. There should also be a focal point to which the eye is drawn.

What Will You Do with It?

16. Now that you have finished, decide on your output mode. If this image is going to be part of an onscreen presentation, save it in the format most compatible with the presentation software. If this image is to be printed, consult your printer resolution and type.

17. If you are using a "layers" functions, merge the layers together. This will dramatically decrease the size of your file. Remember to save your image both before and after this operation, just in case.

18. Print the work on your best paper and at your highest resolution. Let it rest for half an hour and then trim the white borders. Mount the paper on foam board using spray adhesive or rubber cement (see Figure 16.15). Frame it in a purchased or handmade frame.

Cross-Reference

See the section "Framing and Matting Photographs like a Pro" in Chapter 14 for instructions on making a frame.

Figure 16.15 Mounting the image on foam board

Creativity

Use these techniques to come up with a unique holiday card. Combine a solo photo of each family member with a picture from last year's holiday season. Or scan a favorite family holiday decoration and combine that image into the photo.

Trim the foam core to a size slightly smaller than the image, and wrap the image around the sides and glue firmly into place. Make several of these three-dimensional objects in varying sizes by keeping to the 2-inch grid. Hot-glue them to a larger piece of foam core board covered with a rich fabric, and frame this image under glass — it will be a beautiful object that everyone will enjoy.

Flip Books That Catch Your Eye

Did you ever see one of those cute flip books with funny little scenes in them? Here is a way to create a great version for any occasion! Before you begin, select a photograph of an outdoor scene. Then select an object you can use as the animation in your flip book — something that relates to your scene. A bouncing ball is perfect for this book, and we'll use that for our example, but you can look for other images. How about a butterfly or a screaming jet airplane? Find an image in a photograph or a postcard, for example.

You will need to edit and adjust the picture of your moveable object in several steps, all of which are described in the project instructions that follow. First, you will scan the ball and then clean out the background. Sometimes the object you want may be partially obscured by another object, such as a person's hand, or it may be resting on a surface that hides part of it. So, you may have to edit the image so that it forms a complete circle. Once you complete these steps, you will edit the ball to create the illusion of movement across your background picture.

MATERIALS

Photo stock paper — fairly firm

Utility knife or rotary cutter and self-healing mat or scissors

⅛-inch or ¼-inch hole punch

Grommet or button and leather or waxed twine lacing, 6 inches long

Two pictures to scan — one for the background and one for the object that will "move"

Card stock paper in a coordinating color

Image editing software

Paint and/or draw program

Preparing the Background

The easy part comes first: scan a background photograph. Look for a scene that has a nice, flat area. This will create a realistic surface on which to bounce your ball. Scan the ball image, clean it up, and start to combine the two. Clone and selection tools will help you in this process. See your user manual for details. Resize the ball so it looks natural in the picture. It must be small enough to show off the bouncing effect and large enough to be recognizable when you watch the flipping action. You will make several scenes; in each one, the position of the ball will change slightly. This technique creates the optical illusion of movement.

1. Scan the background picture and the picture of the ball at a resolution appropriate for your final output onto high-quality paper.

2. Use your software tools to erase all of the background and any objects that obscure the ball. If the ball is missing a section, use your clone and selection tools to replace that part of the image.

3. Resize the ball image to ½ inch in diameter. Save this in the same format and at the same resolution as your background picture.

4. Using an image editing or paint software program, open your background image. Crop the image so that it is 2 inches high by 4 inches wide. Adjust the color and clean up the image.

5. Make two pages of ten images each: two images wide and five images high (see Figure 16.16 for positioning). If you are using a paint program, make sure that your paper or canvas size is set for an 8½ × 11-inch paper size. This provides a large white area around your 2 × 4-inch scanned image. Select the image and copy and paste it nine more times, arranging each new pasted image as in Figure 16.16.

Tip

You can also save this image in a format that your page layout or draw program will accept. Then open a new document in that program, insert this scanned image into position, and copy and paste it nine times to complete the page.

6. Save this image and call it "page 1." Using your Save As command, save it again, calling it "page 2." Now you have 20 background images with which to work.

Figure 16.16 Pasting additional images

Adding the "Moving" Object

7. Open your scanned image of the ball. Select just the ball and copy it. Bring your background image to the front and paste the ball onto this page. Position the ball in the upper-left picture. Place it as shown in Figure 16.17.

Figure 16.17 Positioning the ball

8. Paste the ball on image number two, moving it slightly lower and to the right from where it was in image number one.

9. Repeat this process, and continue to move the image in an arc towards the lower-right edge of the image. To give a realistic effect, make the ball bounce, hit the surface, and bounce back up by arranging the progression of images as in Figure 16.18.

Figure 16.18 Making the ball bounce

10. Continue to lay out the moving ball, arranging it so that the ball action is spread out over 19 of your 20 images.

11. On the twentieth image, in the spot where the ball would have been, replace the spot with a drawn circle and a small message saying "Smile!" Color the text and the circle to contrast with the colors of the scanned image of the ball so that the final surprise will catch the eye of the viewer.

Printing and Binding Your Flip Book

12. Print the two pages on your highest quality paper and at the highest resolution that your printer supports. Cut apart the 20 images and assemble them in order. Punch two holes in each left-hand side, ¼ inch from the left edge and ⅜ inch from the top and bottom.

13. Create a cover for the book. In your word processing program, draw a box that is 2⅛ by 4⅛ inches. Type the words "My Flip Book" in 48-point type, centered and colored to coordinate with your project. Type the date of the book's creation and place a copy of the ball on the cover in the lower-right corner. Print this image on card stock.

14. Cut out this front cover and a second piece of the same size, 2⅛ by 4⅛ inches, for the back cover of your book. Mark where the holes of the insert pages will fall on the cover stock and punch two corresponding holes in the cover.

15. Run your leather lacing or waxed twine through the holes and your decorative button. Tie a square knot to anchor.

16. Flip through your pages gently to loosen them. Be careful not to crease any of the pages in the early run-throughs, as creasing will damage the illusion of movement.

Creativity

Here are some other ways you can use this technique. Try putting two people's figures in a flip book on a nice, romantic background. Have them come closer and closer together until they meet and are replaced with a big heart and a message of love. Very romantic! If you have a program that creates a morph of two objects, you can separate the images and attach one to each flip page. Watch a great animation of your dog morphing into your cat — or a baby picture morphing into an ancestor. This fun technique points out family resemblance.

Moving On

Creativity is enhanced by the variety of electronic devices available. Step out of the prepackaged mold and make your own statement. In chapters that follow, we show you how to put a spin on the holidays, or change the look of a Web site, and we also provide a long list of resources to help you on your way. Scanning is one key to making your personal life more fulfilling.

Seasonal Projects

IN THIS CHAPTER • A banner for any occasion

• A festive Thanksgiving table

• Enjoying the winter holidays

There's nothing like a looming holiday to get the creative juices going. Whether it is for work or pleasure, the cyclical calendar of the year presents multiple opportunities to personalize, create, and give gifts, mementos, and other expressions of your care and concern.

Using a scanner means that you can grab images from many sources and create lovely projects that will bring compliments and appreciation from all the recipients.

Don't forget that many projects in this book can be styled to suit a particular holiday. The creativity lies with you — the owner of a scanner and now an ace at getting great scans from a variety of materials.

Use your scanner to focus your efforts. Think about what vision you wish to project — this will surely suggest a variety of objects that have scanning potential. For example, if it is an Easter or spring project, think about pastel colors. What do you have at your fingertips that represents this palette? Work from this direction and you will begin to see the abundance of sources for your projects.

If you can't find an appropriate image to scan, draw or paint it yourself and scan it. And if you simply want color and texture, scribble or sloppily paint a surface, scan it, and use your image editing features to turn it into a veritable work of art.

Instructions for Making a Quick Banner

You can buy all sorts of software for making banners, but such software works best with continuous-form paper. If your printer does not have a continuous form switch, the following project helps you to create an easy, sturdy, and fun banner.

MATERIALS

Plain bond paper (in various light colors for a festive touch)

String or raffia (this rough natural fiber used for ties and bows can be found in crafts stores in different colors)

Images to scan

Stapler or tape

Embellishments such as self-stick gold stars, ribbons, and so forth (optional)

Pick a Theme

First, decide what your banner will say. Ours is a birthday greeting. The banner can, theoretically, be as long as you want, but the practical length would be about twenty feet, which accommodates a saying of up to about 25 letters. If you have more characters than that, make two banners!

You will create an image for each letter in your slogan. Hand-drawn or images culled from copyright-free clip-art books can be scanned, manipulated, colored, and printed. If you have a black-and-white printer, create outlines of each letter and, after printing, color them with markers or other art supplies.

Creating the Characters

1. Hand-draw or locate scannable clip-art images of the alphabet. Scan these and save them at a resolution that best suits your printer. Save them in a format that can be inserted into a draw or page layout program.

2. Scan images that you wish to use to embellish your banner. Save these images in the same format and resolution as your alphabet.

Cross-Reference

See Chapter 4, "Resolution, Interpolation, and Sharp Images," and Chapter 10, "Optimizing Color," for more information on resolution and file formats.

3. Insert the first character of your text. Resize the image so that it fills the page.

4. Leave a blank area approximately 1½ inches at the top for the fold. Of course, keep in mind your printer's specifications for margins.

5. Add other images, as desired.

6. Save this page. Open a new page and insert the next character. Adjust the size and color to suit. Save this next page, calling it something slightly different from the first page (maybe just the character it represents).

7. Continue to create a new page for each character of your text. Put other scanned images on the pages, as desired. You needn't make a blank page for spaces, but do make a page for each punctuation mark, such as exclamation points, commas, and periods. See Figure 17.1 for the pages we created.

Print Your Banner Characters

8. When you have completed the text, one character to a page and in the optimum size and best color scheme, print the entire set on your best paper.

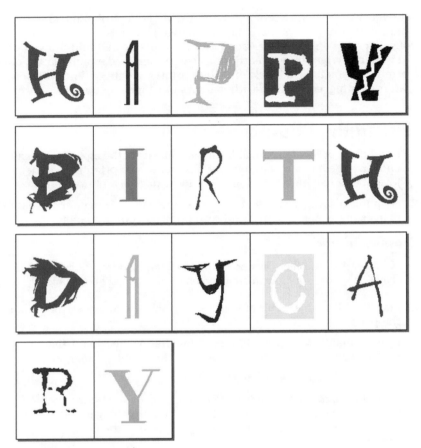

Figure 17.1 Lining up the pages

String 'Em Up

9. Using raffia or strong kitchen twine, cut a length of about one foot per character plus about two feet extra. So, if you have 22 characters in your banner, cut the string to a length of approximately 24 feet.

10. Take the first piece of paper with a character printed on it and fold over the top by 1 inch. Then place the string inside this flap and staple or tape the flap so that the paper forms a channel through which the string runs (see Figure 17.2).

11. Add the next piece to the right of this page.

Figure 17.2 Assembling the banner

12. Continue to add the pages until you need to insert a space. For spaces, simply use a blank piece of paper and continue on your way.

13. Complete your banner and check to make sure you have all the characters and punctuation in the right spots.

14. To hang the banner, use thumbtacks at each end and tie the string to it. If your banner is long, add a thumbtack in the middle to give support. If thumbtacks won't work on the surface on which you're hanging your banner, substitute suction cup hangers that can be purchased at a hardware store.

Creativity

In some software, you can convert a text character into an outline, which means you can then fill it with patterns, gradients or even images. Take advantage and make some really wild text. Scan your images and insert them into the outlines.

You could graduate the size of the text on each page to create an effect of a receding or sculptured greeting. Make each character a slightly different size from the next. When you hang this, it will have an optical effect that will really catch the eye.

When you have printed the greeting, you may choose to add embellishments such as glitter, gold leafing, beads, ribbons, and other items that add dimension and fun. One great idea is to place a bead on your string after each letter. You could make spaces in your banner by adding two beads spaced about 10 inches apart to create a gap between words.

If you've created a banner for the kickoff of a new year at your company, have everyone sign the finished work and rehang it in the office for continued inspiration. If your business is goals-oriented, have everyone sign the banner with his or her commitment to the coming year's accomplishments. This project is great positive reinforcement.

A Festive Thanksgiving Table

Holidays are a time for fun and traditions. We are establishing our tradition with a lovely coordinated tablecloth, napkins, and place cards. We've chosen to do this for Thanksgiving, but you can adapt this project to any holiday or special occasion. The following instructions are for one 42×42-inch tablecloth and eight 10¾-inch square napkins.

MATERIALS

2 yards of 45-inch unbleached cotton muslin, or any other appropriate fabric, or pre-made, plain tablecloth and napkins

T-shirt transfer paper (approximately 10 sheets)

Scrap fabric

Iron

Firm, flat ironing surface

Scissors

Utility knife

Straightedge

Cardstock

Creating the Art

1. Find some holiday-appropriate art. We used Victorian black-and-white drawings found in a royalty-free collection. The transfer paper creates a mirror image so remember to reverse your image. Scan each one to the approximate size you will need and save in the format that is correct for your image editing software. See Fig 17.3 for the scannable art that we used.

2. Color tint as needed. We stayed with a fall "harvest" look — browns and oranges.

3. After you have achieved the effect that you want, save in a format suitable for your draw or page layout software.

4. Now you can lay out your tablecloth and napkin design. We made a square tablecloth, using 45-inch fabric that, when hemmed, was 42 inches. So a comfortable layout scale worked out to ⅙ — or 7 inches square. This is the time for you to adjust our design to suit your table and your family.

Figure 17.3 Choosing holiday art

5. Open your draw or layout program and draw or indicate a 7-inch square. Place each of your elements on the document and size them to fit, arranging them in a pleasing design. Note the percentage that you reduced each element to fit the design. For example, in our layout we reduced the turkey to 40 percent of its actual size (see Figures 17.4 and 17.5).

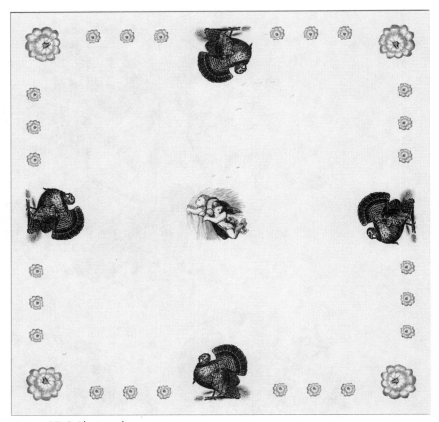

Figure 17.4 Placing the images

6. Once your design is set, open another page and again, begin placing each element. This time they need to be the actual size. By multiplying the percentage in the layout (40 percent for the turkey) by 6, you now have the actual size (240 percent) you need for final output. Continue to place and arrange the actual-size elements, trying to make the best use of the printable area as possible (see Figure 17.6).

7. Print the number of pages needed to complete the project on the T-shirt transfer paper, plus a couple of test images.

Figure 17.5 The napkin

Figure 17.6 Completing the layout

Making the Tablecloth and Napkins

8. Cut one 45-inch square and eight 11¼-inch squares from the muslin. Hem the tablecloth 1½ inches all around: fold over ¾ inch, press, and then fold over another ¾ inch. Stitch the hem. Hem the napkins ½ inch each side: fold over ¼ inch, press, and then folder over another ¼ inch. Stitch the hem.

9. Iron the hems flat.

Applying the Transfers

10. Carefully mark lightly with pencil (it washes out if any shows when you are done!) where each transfer is to be placed. It is better to plan carefully at this stage than to have to start over again.

11. Trim each transfer carefully, as close to the image as possible, leaving a small tab to aid in removing the backing.

12. Prepare a firm ironing surface and preheat your iron. Remove any water from the iron and set the temperature gauge to the hottest setting.

13. Arrange the scrap fabric on your surface, iron it smooth, and place one of the test transfer papers on it, image-side down. Make sure that you have a good 2-inch margin of fabric on all sides.

14. Begin ironing the test image on the scrap fabric. We have found that gently anchoring the image with short all-over pressure, and then returning to iron in a gentle, circular, up-and-down motion works best. Follow the manufacturer's directions as to the length of ironing time. Be careful not to iron over your small removal tab.

15. When the image is completely fused into the fabric, pull the corner tab while it is still very warm and remove the backing paper. Re-apply the iron if it isn't warm enough to come off easily. Try not to force the paper too much — you want to leave all of the image on the fabric! Adjust your designs as necessary. If you are satisfied with your results, proceed. If not, retest the techniques until you are consistent and successful. If one image is close to another, be sure to cover the already-transferred image with some scrap fabric to protect it.

16. Using your markings as guides, carefully place and iron each element. Now you have a beautiful tablecloth and eight napkins ready for your guests!

Turkey Place Cards

17. Open a page in your draw or page layout program. Divide the printable area of your page into thirds. Place the turkey that we used for the table-cloth in the first section. Size the image (about 2 inches high) and center it.

18. Draw a 1 × 7½-inch box to sit just under the turkey's feet. Fill the box with a color (we used a dark brick-red).

19. Centered within that box, place a text line that will be the guest's name. Size it as large as you can for readability, and choose an attractive font (we used Caslon Antique). Color the text a bright yellow-gold.

20. With a line, indicate a ½-inch cut ½ inch from each end of the base. One side cuts from the top; one side cuts from the bottom. This will enable you to interlock the ends to form the base when it is trimmed.

21. Group all of these elements. Copy and paste two more times to fill the page (see Figure 17.7).

Figure 17.7 Laying out the place cards

22. Type each guest's name, saving the first page when it is complete; then use the Save As command to save the additional pages needed in order to make one image for each guest.

23. When you have completed all of them, print them on cardstock.

24. Let the ink dry completely, and then trim each place card. Trim the base with a straightedge and utility knife and then cut carefully around the turkey with either a utility knife or scissors.

25. Make the cuts on the two ends. Bring the ends of the base around and slip the cuts together, keeping the ends on the inside (see Figure 17.8).

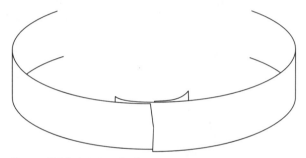

Figure 17.8 Joining the base

26. Voilá. A place card for each person!

Creativity

The place cards can also be used as napkin rings. And you can make them for any occasion: Mother's Day, birthdays, and for no reason whatsoever. Scanning small images to include can be fun — inside jokes or sweetly sentimental messages are great for a special Sunday brunch out on the patio.

First-birthday party tables can be set with these sweet mementos. Make very special ones that can be passed down, adding a name or photo each time it is used. Special occasions can be created for anyone — with the honoree's photo in the center of each place card or napkin ring. Don't stop here. There are so many ways to make a special occasion even more special.

Creating a Customized Company Christmas Card

You can buy preprinted holiday greetings cards with your company name stamped inside, but now that you have a scanner, why not personalize things a bit more? Make a wreath using photographs of the people who work for your company, scan an image of a red ribbon, and create your own greeting. People won't forget this card.

MATERIALS

Image editing software

Photographs of your company's products, buildings, or people

A red ribbon tied into a bow or a photograph of a bow

High-quality paper

Bone folder

Purchased envelopes or paper to make your own

Scissors

Glue

Ruler

Smile Everyone

Start by collecting photographs of everyone. Remember to ask permission to use the pictures on the company card. Once scanned, assembly is simple. Sheets of 8½ × 11-inch paper and purchased envelopes are all you need. Of course, you can always take the extra step and make your own envelopes, too.

1. Scan photographs and save them all at the same resolution and in the same format — one that can be imported into your page layout software.

Cross-Reference

See Chapter 4, "Resolution, Interpolation, and Sharp Images," and Chapter 10, "Optimizing Color," for more information on resolution and file formats.

2. Scan a bow or a picture of a bow. Clean up the scan and save it at the same resolution and in the same format as your photographs.

The Layout

3. Open your page layout software and draw guidelines as in Figure 17.9.

4. Draw a circle and place it on your page. Insert your first scan of a photograph of a face. Position it along the circle.

5. Insert the next face, overlapping it on your first face.

6. Continue to insert and overlap pictures until you use all of your photos.

7. Insert the bow at the bottom of the picture. See Figure 17.9 for our layout.

8. Using your text tool, type a greeting. Style and place the text to suit your layout. Our "Happy Holidays" text fit best in the middle of the wreath.

Figure 17.9 Designing your holiday card

The Message Inside

9. The inside message is positioned upside down so that it will print properly after folding. To do this, type and style the text to suit your layout. Use your rotate tools to turn it 180 degrees from its original orientation.

10. Lay out text and an image, if desired, for the back of the card. Your company logo or other device would be perfect.

 Cross-Reference

See Chapter 15, "Projects for the Home," and specifically the projects called "Quick and Clever Greeting Cards" and "Greeting Card Poetry and Imagery" for more ideas.

11. Print as many copies as you need, plus about 10 percent extra, on your highest quality paper.

12. Using a bone folder, score and fold into quarters.

Making the Envelope with a Return Address

Now that you have such a pretty card, you can't let the envelope be just a boring old white. Does your printer accommodate printing on envelopes? If so, dress the envelopes up to match your card.

If you are making your own envelopes, use our template shown later in Figure 17.10. For other sizes, adjust your measurements.

Return Address

13. In your image editing software, open the image you have selected for this. We found a wreath. Size this to fit and save this, calling it "envelope image," in the format and at the resolution best suited to your setup.

14. Open a new page in your page layout software. Insert this scanned image in the upper-left corner, ¼ inch from the top and left edges. See Figure 17.11 for our example. Check to see if there is an envelope template for your software or printer.

Tip

To check positioning, print a sample of your image at low resolution. Hold it on top of a piece of your envelope paper and hold both up to the light. Take accurate measurements to reposition your image in the correct spot. Also, cut pieces of paper the size of your envelope and use them to test positioning.

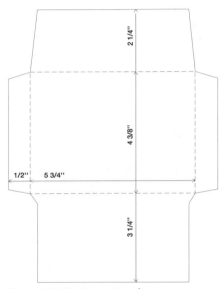

Figure 17.10 Preparing the image

15. Using your text tool, type the return address information. Position against the scanned image. Save this as "envelope return address."

Tip

In Step 15, you can experiment with all those great fonts you have on your computer.

Make Your Own Envelopes

16. Using the template in Figure 17.11, plan your layout to include cutting lines as well as return address information.

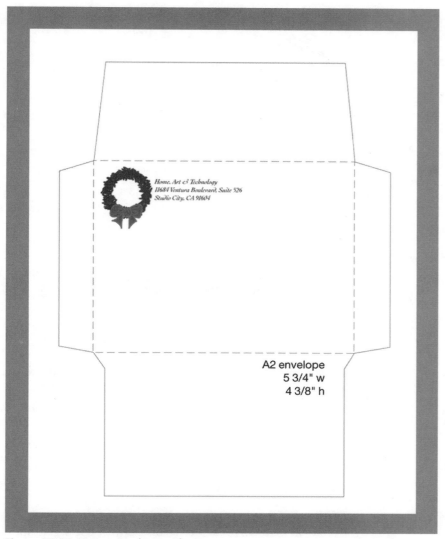

Home, Art & Technology
11684 Ventura Boulevard, Suite 526
Studio City, CA 91604

A2 envelope
5 3/4" w
4 3/8" h

Figure 17.11 Laying out the envelope

17. Using the same image and address as you created above, position these elements as shown in Figure 17.12. Print as many as you need.

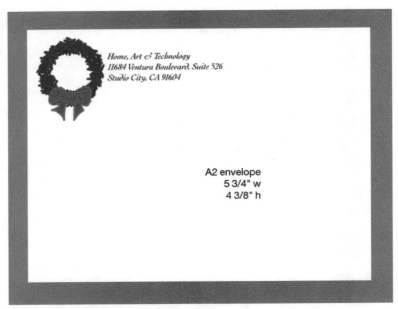

Home, Art & Technology
11684 Ventura Boulevard, Suite 526
Studio City, CA 91604

A2 envelope
5 3/4" w
4 3/8" h

Figure 17.12 Positioning the elements

18. Cut out the envelopes using scissors or a utility knife.

19. Score and fold along the dotted line, using a bone folder and a straightedge.

20. Fold the side flaps, apply glue, and fold the back of the envelope. Press firmly. Allow to dry thoroughly.

And the Envelope Please . . .

You are ready to sign and send.

21. Sign the cards and slip into your envelopes. Use self-stick dots or decorative stickers to close each envelope, or just use a glue stick to secure the back flap.

Creativity

You could make a card that uses your company logo. This would work especially well if your logo contains red or green. If not, think of some other appropriate images. Experiment with shaping one or all of the edges of the card. You can buy decorative edgers at a crafts shop.

Cross-Reference

See Chapter 13, "Projects for the Office," for information about making your own logo.

You could also make a two-fold card. Orient your paper horizontally and divide it into three vertical panels. Place the main image at the right-hand side. Open a second page and put your greeting on either the center or right-hand side, according to your preference. Print on both sides of the paper, and you have a neat design.

You could also cut the top edge of the paper on an angle. When folded, this technique creates an effect well suited to a festive card. Consider searching for the specialty papers that have two different colors — one on each side (duplex paper). Another way to maximize the punch of this piece is to fold your piece like doors, with the message inside. Color and movement give your card extra appeal.

Cards for Christmas or New Year's Day are just the beginning. Most companies have some sort of kickoff celebration — either yearly or based on a move to a new building or on the company anniversary. Make greeting cards to celebrate these events. Scan seasonal photos or special times and combine them in your page layout. Also consider scanning handwritten documents, award plaques, or other mementos.

Moving On

In the next chapter, we move up a notch on the complexity scale: new printing surfaces and materials. We aim at creating a more personal home environment. Remember that any of these home-oriented projects could also be reconfigured to spark some business ideas, so make sure to check them out!

Projects for Web Sites

IN THIS CHAPTER • Making text out of images

• Designing textured backgrounds

• Enhancing with banners, buttons, and image maps

• Laying out your site

Over the last several years, the Web has grown by incredible leaps and bounds. The beauty of the Web, of course, is its ability to present information graphically and dynamically. As with any new frontier, people are still discovering what works and what doesn't, and a tremendous amount of testing occurs every day. This chapter provides fundamental design principles for Web content creation. Your goal is to attract an audience and get them to act in some definitive way, either by buying a product or by absorbing some information. These two goals are similar and the benefits of using your scanner become readily apparent. You can easily adapt any of this chapter's four ideas to your purposes. Study the following information on how the use of graphical images will affect your text message, page layout, and other decision points. Graphics have the biggest impact on creating a well-tuned page, so consider these items:

■ What's the purpose of your page? Keep your overall style in mind. Is this going to be a funny, quirky, personal site? Do you need to convey serious information for a business? Are you providing a service, a product, information, or pure entertainment?

■ Who do you want as an audience? Knowing something about your intended viewers helps you plan the way you appeal to their senses. Everything about your site will be tailored to the demographics of your target audience.

■ How do you plan to present the information? In our culture, the eye is naturally drawn to the upper-left corner. Use this to your advantage. In order to capture a casual reader's attention, put the eye-catching content toward the top. If you have more information than one page can hold, break it into logical chunks.

■ Will you link to other sites? What will you use as an easy-to-understand method of getting viewers to click those links? Think this through — an overly complicated scheme is confusing; one that is too simple may not be intriguing enough. Graphics can be your key ally here.

■ How do you find the balance between the number of pictures you use and performance? If your page doesn't load quickly, people will simply leave your site. Your target audience influences this balancing act, as well. If you are aiming at the techno-proficient power users who collect plug-ins like dogs collect fleas, by all means, go ahead and load up your pages! If you want to reach a more conventional audience, skip the fancier, load-intensive flourishes and keep your graphic images as small as possible. Some of these people still have text-only readers!

Start with your overall message, mission, and style. Decide on colors and the main images you will use.

You can spend thousands, even hundreds of thousands of dollars for an exciting, animated Web site with lots of Java applets and frames and other jazzy items, but why? Your scanner and some basic HTML or Web authoring software are all you need to get started. This chapter does not teach you HTML, the language used to create Web pages, but check out the following IDG Books Worldwide offerings for more information on HTML:

- *HTML 4 Bible*, by Bryan Pfaffenberger and Alexis D. Gutzman
- *HTML 4 for Dummies (with CD-ROM)*, by Ed Tittel, Natanya Pitts, Mike Wooldridge, and Chelsea Valentine

Many Web sites also provide ideas and resources on building HTML for your pages. A good learning site about HTML and creating Web sites is located at `http://www.geocities.com/Heartland/Plains/6446/helpmap.html`. You may also want to look at a Netscape site that contains a wealth of information, links, and forums: `http://netcenterbu.builder.com/QuickReference/?tag=st.bl.3881.edt.bl_QuickReference`. Lead your viewers with simple graphic images you either create from scratch or edit from your source materials.

This chapter focuses on what to scan and how to scan it for best use on a page. Once you have your scan, we discuss some clever tricks that maximize the impact of your scans. We also introduce techniques for creating buttons, banners, and textures.

By showing you how to use graphics to create a sense of excitement, you will be prepared to meet the goals of your site: information and action.

Web Site Dress-Ups

You have seen some cool Web sites and you figure that some of these ideas must be easy enough to accomplish on your own site, right? Well, here's your chance. Your scanner comes into the picture as a two-pronged aid: an easy way to capture images and a starting point for making textures and backgrounds. This section shows you how to take a simple photograph and style it so that the resulting image is interesting and loads quickly. We also give you a couple of ideas on how to present the photograph as a focal point that enhances your message. Let's make a real statement.

One of the universal goals for publishing on the Web is to keep those images small! Most people will be viewing your pages on monitors with resolutions of around 72 ppi (pixels per inch) and approximately 15 inches diagonally. After considering room for menu bars, scrolling bars, and other objects, you will have an area approximately 8 inches wide by 5 inches deep with which to work. Aim to keep the total size of images used on a single page at around 50K or less. Calculate this target by multiplying the resolution (72 ppi) by the height and width of each image. As you can see, two to three images can easily meet this target. Reduce file size by using "indexed" colors — check your image editing software for details.

For faster page loading, specify the height and width attributes for each image in the page. That way, the browser sets aside a defined area for the picture and doesn't have to stop to calculate spacings. Height and width are expressed in pixels.

To scale an image for your overall page dimensions, think in terms of your viewer's screen size. For HP scanners, set the destination to Screen ⇨ Image File, or pick 75 (instead of 72) ppi. Then scale the image to the number of "pixels" you want for width and height. Think in terms of filling up a computer screen that is one of three sizes: 640×480 pixels, 800×600 pixels, or 1,024×768 pixels. If you think most of your visitors will have a 1,024×768 display, make your images somewhat smaller. If you want your site to work well on 640×480 displays, then make the image less than 640×480 (maybe 600×400 or 550×350).

Because you cannot control what type of equipment each viewer is using, the developers of the Web have come up with a limited palette of colors that are "browser-safe." Use these colors for text, backgrounds, and large expanses of a single color in an image. Check out the Web sites that show you these browser-safe colors — a good site is http://www.lynda.com/hex.html.

Almost all Web site developers use one of two formats for graphics: GIF (CompuServe Graphics Interchange Format, which will show up as a .gif extension in your file window) and JPEG (Joint Photographic Experts Group, .jpg extension). The JPEG format works best for photographs and continuous tone images. JPEG images can also be compressed, with fairly good control over these mathematical compression techniques. A common Windows file format for graphics is bitmap (.bmp), which can be converted in some software programs to the JPEG format.

The GIF format works best for vector images, line-art drawings, most logos, and screenshots. GIF files sometimes "dither" solid areas of color into a variety of tones and may not display as well as JPEG images. On the other hand, GIFs usually appear faster because they were designed for compact file size. The original GIF design standards were based on an environment for which downloading time was a major consideration. The trick for large, slower-loading graphics is to create two images, one at a low resolution and one at your final resolution. The low-resolution image, thanks to HTML, is displayed while the final image is loading. Refer to your HTML manuals for more information.

What Does Text Have to Do with Graphics?

As you create your Web sites, one of the fun decisions you get to make is what font to select. Before you tie all of your design considerations to this font decision, consider this: Most Web browsing software enables the user to set a default font that overrides any decisions you are about to make. Even though you will make default font decisions, the ultimate master is your viewer. Browser software such as Netscape Navigator uses a proportionally spaced font such as Times Roman as the default for text. If you want to control exactly how the viewers see your text, that text must be delivered as an image. Because of size limitations for downloading, you can see that this problem radically limits the amount of text that you can style. Save it for the headlines on the page.

Think of text in a new way: as image, focus, and entertainment. Your viewer receives an overall impression of contrast and pattern on your page. After this first graphic scan, the viewer moves from being a "viewer" to being a "reader" as they spend time deciphering the blocks of text. Catch them in the viewer stage and make it easy to woo them into the reader stage.

Use white space to show off and guide people visually to a highlight on your page. There is no need to restrict images in boxes with extraneous blank lines and horizontal rules. Give the viewer a wide-open feeling. These guidelines are especially important if you are selling a product: Capture the visitor's interest visually, and then move to the details.

One More Thing Before We Get Started . . .

Graphics may not show up properly in two situations:

- When the path to the directory where your image resides gets broken
- When your viewers use a text-only Web browser or when they turn graphics off

Provide an alternative by including text descriptions to your graphics. Otherwise, your viewers will see a generic placeholder image instead of informative text.

Tip

A *thumbnail* is a small version of your picture that can then be linked to a larger version. If you must use multiple large pictures, put a thumbnail of the picture on your page. The viewer can then click the thumbnail, and the larger picture appears. The disadvantage is that your viewer will be required to take one extra action to see your efforts, although this is mitigated by the quick load time. Upload both the picture and the thumbnail to your file directory.

MATERIALS

Image editing software

Draw program or page layout program

Photographs

Plain bond paper

Pencils, markers, or other drawing implements

Preparing the Photographic Images

Because the Web is such a visual medium, you need to master how to make your images look great onscreen. Take your time — practice and test as many methods as possible. Select a main image that will give you versatility. Spend the extra effort to make a good scan because you will use it in a variety of ways. Then scan some additional items to give yourself some flexibility as you proceed. The photograph used as an example in this section will become part of our Web site makeover in the section "Making Your Home Page Stand Out," later in this chapter.

1. Scan the first picture at a resolution appropriate for your intended audience. Remember that 72 dpi is about the highest resolution that most monitors use for display.

Cross-Reference

See Chapter 4, "Resolution, Interpolation, and Sharp Images," and Chapter 10, "Optimizing Color," for more information on the technical aspects of scanning.

2. Open the photo in your image editing software and correct any imperfections. See our example in Figure 18.1.

Figure 18.1 Beginning to prepare the image

3. Plan your photo placement on your page. Remember that most monitors use a horizontal page orientation. In our culture, we scan the page from top left to bottom right. Place the most important piece of information, or most eye-catching part of your image, in that upper-left quadrant.

Decorative Edges for the Photograph

Once you have a good scan, think about how to break it out of the traditional rectangle. Change the appearance of one or all four edges so that the picture takes on a different style. This technique involves scanning a piece of paper whose edges have been cut, torn, or otherwise manipulated. These scanned edges are applied to your photograph and the new image is saved separately.

4. Tear a blank piece of paper so that all four edges are slightly irregular (see Figure 18.2).

Figure 18.2 Creating irregular edges

5. Scan this piece of paper in black-and-white line-art mode. Save this image in the same file format and at the same resolution as your photograph.

6. Open your photograph in your image editing software and create a new channel.

7. Copy and paste your torn-edge scan into this channel. Change the size to match your photograph.

8. Drag the torn-edge scan until it covers your photograph entirely and creates a pleasing composition.

9. Select the background, invert the selection, and delete this selection. Your photograph now has a decorative edge.

10. Save this image as the final image for uploading to your site.

Creativity

Here are some other edges to try:

■ Use decorative scissors to cut designs along the four sides of your paper. Scan an old Polaroid photograph and use only the deckled edge.

- Look for decorative edge rulers available in scrapbook supply stores. These rulers work as follows: Use thin paper, hold the ruler over the edge, and tear the paper against this edge.

- Look for any slightly irregular edge as a potential source for creativity.

Making Text Out of Images

This technique enables you to create text that is actually an image. Your viewers cannot edit the text, nor can they copy this image as text to another application. However, the image will always appear exactly as you create it. Different browser default-text settings, colors, or font choices will not affect its appearance.

Scan your text of hand-drawn images, or style the text in your draw or page layout program. You can also scan a photograph to use as the basis for your image creation (see our example in Figure 18.3).

Figure 18.3 Starting with a scanned image

Create a design that can be made into a picture, headline, or banner. Use a style that reinforces the theme of your site. If you are selling a tangible product, think about using the product itself or the colors from your packaging.

1. Hand-draw a letter. Make it as decorative as you wish. See our example in Figure 18.4.

Figure 18.4 Using a letter as the starting point

2. Scan this creation and save it at 72 dpi in either the JPEG or GIF format, depending on the type of image you have created.

3. Use this image as the opening capital on your text page. See Figure 18.5 for an example of a finished image. We placed the image of the letter first and then used our page layout software to flow the text around it.

Figure 18.5 An opening capital

Creativity

Think of this topic in two ways: What leads people to buy your product and what makes a visually arresting page? The two points can come together with a little forethought. Use unusual cropping for your images. A few possibilities include creating polygons, cropping on the diagonal, or cropping a picture tightly to create mystery. Draw a letter form and fill it with images of your company, product, or other related elements.

Plan to constantly change your site to keep it fresh. People will tire of your site and stop visiting without new site content. However, you don't have to do a complete makeover every week — major changes also frustrate viewers. Unless there is a compelling reason for a complete makeover (as we show you at the end of this chapter), create small, incremental changes to your site. Give visitors enough change to whet their appetite but keep enough familiarity to help them feel at home.

When you create your original scans, make variations that can be plugged in at specific points. Adding a holiday flavor is effective. Scan in small seasonal items and store them. Upload them at the appropriate times, and then clear them out when the holiday is over. This strategy encourages people to check back and see what's new at your site.

Fun Backgrounds and Textures

Making beautiful backgrounds out of humble beginnings is a great creative experience. When used wisely, these backgrounds point to your message in a subtle and cohesive way. Key your background to your audience and make the whole experience blend together. For a successful background, keep contrast and pattern in mind. Light text is hard to read unless the text is set against a uniformly dark background. Dark text will need a light background to ensure legibility. Test your images on top of your selected background — you do not want the background to be distracting. Beware of the busy backgrounds that make it hard to read the text. If you are selling something, keep the focus on your product.

Color

Thoughtful and consistent use of color in backgrounds pulls your pages together. Look for the dominant colors in your materials and pick one or two tones with which to work. Cool colors are generally easier because they blend with objects such as the menu bar. Warm colors are a little trickier because the yellow undertones are less common in either the Windows or Macintosh operating system presentation. In general, light pastel backgrounds are best for reading large amounts of text. If your site is graphic-intensive, a black background can make your photos look good and give your pages an elegant, art gallery effect. A tiled background may create a feeling that the image is floating, but any text you apply over a tiled background may be difficult to read. Using a white background can make text look good and give your document a great graphical look, but if you have a lot of pages, it can be tiring for the eyes.

In this section, we will show you how to make different background patterns, downsample an image to create a cool pattern, and scan other resources to make wonderful additions to a page.

MATERIALS

Image editing software

A variety of fabric samples

Plain bond paper

A colored marker or other craft tool

Photograph or other image to scan

Japanese rice paper or other handmade paper

Wrinkled piece of paper

Using Fabric for Backgrounds

Fabric may not seem like a logical starting point, but with a few editing tools you can really have some fun. And it isn't just fabric — there are so many everyday objects that you can scan and turn into something completely different. Your imagination will overflow after you try a few of these ideas.

Take three or four pieces of patterned or loosely woven fabrics. Scan them "as is," and then start to play with them. Because your scans are different from our examples, try several techniques to find out what works best. The key is to notice the dominant feature in each fabric — is it the color, the printed design, or the weave? The first technique in this section is great for playing up colors, the second is good for patterns, and the third is great for texture enhancement.

Coloring Your World

Find a bright piece of fabric in which one or two colors dominate. Figure 18.6 shows our piece. We manipulated the sample to play up the gold and brown highlights.

Figure 18.6 Choosing a piece of fabric

1. Scan your fabric sample at 72 dpi and save it in a format compatible with your image editing software.

2. Open your scan in your image editing software. Correct the color balance and any other imperfections.

3. Most image editing software offers an effect called "posterize," which flattens out the image. Apply this to your scan for an interesting, reduced-color look.

Creativity

An alternative method is to scan the image in indexed color mode, which uses only 256 colors. These changes to the color scheme mean that the image begins to flatten out. Instead of rendering your photo in millions of colors, the software interpolates mathematically and substitutes one of these 256 preselected colors for any tone that falls outside this range. A side benefit of indexing your colors is that the file size shrinks. Your 1MB file reduces to about 350K. Because less information is necessary, the file doesn't consume as much storage space.

For fun, change to 3-bit color. Notice the effect on your photo. You are now using only eight colors: six plus black and white. The photo will now have an almost abstract quality because it is reduced to a few tones. Explore the options provided in your software. Figure 18.7 shows the effect of indexing color on our photograph.

Figure 18.7 Indexing color

Designing New Patterns

If your fabric has printed designs, you can convert them to a new image with a couple of tricks. The first method reverses all of the colors, making a negative image out of your positive. You've seen this effect with X-ray pictures and photo negatives, but using it on fabric can create some outstanding new designs. The second project involves taking the image to 8-bit indexed colors, and then changing the color table mode to system colors, which changes your image radically. This function was originally developed in order to map continuous tone photographs to colors that work in limited-palette software, such as Persuasion, but here we find new uses for it.

1. Scan your image and save it at a resolution and in a format appropriate to your Web authoring and image editing software. Open the image in your image editing software. We used the same fabric that we scanned in Figure 18.6.

2. Select the entire image and invert the colors, using either the "Negative" effect in many software programs or the "Invert" command in Photoshop. The colors may look a little bright if your original image was on the soft side. If so, adjust the brightness and contrast controls to bring it in range.

3. Save this new image in either JPEG or GIF format.

A second method takes advantage of the capability to save your scan as an indexed color file by substituting system colors for the original palette. This process requires software like Photoshop, so check your owner's manual.

1. Scan your image and save it at a resolution and in a format that works well with your software.

2. Open your image in Photoshop or other similar software. With some HP scanners, you can make your original pass at the image to scan as indexed color. For others, convert the image to "index color" mode, or 256-color mode. When the software converts your image to indexed color, it will look identical to the normal RGB mode.

3. Now comes the big change: Select the color table and change the table from Custom colors to System colors. Wow! Each of your original colors gets mapped randomly to a new color and surprises abound. Figure 18.8 shows an example (because the figure is in black and white you won't see all the detail – just trust us!). Have fun with this technique.

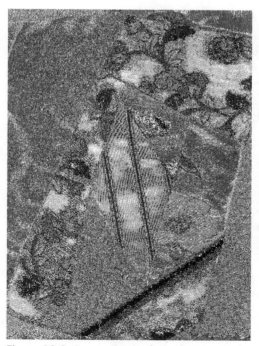

Figure 18.8 Surprising results with system colors

Texture Generating in Minutes

Look for loosely woven fabrics for this project. We used a hand-woven shawl in a soft cream color. Try these steps for a way to spark your imagination. First, change the brightness and contrast to make it look like a burlap sack. The second trick involves downsampling the picture, and then upsampling it until the fabric weave looks like a computer-generated texture. These two techniques can be accomplished with even the most basic photo image editor so test them and then explore other options in your software. Remember that you can undo anything you don't like with the click of a mouse.

1. Scan your image and save it at a resolution and in a format that works best for your software.

2. Open the scan in your image editing software. Decrease the contrast so that the entire image appears less detailed. You will probably need to adjust this control several times, previewing the image until you are satisfied.

3. Adjust the brightness control to darken the image as well, which creates a rough texture. See Figure 18.9 for an example of this technique.

Figure 18.9 Darkening the image to create a rough texture

Tip

The difference between contrast and brightness controls is as follows: Brightness is the lightness or darkness of an image; contrast is the way we perceive the range in tones from darkest to lightest. Low contrast will bring you to an all-gray image, whereas high contrast will make everything either black, white, or a primary color.

When you want a soft texture, the following is a quick trick. All software lets you reset the number of pixels per inch. By making this change repeatedly, you alter your image to a cloud-like pattern. After you execute this technique, you may want to adjust the color balance.

1. Scan your fabric and save it in the format most compatible with your image editing software.

2. Adjust the image-size dpi or pixels per inch to around 4 dpi.

3. Save the image, and then adjust the image size again. This time, select 100 dpi. Save this. If the resulting image is not softly patterned enough for your needs, repeat this process several more times, selecting numbers between 4 and 100 for each image resize. Figure 18.10 gives you an example of the image after several changes in dpi.

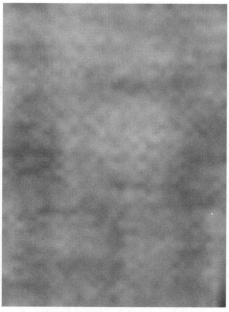

Figure 18.10 The image after several changes

A Pen, a Scanner, and an Idea . . .

Quick ideas are often the best. For the following idea, spontaneity works to add freshness and surprisingly sophisticated results. Scribble on a piece of paper using a marker. Any scribble will do, so don't worry if you aren't Michelangelo. Scribble, scan, and play. Sounds like fun, doesn't it?

1. Using a colored marker, scribble on a piece of white paper. Scan this drawing at around 100 dpi.

2. Open the image in your image editing software. Change the image size to between 8 and 10 dpi.

3. Apply the Noise filter to your entire image. This filter adds extra bits of color and texture to an image. Even though you started off with a two-color image, you will now have a beautiful rendering of soft pastels mathematically calculated from your original scan.

Creativity

Use this image in a variety of ways, depending on your needs. Clip a part out of the overall image and use it as a button or a place marker. Make two or three passes with the noise filter and notice that the effects are cumulative. A beneficial side effect of this technique is that the resulting image is fairly small, which is good for Web sites.

Plain Old Downsampling

A variation of the preceding project is to take a scan and simply change the dpi until it loses the original look and turns into an abstract pattern. A nice way to do this is to place a downsampled image next to one scanned at around 72 dpi. If they are laid out right next to each other, the effect can be very sophisticated. The best images for this technique are scans with lots of all-over color. If you scan an image, you may need to use your "sharpen" effects to define the colors and make them stronger.

1. Scan your image at 72 dpi and save it in the format that best suits your software configuration.

2. Open the image in your editing software and crop it in half lengthwise.

3. Save this image with a new name.

4. Reopen the original image and crop it so that you include the half that was not saved in the first job.

5. Change the image size dpi to 8 dpi. Save this new image with a different name.

6. In your HTML or Web authoring software, place these images side by side, as in Figure 18.11.

Figure 18.11 Placing the images side by side

Scan Whatever You Can Find

If you want some really fun images, look around the room. What's the first thing you see that you could put on your scanner glass? Try it — just so long as it won't leak, crack, or spill, it is fair game for a scan.

This project involves scanning unusual papers and other surfaces for backgrounds. Try these and then branch out. Japanese rice paper and other specialty products can be found at artist supply stores and fine stationers.

1. Place a piece of Japanese rice paper on your scanner glass. Scan this paper and save it at 72 dpi and in a resolution compatible with your image editing software.

2. Open the scan in your editing software and adjust the color balance. Remember to make the colors softer if you are going to place text over them.

3. Decide where to crop the scan and save it. Figure 18.12 shows you a small sample from our image library.

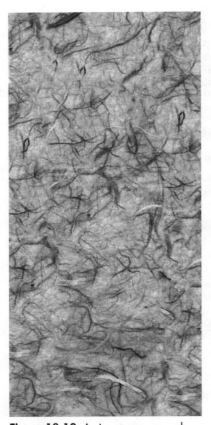

Figure 18.12 A rice paper sample

Now, let's try something more adventuresome. Pull out a wrinkled piece of paper from the trash. If you can't find a suitable piece, make your own by taking a blank piece of paper and crunching it up. Smooth it out, place it on the glass, and scan.

1. Scan a piece of wrinkled paper. Save it at 72 dpi and in a format appropriate for your software.

2. You may need to adjust your contrast and brightness controls before you get a finished scan with enough detail. Experiment until you are satisfied with the results (see Figure 18.13).

Figure 18.13 Experimenting with wrinkled paper

3. You can use this scan as it is or take it a few steps further to create a dense pattern.

4. Adjust the brightness and contrast controls until you achieve a high-contrast image.

5. Using your magic wand tool, select the white background. Invert the selection so that only the high-contrast wrinkle pattern is selected.

6. Create a new layer, and copy and paste this selection to the new layer.

7. Rotate this selection 180 degrees. Merge the layers together to make the file smaller.

8. Continue to select the colored sections, and copy, paste, and rotate them to create a more complex overall pattern. Save this in the format and at the resolution best suited to your project. Figure 18.14 shows you an example of the final result of altering a piece of plain bond paper.

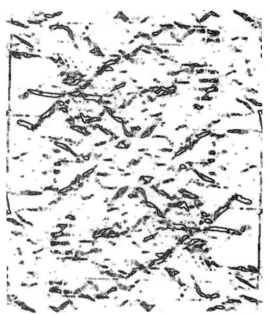

Figure 18.14 A pattern made from plain bond paper

Creativity

And one more idea — scan some tin foil. Figure 18.15 shows what tin foil can look like once it has been scanned. Then try plastic wrap. What about the paper or plastic bags that come with groceries or clothing purchases?

The filters that add pattern or special effects to your design are the ones that will work best here. One of the easiest effects is to invert the colors — turning each tone into its opposite color. Red becomes green and vice versa.

You can also blur filters to soften the entire image. These filters obscure the distinction between color areas and create soft overall patterns.

Another idea is to make a small section of an image into a big scan. Scan your image, preview it, and set the dpi to around 400. Scan only a small part of the overall picture and notice how this provides you with some interesting possibilities. As an added side benefit, your image size remains small because you are only using a small section.

When you have some spare time, try taking an image and running all of your special effects against it. Test even the most unlikely sounding combinations — this is how we found some of our favorite creativity tools. Software functions are created to solve specific problems and challenges, but serendipity comes into play. Experiment and expand your horizons.

Figure 18.15 Using foil for a pattern

Make Your Images into Banners, Image Maps, and Buttons

This section covers several areas: creating banners, making image maps or buttons for navigation, creating clever animations, and styling the head of each page.

Have you heard of a Web graphic called an image map? An *image map* is a graphic in which a number of links can be activated by touching the mouse on the different parts of the image. Clicking on one area of the image takes you to a specified page, while clicking in another spot takes you to a different page, and so forth.

Headers are a consistent way of designing the top of your Web page to allow viewers to grasp the point of your site immediately and to preview what subsequent pages have to offer. The challenge for a Webmaster is to think three-dimensionally. Where was the viewer before they saw this page? Where might they go next? Give your viewers constant clues to orient themselves properly. This orientation is especially crucial when you are drawing people in via a banner at another site. Once they drop down the funnel into your site, help them get their sense of balance again.

Another great idea is to add motion to your site. A number of animation software programs can add an extra bit of pizzazz to a site. Look for a program that is for entry-level users since you don't need to make things any more complicated than is necessary. Here are a few you might look into: GIF Construction Set (shareware — check `http://www.mindworkshop.com/alchemy/alchemy.html`), Ulead's GIF Animator, Adobe Live Motion, or Adobe After Effects.

MATERIALS

Image editing software

Draw program or layout software

Photographs or other images to scan

Making a Banner

What is a banner? It is an ad placed on someone else's Web site. When a viewer clicks on the banner at that site, they are whisked off the original site and onto your doorstep. For this quick project, think about what the banner does. These skinny little pieces of advertising must be catchy and informative. You need to communicate in a visual context so plan your message thoroughly in advance. What an exciting opportunity to see how much you can say in such a small space. The typical dimensions are around 1 inch high by 6 inches wide, or around 468 pixels by 60 pixels. Your host site administrator will provide the exact dimensions. Not your usual blank page format, is it?

If you think in terms of the height-to-width ratio, you will begin to see the creative possibilities: photographs usually have a ratio of 1 inch wide to 1½ inches high. On the other hand, a banner is a 1:6 or 1:7 ratio. How do you stretch a photo or a scan to cover this space? By thinking creatively.

The following project shows you how to use photographic images to speak to your audience. If you calculate the old adage about a picture being worth a thousand words, let's plan on a very talkative ad.

Dimensions Are Everything

Start by deciding what image or part of an image you can show in your banner. Close cropping is essential. Scan your image and decide what colors can be used in the rest of the banner to make a seamless background. Then add a bit of focused text. Save this and be ready to send it off to the Webmaster for your host site. Watch how fast a good ad can draw viewers.

When you change a canvas size in Photoshop, it surrounds the image with white background. Clicking inside the grid called "Placement" (in your Canvas Size window) allows you to determine the distribution of this white space. For these projects, we will select the image to be placed at the extreme upper left of the canvas.

1. Scan the image of your choice, saving it at around 72 dpi and in a form compatible with your page layout or image editing software.

Cross-Reference

See Chapter 4, "Resolution, Interpolation, and Sharp Images," and Chapter 10, "Optimizing Color," for more information on the technical aspects of scanning.

2. Change your canvas size to 468 by 60 pixels. Make sure that the image is set to appear at the left-hand side of your canvas.

3. Select an interesting section, using as much of the image width as possible. Think as if you were looking through slats in a blind — what looks intriguing? Notice how the whole look of the image changes when it is cropped tightly.

4. Now you have a great expanse of white space to the right of your image. Using a magic wand tool or eyedropper, select a suitable color out of the background of your cropped image and fill the white expanse with this color. Use your bucket, brush, airbrush, or other tools to complete this task.

5. Open your text tool and add a few words to entice people. No need to over-emphasize the "click here" instructions. Simply tell people what they will get when they click; for example, "Click to order books."

6. In the remaining space, add another graphic image, if you wish. Use your image editor to determine which image appears where. Remember you are encouraging people to enter this portal into your site, so think of it as a half-opened door. Our example banner in Figure 18.16 shows off this horizontal technique.

Figure 18.16 Using a horizontal design for an effective banner

Taking an Upright and Making It Read Horizontally

Because these spaces are so horizontal, it becomes a challenge to work with vertical images such as a person's face, a building, and many other everyday objects. Here are a couple of suggestions on how to take an upright piece of art and find a way to crop or convert it. Start with an image that is taller than it is wide. The first example that follows uses a person's face, while the second uses a key. See how close cropping heightens the impact and how unusual angles can lead to different interpretations.

1. Scan the image at 72 dpi and open it in your image editing software. Refer back to Figure 18.1 for the source image.

2. Human eyes are evocative. Crop a horizontal section in your image that includes only a pair of eyes, as in Figure 18.17.

3. Save this crop to be inserted in your banner.

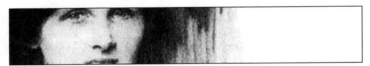

Figure 18.17 Close cropping to create a horizontal image

Another approach rotates or shows your image in motion. For this example, we use a simple, everyday object: a key. The first image shows you the original scan, while the second rotates and crops it. Each change in position changes its meaning.

1. Scan your object and save it at 72 dpi and in the format you will use for your Web site. Crop this into a tight rectangle. Figure 18.18 demonstrates this close cropping.

2. Open the image in your image editing software, immediately saving it as a different document name, in this case, "key 2."

3. Change the image size so that the height is 1 inch. Now your key will be fairly small but still upright.

4. Change the canvas size to reflect the final dimensions of your banner, in this case, 1 inch by 6 inches. Make sure to select the placement to be the left-middle square in your placement grid. Save this. Notice the placement of our image in Figure 18.19.

5. Open the original scan again and save it with a new name. This time, rotate the object 90 degrees clockwise. Change the image height to 1 inch and change the canvas size as before: 1 inch by 6 inches wide. Select the leftmost position for placement. Save this. Figure 18.20 shows the horizontal example.

Figure 18.18 Cropping an object into a tight rectangle

Figure 18.19 Placing the image

Figure 18.20 A horizontal placement

6. Here is a third view. Open the original scan and save it using a new name. Rotate the image 45 degrees clockwise and crop it so that it forms a diagonal that will fill the left-hand side of your banner. Change the image size to 1 inch high.

7. Change the canvas size to 1 inch high by 6 inches wide and select the left-hand position for placement. The diagonal placement and resizing are shown in Figure 18.21.

Figure 18.21 Changing to a diagonal placement

8. Save this. Now fill the background as in the above example or see the next project for another idea on how to create an integrated layout.

Building Overlapping Images

One photograph is rarely long enough to fill your banner. It may take two or three images to complete the whole. Here are two ways to combine images so that they overlap and become part of an integral design:

1. Scan your images and save them at 72 dpi in the format you plan to use for the banner.

2. Open your first image in your image editing software and position the image on a canvas size of 1 inch high by 6 inches wide, placing this first image at the left-hand side of the canvas.

3. Fill the right-hand side of the banner with a compatible color.

4. Open your second image and size it as necessary to fit the overall design.

5. Place this second image on top of the banner, blending with the background. Figure 18.22 shows two images smoothly placed on one banner.

Figure 18.22 Using two images in one banner

Animate That Idea!

The best use of animation is to focus your viewer's attention on a particularly challenging concept. Our animation is whimsical to add a touch of gentle humor to a non-business site. We tested many concepts before figuring out the one that seemed to work best. We tested this on colleagues, friends, and users to check for consistency of performance under a variety of conditions. Keep it simple and overstated in order to catch the viewer's attention.

1. Plan the animation cycle. How big is your space? How well will your images read at that constrained size? What do you want your animation to accomplish? Draw up a storyboard on paper.

2. Scan your images. We used a background image that fades in, copy that moves into place, and four books that fade in. Save them in a format and at a resolution that is most appropriate for the software you are using.

3. In your animation software, create a "frame" for each step of the animation. Each frame changes or brings in the elements you are using. Figure 18.23 shows our frame-by-frame animation.

Figure 18.23 Frame-by-frame animation

4. Set up your sequence of timing. How long will each image be visible and how fast will the animation move?

5. Save this group of images and animation information.

6. Test your animation. Most software allows you to simply drop the animation onto your desktop, where you can double-click it to run it in trial mode.

7. Upload the files and test your animation from the Internet. Be especially critical of the speed. If the files are too large, the speed slows down and the animation will lose its fluid motion. This jerkiness may not be a showstopper for you, but it does help to see the results in real-time. Ask a few others to test the animation on their Internet connections and compare notes. Adjust the animation as necessary.

Creativity

We have some great effects that can be easily imitated — see below for our sequence. Morphing software can help you create a seamless transition between two images. Morphing software takes two dissimilar images and through a number of mathematical calculations over a predefined sequence of steps, the software calculates minute differences between the two and creates a series of in-between images that allows one image to change into another.

You can also use animations as teasers in a banner. Catch the viewer's eye and include a "Click here" image in the middle of the animation. Watch the "click-throughs" start to happen.

Image Maps and Hot Buttons

Two distinct approaches exist for creating graphic buttons for viewers to click:

- One large graphic with hot areas for the links to other pages

- Separate hot buttons that provide graphic communications about what the link will be

Both approaches are fun to create. Going back to our original premise, we remind you that you must know your audience and make your choices consistent.

An image map is one big button in which separate links are tied to specific areas of the image. Use the books or Web sites mentioned at the beginning of this chapter for more information on the HTML that makes these maps work. You may also want to take advantage of software such as Webmap for the Mac environment or Mapedit for Windows. These resources will help you to select the boundary areas of your image map.

The buttons also need specific HTML code to function. Always rigorously check each link you create. Test the links on your own machine, and then make sure others who use different browsers and platforms have tested every pathway. There can be unpleasant surprises on the way to a successful site, so check it out.

Making Your First Image Map

This is going to be interesting so get ready! What you need is a picture that relates to your site. It needs to be divided into distinct regions where you can place text to indicate what happens when you click. Look for a picture or object that will fit the horizontal monitor format. A simple graphic that is about 2 inches high by

4 inches wide would be perfect. Look for an image that breaks down into specific areas. Your viewer will be clicking on what they perceive is the hot spot, so make it obvious. Images with polygonal areas work well. Light colors work best unless you place light-colored text on top. Got something in mind? Let's go.

1. Determine how many links you have. You will assign a distinct area of your graphic to each link. Plan your layout on paper first, ensuring that there is logic to the link placements.

2. Scan your object or image and save it at 72 dpi. Save the image in either JPEG or GIF format, depending on the type of image it will be. See the section "Web Site Dress-Ups" earlier in this chapter for more information about JPEG and GIF formats.

3. Open the scan in your image editing software. Adjust the color balance and contrast/brightness of the scan and clean up any imperfections. Clean out extraneous background details. Save this.

4. Determine the areas that will be hot for each link. The mapping function enables you to set coordinates or points for polygons, rectangles, circles, or points, so plan your image accordingly. Figure 18.24 displays an interesting image map.

5. Using your text tool, select a color, style, and size that suits your overall theme.

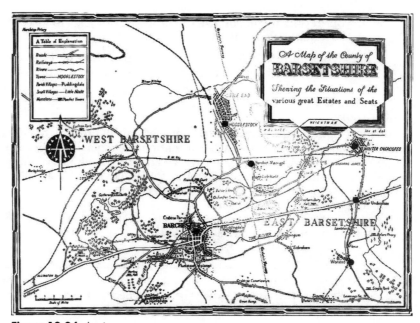

Figure 18.24 An image map

6. Add text in the appropriate areas, according to your plan. Make sure you spell-check all of the text before you save each change.

7. When your design is complete, save it in the final format for your Web site. In your HTML file, include the address of the image and the proper HTML tags for navigation.

Button, Button . . .

We love making buttons. Each one is a little work of art: a jewel at 72 dpi. You can use just about anything for inspiration. Visual puns are always great. If you are creating this Web site for your company, why not use a graphic of your product as a consistent button device? If you want to stretch your creativity, gather everything you can think of that relates to your site. Because 72 dpi does not leave a lot of room for clear details, test your ideas carefully. Have a third party look your ideas over to ensure that they translate to another set of eyes.

1. Scan a number of small objects or images. Save them at 72 dpi and in either JPEG or GIF format.

2. Open the first image in your editing software and crop the image around the outside edge. If this is a polygon, select the background and delete it. View the image at 100 percent and decide whether there is enough visual information to allow a viewer to decipher your meaning. Adjust the image as necessary and save it.

3. In your HTML document, use the proper HTML tags to insert the button in the required spot with the correct linkage.

4. Test your buttons before and after you upload the files because you want viewers to have full access to your site from day one.

Creativity

You may want to experiment with other methods of creating banners. Try an old trick — an open door. Nothing gets attention like a partially open door. Another approach is to look for strong horizontal lines. Think about a shoreline, a long landscape, a hand, or a bed. Remember, this is like creating an Alice in Wonderland attraction: When the viewer clicks on your banner, they fall through the looking glass and into your world.

As for buttons and image maps, begin to create a library of images — you never know what may be useful someday.

Cross-Reference

See Chapter 12, "Getting Started with Scanner Projects," for more information on image libraries. The section "Now Where Did I See That Great Picture of Paris" discusses how to organize your images.

Making Your Home Page Stand Out

The fact that the Web contains millions of pages is a great reason to strive for excellence. Your scanner gives you the edge you need. Beauty and brains are what you want. Scanners enable you to create a visual image much faster than illustrations, words, or any other medium. Think pictures, think big, and think motion.

Pages that don't get updated frequently are sometimes referred to as cobweb sites. Don't let that happen to your company! With new graphics and a more engaging look, you can attract more viewers.

This section prepares a makeover of a site for the literary society of a World War II-era British novelist. The site reflects a 1940s sensibility and a cool gray-to-brown palette reminiscent of the wartime.

We also added a section to sell memberships and merchandise such as articles, books, calendars, and coffee mugs. For businesses, consider what your customers want at your site. Are they looking to order products or gather information? If this is an informational site, do you want to offer some take-away or downloadable information? A fun personal site has a different mission to communicate about who you are and what your interests are. Links to your favorite sites may be most important here.

Concentrate your efforts and use visual materials to send the right message.

MATERIALS

Image editing software

Photographs, images, and small three-dimensional objects to scan

Web authoring software or text processing program for HTML

Gathering and Scanning Your Materials

First, gather your materials. Remember to review the purpose of your site to focus yourself on what is important. Build a treasure chest of text, data, images, objects, and electronic resources. Don't worry about having too much stuff or too little organization at this point. You want lots of choices to encourage experimentation. Include some three-dimensional objects. We first scanned the author's photograph for our main page. Refer to Figure 18.1 for this scan.

 Cross-Reference

Chapter 12, "Getting Started with Scanner Projects," covers the process of building a library in the section "Managing All Those Images."

Look for flat or shallow items, such as key chains or small toys. Humor and visual links are great sources for inspiration. Scan objects and materials from a wide range of sources. Scan any documents or letters that you don't have in electronic form. Save these materials in the best resolution and file format for your particular setup. Use a naming convention that will be easy to follow.

Warning

Make sure all of your materials are copyright-free.

1. Place a three-dimensional object on your scanner glass. Follow your manufacturer's directions for placing the scanner cover in position when scanning an object with some depth to it. Preview the scan carefully, making sure to position, size, and save this in the format that works best for your image editing software.

2. Open the scan in your editing software and erase all extraneous background. Size the image and save it.

3. Repeat this process for each three-dimensional object. Remember to size them relative to each other and your expected final output. All the resolutions must be the same in order to combine them properly in a final image.

4. Scan any documents that will be included, saving them in the format and resolution that allows best legibility. Test carefully, as large amounts of text quickly become illegible.

5. Scan any photographs or other images you will be including in the site. Save these at 72 dpi and in the format most suited to their display.

Combining Electronic Images

Couple a scan of a three-dimensional object with one of the text scans. Look for ways to add humor or to reinforce your product positioning.

6. Open the image you plan to use as an underlying background, and then open the scanned, three-dimensional image you want to incorporate.

7. Select only the image you want to combine. You can do this by selecting the background with the magic wand tool and inverting the selection, or by using the eraser tool.

8. Copy and paste just the object, not the background surrounding it. If you are unfamiliar with this operation, consult the manual for your image editing software.

9. Continue to combine images and objects, saving each separately. Figure 18.25 provides an example.

Laying Out Your Site

Decide on the method of presentation. Our site originally had a main page with several subsidiary pages. We broke down the information into chunks so that related materials were kept together. Our old site had too much text and not enough graphics. See an example of one of our original pages in Figure 18.26.

Figure 18.25 Combining several images

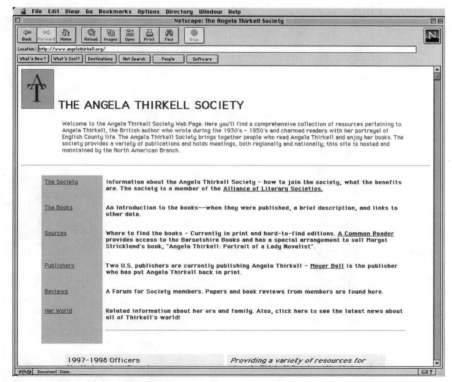

Figure 18.26 The original page

Now we will build a more visually appealing site, with images that illustrate rather than text that lectures:

1. On paper, lay out some rough samples of each page, taking into account the dimensions of the average monitor, which is between 13 and 15 inches diagonally.

2. Plan for a header section that previews the page, navigation aids at the bottom of the page, and enough white space to keep viewers from tiring easily. When in doubt, break the page into two smaller pages.

3. In your page layout software, build a mock-up of your pages, but do not code your HTML yet. Open scanned images and place them as your rough sketches indicate. Place text mock-ups as well. Test out this "page" from a visual perspective. See our example of a mock-up page in Figure 18.27.

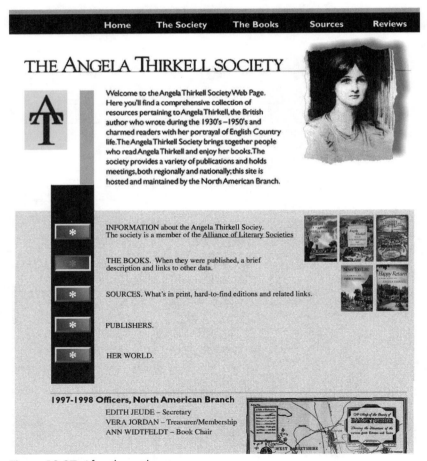

Figure 18.27 After the makeover

Creating Your HTML

4. Create your top navigational bar area first. Make sure that you have links to every page you offer.

5. Write the HTML for the "sweet spot" — the area seen by every browser. This area is the 640 by 480 pixels space. If you have more information, allow the information to scroll, making sure there are visual clues to the scrolled materials.

6. When you are satisfied with your layout, test your HTML, checking all of the image maps, links, and buttons.

7. When ready, move to the next section!

Printing Everything

Printing everything out seems illogical. Why print what is going to be viewed? Two reasons:

- On paper you see errors that your eye didn't catch onscreen.

- You will see what your pages look like when people print them.

Spell-check carefully and determine whether your layout makes sense when printed.

8. Print all of the pages on scrap paper. Make careful note of whether the entire width of the document will print properly.

9. Review for accuracy, legibility, and format. Adjust your HTML and images as necessary.

Assembling Your Production

And now for the finale: Upload your files and test them. Take testing seriously. Because the people who are most eager to use your services will click through your site first, make sure you give them a very clean offering, even if it means a delay in opening your site for business. You wouldn't open your office if the lights didn't work reliably, would you?

Creativity

The best way to get some ideas is to surf the Web. There are even sites that point you to good sites! Check out `www.coolsiteoftheday.com` and `www.library.cmu.edu/Unofficial/WebCourse/webdesign.html` for some good ideas.

The best creativity drivers are your customers — your viewers in this case. Query them and ask them what works well at your site. Don't rely on mail-in comments alone; call some people to ask about their impressions of your site. Most people will be willing to volunteer their reactions.

Take time to notice what you like on the Web. Navigational strategies are generally less than optimal so pay particular attention to sites that work well. What can you do to improve yours? Could you scan objects that are color-coded or are a visual reference to their location? Think about using scans of objects that represent pages. Building blocks, steps and ladders, the ABCs, or any other sequential or organizing objects can help you to give your viewers the right frame of reference.

Moving On

Scanners can improve your effectiveness in communicating. Ours is an increasingly visual world and your skills at capturing, manipulating, and presenting slices of life will add to every project you undertake. Whether for home, office, or school, use your scanner to increase your range of options. Try projects in this book, use the knowledge to maximize your investment, and begin a journey of pixels that is never ending and always changing.

Resource Kit

Because so many of the projects in this book use arts and crafts materials, this appendix gives you specific places to find these items via mail order. In addition, a tremendous number of resources are available for hardware and all sorts of software add-ons, including Photoshop tools. Because there are many sources of information as well, we have divided the resources into three sections:

- Art and craft supplies
- Hardware and software sources
- Resources for learning

Art and Craft Supplies

BagWorks

BagWorks sells canvas products — from canvas totes to vests, aprons, pillows, and window treatments. These are great surfaces to use for the T-shirt transfer process.

> 3301-C South Cravens Road
> Fort Worth, TX 76119
> 817-446-8080
> 817-446-8105 Fax
> email: info@bagworks.com
> www.bagworks.com

Creative Paper Collections

This is a great specialty and exotic paper resource. The company offers over 180 specialty papers, cardstock-weight paper, and greeting cards, most with matching envelopes. Many of these papers and envelopes are compatible with inkjet printers. Call for specifics.

> 12335 Santa Monica Boulevard, #301
> West Los Angeles, CA 90025
> 323-965 2581

CTI Paper USA, Inc.

Great papers for the craft industry. Call for a retail source near you.

1545 Corporate Center Drive
Sun Prairie, WI 53590
800-284-7272
608-834-9900
608-834-9800 Fax
www.thepapermill.com

Daige, Inc.

Rollataq is a permanent adhesive system that doesn't require sprays or dry
mount supplies. It creates a strong, permanent bond in three desktop sizes
(12-inch, 24-inch and 36-inch) and a hand-held model.

1 Albertson Avenue
P.O. Box 223
Albertson, NY 11507
516-621-2100
800-645-3323 Customer Service
516-621-1916 Fax
www.daige.com

Daniel Smith — The Catalog of Artists' Materials

Great products, including the company's exclusive iridescent watercolors. Very
professional and helpful staff.

4150 First Avenue South
P.O. Box 84268
Seattle, WA 98124-5568
800-426-6740
800-426-7923 Mail Order
800-238-4065 Fax
e-mail: sales@danielsmith.com
www.danielsmith.com

Design Vinyl Company

This company makes scrapbooks and has a new product called "The Keepsake
Keeper" that allows you to save three-dimensional objects in your scrapbooks.
There are plastic bubbles on the page so your keepsakes are protected and yet
completely visible. Call the company for a retailer near you.

2270 Bridger Road
Salt Lake City, UT 84104
800-343-3778
801-975-0562 Fax
e-mail: dvesop@xmission.com
www.xmission.com/~dvesop

Dick Blick Art Materials

Art supplies mail order catalog.

P.O. Box 1267
Galesburg, IL 61402-1267
800-933-2542
e-mail: info@dickblick.com
www.dickblick.com

Hygloss Products, Inc.

A source for quality arts and crafts papers, including Velour Craft Paper, which has a soft finish and will feed through most inkjet printers. Call for sources near you.

402 Broadway
Passaic, NJ 07055
800-444-9456 Office
973-458-1745 Fax
e-mail: info@hygloss.com
www.hygloss.com

Lucky Squirrel

Supplier of clear, translucent, white and black PolyShrink plastic.

1635 Menaul NW
Albuquerque, NM 87107
800-462-4912 Orders
505-345-9455 Office
505 342 9618 Fax
e-mail: mail@luckysquirrel.com
www.luckysquirrel.com

Midwest Products Co., Inc.

This company sells quality wood products for crafters. Experiment with the T-shirt transfer process on these wooden objects or use clear gloss self-adhesive papers to decorate their surfaces. Call for a retail source near you.

400 S. Indiana Street
P.O. Box 564
Hobart, IN 46342
800-348-3497
www.midwestproducts.com

Multi-Ply Wood Design, Inc.

Wood products made of white birch plywood are presanded and come in many sizes. Multi-Ply offers round plates, trays, shaped plates, and album covers.

46 Grey Street
Fredericton, NB
E3B 1V7
Canada
800-550-2325 Orders
800-550-8220 Fax
www.multi-ply.com

Nasco Arts & Crafts

Great source for schools and institutions.

901 Janesville Avenue
Fort Atkinson, WI 53538-0901
800-558-9595
e-mail: info@enasco.com
www.enasco.com

Paper Access

Specialty papers for the crafter.

23 West 18th Street
New York, NY 10011
800-PAPER 01
212-463-7022 Fax
e-mail: info@paperaccess.com
www.paperaccess.com

Paper Direct

Paper Direct sells a variety of special papers with preprinted designs, and in a variety of colors. It also offers some extra fun stuff that your imagination can go to work on.

PaperDirect Internet
1025 East Woodmen Road
Colorado Springs, CO 80920
800-272-7377
800-443-2973 or 719-534-1741 Fax
e-mail: PDI-CustomerService@currentinc.com
www.paperdirect.com

Pearl Paint Company, Inc.

Pearl is a great source for all things artistic — fine arts, crafts, frames, and so on. The company now has several stores across the U.S. in major cities, but you can also reach them via their 800 number.

308 Canal Street
New York City, NY 10013
800-451-PEARL
e-mail: Pearlsite@aol.com
www.pearlpaint.com

Phoenecian Papers

Handmade, wood-free, recycled papers and envelopes. The company sells beautiful papers with flower petals worked into the paper. There are sets of cards and envelopes as well as bulk papers and folders.

20 Meadow Lane
East Windsor, NJ 08520
800-875-1500

Plickety Plunk Press

Learn the art of genuine bookbinding using the tools and techniques of professionals. The Bookmaker kit as well as other fine bookbinding tools, kits, and supplies are available from this wonderful company.

P.O. Box 37
Caliente, CA 93518
805-867-7007
805-867-7003 Fax
e-mail: plunki@aol.com
www.plickityplunk.com

PromoGraphics International, Inc.

Digital printing on T-shirts, caps, mousepads, canvas bags, and other items.

4980 Southwest 52nd Street, Suite 118
Davie, FL 33314
954-797-9600
954-797-7173 Fax
e-mail: info@promographics.com
www.promographics.com

Quill Corporation

This is a source for high-quality, full-color papers that work in laser printers, inkjet printers, or copiers. Call for a free catalog and sample.

100 Schelter Road
Lincolnshire, IL 60069-9972
800-982-3400
www.quillcorp.com

Saro Trading Company

Saro offers fabrics that can be used in the T-shirt transfer process to make romantic and beautiful projects. The company carries linen napkins, Battenberg lace, and other items of very high quality.

720 W. Broadway Street
Glendale, CA 91204
800-662-7276
800-662-2361 Fax
www.saro.com/

Sax Arts & Crafts Catalog

Mail order source.

P.O. Box 51710
New Berlin, WI 53151
800-323-0388
e-mail: info@saxarts.com
www.artsupplies.com/

Sunshine Discount Crafts

Arts and crafts materials.

P.O. Box 301
Largo, FL 34649-0301
800-729-2878
www.sunshinecrafts.com

The Paper Patch

Specializing in acid-free printed background papers and other specialty printed papers. Call for a retail source near you.

P.O. Box 414
Riverton, UT 84065
801-253-3018 Office
800-397-2737 Orders
801-253-3019 Fax
www.Gonscrappin.com

Wisconsin Lighting

The company sells a product called "The Luminator." Print a scanned image and self-laminate it to a lampshade.

800 Wisconsin Street
Eau Claire, WI 54703
715-834-8707 Orders
715-834-2608 Fax

Hardware and Software Sources

Club Mac

Mail order source for Apple Macintosh supplies.

7 Hammond Drive
Irvine, CA 92618
800-258-2622
714-768-9354 Fax
www.clubmac.com

Chroma Graphics, Inc.

Software tools for Photoshop — selecting objects, blending colors together, changing colors.

577 Airport Blvd., Suite 730
Burlingame, CA 94010-2020
650-375-1100
650-375-1118 Fax
www.chromagraphics.com

DTP Direct

A mail-order source with a graphics twist.

800-395-7778
www.dtpdirect.com

Educorp Direct

CD-ROMs and diskettes with software, shareware, and games.

914-347-2464
www.eduss.com

EyeWire

Innovative stock photographs, software, clip art, and fonts.

8 South Idaho Street
Seattle, WA 98134
800-661-9410
800-814-7783 Fax
www.eyewire.com

DsgnHaus, Inc.

A great resource for high-quality, professional-level fonts, software, and clip art.
Check out the company's online magazine.

1375 Kings Highway
East Fairfield, CT 06430
800-942-9110
203-367-1860 Fax
e-mail: fhsales@dsgnhaus.com
www.fordesigners.com

Hewlett-Packard Company

Premier provider of scanners, computers, printers, supplies, and services.

www.hp.com

Publisher's Toolbox

Desktop publishing and graphics-related products.

2310 Darwin Road
Madison, WI 53704 3108
800-390-0461 Orders
608-243-1253 Fax
www.pubtool.com

Zones.com

Mail order source for Apple Macintosh and Intel-based computers and supplies.

707 South Grady Way
Renton, WA 98055-3233
800-248-0800
206-430-3500 Fax
www.zones.com

Font Sites

There are hundreds of sites where you can shop for and download new fonts. Some of these sites have free fonts, but most of them charge, in a variety of ways, for their products. We have listed three sites that are easy to navigate and offer quality products. Any search engine in your browser will help you locate others.

Adobe Systems
www.adobe.com/type/main.html

The Font Site
www.fontsite.com

The Font Pool
www.fontpool.com

Resources for Learning

Adobe Systems Incorporated

Adobe Systems offers *Adobe Magazine* to all registers users of its products (Pagemaker, Photoshop, Illustrator, Persuasion, and others). A valuable source for design ideas and technical help.

411 First Avenue South
Seattle, WA 98104-2871
800-272-3623
206-470-7693
206-470-7106
www.adobe.com

Creating Keepsakes Scrapbook Magazine

A nice magazine for interesting and family-oriented scrapbooking projects. Crisp, clean graphics and easy-to-follow instructions.

354 South Mountain Way Drive
Orem, UT 84058
888-247-5282
e-mail: CreatingK@aol.com
www.creatingkeepsakes.com

Dynamic Graphics Magazine

Monthly service called "Clipper," for clip art in electronic and paper format in TIFF and EPS images, with a monthly how-to magazine and training on CD-ROM. Great magazine, *Dynamic Graphics*, for small-office and home-office desktop projects and information. *Electronic Design* is aimed at the graphics professional and shows specific projects and techniques.

6000 N. Forest Park Drive
P.O. Box 1901
Peoria IL 61656 9941
800-255 8800
800-488 3492
www.dgusa.com

HOW Magazine

Design magazine that covers creative and business issues, practical information, and inspiring works.

P.O. Box 12575
Cincinnati, OH 45212-9927
800-333-1115
e-mail: editorial@howdesign.com
www.howdesign.com

IDG Books Worldwide, Inc.

Our publisher. World-leading media, research, and exposition company.

919 E. Hillsdale Blvd., Suite 300
Foster City, CA 94404
www.idgbooks.com

I Love Remembering Magazine (D.O.T.S. Company)

This is a new magazine for paper crafters. It is an idea book published quarterly to showcase the art of scrapbooking. Lots of ideas.

P.O. Box 680
Pleasant Grove, UT 84062
800-965-0924 Office
801-492-9342 Fax
www.iloveremembering.com

Somerset Studio

This wonderful magazine showcases paper arts. Send in one of your creations — they run readers' works every month!

22992 Mill Creek Blvd., Suite B
Laguna Hills, CA 92653
949-380-7318

Glossary

A

achromatic color

A color with no saturation.

additive colors

The primary colors of light: red, green, and blue, used by scanners, monitors, and other computer devices. When combined, they produce white light.

airbrush

An atomizer tool found in Photoshop and other image editors used for spraying paint.

anti-aliasing

A process used to remove a stair-stepping effect found in diagonal lines of an image by inserting dots of an in-between tone along the edges.

applications program interface (API)

A common interface, like TWAIN, that allows software engineers to write programs, such as scanner drivers, that will operate with a broad range of computer configurations.

array

A grouping of elements such as sensors.

aspect ratio

The relative proportion of the length and width of an image. For example, if you scan an original that measures 4 by 6 inches, it will have an aspect ratio of 4:6, or 2:3.

attribute

Characteristics of a page or character, such as underlining, boldface, or font, that can be captured by an optical character recognition (OCR) program.

automatic document feeder (ADF)

A device attached to a scanner that automatically feeds one page at a time, allowing the scanning of multiple pages.

auto trace

A feature found in many object-oriented image editing programs, such as Adobe Illustrator, that allows you to trace a scanned image and convert it to an outline or vector format.

B

batch

Actions carried out consecutively on a set of files.

bilevel

In scanning, a binary scan that stores only the information that tells whether a given pixel should be represented as black or white.

binary

Base-two arithmetic, which uses only 1s and 0s to represent numbers. 0001 represents 1 decimal, 0010 represents 2 decimal, 0011 represents 3 decimal, and so forth. Binary numbers are used indirectly to refer to color depth, as in 24-bit or 8-bit color.

bit

The abbreviation for binary digit — either a 1 or a 0. Scanners typically use multiple bits to represent information about each pixel of an image.

bit depth

The number of bits used to represent colors or tones.

bitmap

An image represented as pixels in row and column format. Note that Adobe refers to a bitmap as a two-color image.

black

The color formed by the absence of reflected or transmitted light.

black printer

The plate used for the black ink in the four-color printing process. It provides emphasis for neutral tones, detail in shadow areas of the image, and a deeper black than can be provided by combining cyan, magenta, and yellow alone.

bleed

An image that continues to the edge of the page, often accomplished by having the image extend past the edge and then trimming the page to the finished size.

blend

To improve the transition between image areas by smoothing the boundaries between them.

brightness

The intensity of light in an image.

burn

To make a portion of an image darker.

byte

Eight bits, able to represent any number from 00000000 to 11111111 binary (0 to 255 decimal).

C

calibration

A way of correcting for the variation in output of a device such as a printer or monitor when compared to the original image data you get from the scanner.

camera ready

Artwork printed in hardcopy form, which can be photographed to produce negatives or plates for printing.

carriage

The scanner component that moves down a page to capture an image.

cast

A tinge of color in an image.

CCD (charge-coupled device)

A type of solid-state sensor used in scanners that captures light reflected or transmitted by the original.

chroma

Color, combining hue and saturation.

chromatic color

A color with at least one hue available, with a visible level of color saturation.

chrome

Photographer talk for a color transparency.

CIS (Contact Image Sensor)

A new type of image sensor used in smaller, low-cost scanners that has limitations on resolution.

clipboard

A memory buffer that stores images or text so they can be pasted within the same application or other applications.

clone

To copy pixels from one part of an image to another.

CMOS (complementary metal oxide semiconductor) sensor

A new type of sensor used in scanners and digital cameras that is based upon a semiconductor process designed for digital electronics instead of analog electronics as in the CCD. (See *CCD*.)

CMYK

The abbreviation for cyan, magenta, yellow, and black.

color correction

Modifying the color balance of an image, usually to produce a more accurate representation of the colors in an image. Color correction compensates for the deficiencies of process color inks, inaccuracies in a scan or color separation, or an undesired color balance in the original image.

color separation

The process of reducing an image to its four separate color components — cyan, magenta, yellow, and black. These separations are combined using an individual plate for each color on a press. To create a color other than the three primaries plus black, percentages of the primaries are combined. Also the process, inside the scanner, of separating the colors into the three additive components, Red, Green, and Blue – usually achieved using colored filters on the CCD.

comp

A layout that combines type, graphics, and photographic material; also called a composite or comprehensive.

complementary color

The opposite hue of a color, or the direct complement. For example, magenta is the direct complement of green.

compression

Squeezing a file (especially an image) into a more efficient form to reduce the amount of storage space required.

continuous tone

Images that contain tones from black to white and all the tones in between.

contrast

The range between the lightest and darkest tones in an image. In a high- contrast image, the shades fall at the extremes of the range between white and black. In a low contrast image, the tones are closer together.

copyboard

The glass plate that artwork is placed against for scanning.

copy dot
Photographic reproduction of a halftone image in which the halftone dots of a previously screened image are carefully scanned as if they were line art. The same technique can be used in scanning to capture a halftoned image. If the original dot sizes are maintained, the quality of the finished image can be good.

crop
To trim an image or page.

data compression
A method of reducing the size of files, such as image files, by representing the sets of binary numbers in the file with a shorter string that conveys the same information. Many image editing programs offer some sort of image compression as an optional mode when saving a file to disk.

default
A setting used unless you specify otherwise.

density
The lightness or darkness of an image or a portion of an image.

desaturate
To remove color from an image or hue.

descender
The portion of a lowercase letter that extends below the baseline. The letter *p* is an example of a character with a descender.

device driver
A software module that tells your operating system how to control a given piece of hardware, such as a scanner.

diffusion
The random distribution of gray tones in an area of an image.

digitize
To convert analog information, such as a continuous tone image, to a binary form that can be processed by a computer.

direct memory access (DMA)
This term refers to the movement of data directly from memory to some other device, such as the disk drive, without first being loaded into the microprocessor.

dithering
A way of simulating gray tones or colors by grouping dots so they can be merged into intermediate colors or tones.

dot
A unit used to represent the smallest element a printer can image, but sometimes used to represent the resolution of other devices, such as monitors or scanners.

dot gain
The tendency of a printing dot to grow from the original size when halftoned to its final printed size on paper. This effect is most pronounced on offset presses using poor-quality papers that allow ink to absorb and spread.

dots per inch
The resolution of a printed page, expressed in the number of printer dots in an inch. Abbreviated *dpi*. Scanner resolution is also expressed, somewhat inaccurately, in dpi.

downsampling
To reduce the amount of information in an image, usually to make it smaller or to discard some colors when changing bit depth. Also used when reducing the number of pixels in the image, i.e., reducing the ppi or dpi.

dropout color
A color invisible to a scanner during a grayscale scan.

dummy
A rough approximation of a publication used to gauge layout.

duotone
A printed image, usually a monochrome halftone, that uses two different colors of ink to produce a longer range of tones than possible with a single ink density and set of printer cells alone.

dynamic range
The range of densities between the highlights and shadows of an image.

E

export
To transfer an image to another format.

F

filter

An image transform tool used to process an image; for example, to sharpen, blur, or diffuse it. Often this is a plug-in in an image editor, but filters are also built into scanning software or hardware.

FireWire

An advanced serial interface that runs at very high speeds. FireWire is becoming popular for digital video systems.

FlashPix

A new image format that stores images in a series of different resolutions.

flat

A low-contrast image.

font

Originally a group of letters, numbers, and symbols in one size and typeface, although today the term is used interchangeably with typeface.

for position only (FPO)

Artwork deemed not good enough for reproduction, used to help gauge how a page layout looks.

four-color printing

Another term for process color, in which cyan, magenta, yellow, and black inks are used to reproduce all the hues of the spectrum.

frequency

The number of lines per inch in a halftone screen.

G

gamma

A way of representing the contrast of an image, shown as the slope of a curve showing tones from white to black. Also the response of a display device to various values – as in the gamma of the display is 2.2.

gamma correction or gamma compensation

The process of preconditioning or adjusting an image to correct for the gamma of a later device used to reproduce the image, such as a printer or display screen. Without gamma compensation, the image will look too dark when printed or displayed.

gamut
A range of color values that can be represented by a particular color model.

gang scan
The process of scanning more than one picture at a time, used when images are of the same density and color balance range.

GIF (Graphics Interchange Format)
A lossless file format that represents colors using 256 or fewer colors.

gray component removal
A process in which portions of an image that have all three process colors have an equivalent amount of gray replaced by black to produce purer, more vivid colors.

grayscale
Gray values in an image.

H

halftoning
A method for representing the gray tones of an image by varying the size of the dots used to show the image.

highlight
The brightest values in an image.

histogram
A bar-like graph that shows the distribution of gray tones in an image.

HSB (Hue, Saturation, Brightness) color model
A model that defines all possible colors by specifying a particular hue and then adding or subtracting percentages of black or white.

hue
A pure color.

I

interpolation
A method for changing the size, resolution, or colors in an image by calculating the pixels used to represent the new image from the old ones. Interpolation is also being used to increase bit-depth claims on scanners (as in "Enhanced Bit Depth" or "Enhanced Color").

interrupt

A signal to the microprocessor to stop what it is doing and do something else. An action as simple as pressing a key can generate an interrupt.

invert

To reverse an image's tones to their opposite value; to make a negative.

I/O (Input/Output)

Used to describe the process whereby information flows to and from the microprocessor or computer through peripherals such as scanners, disk drives, modems, CRT screens, and printers.

J

jaggies

Staircasing effect seen in diagonal lines.

JPEG (Joint Photographic Experts Group)

A "lossy" format that reduces the size of an image file by discarding some image information.

K

knockout

Area on a spot color overlay in which an overlapping color is deleted, so the background color shows through.

L

landscape

The orientation of a page in which the longest dimension is horizontal.

line art

Usually, images that consist only of black-and-white lines.

line screen

The resolution or frequency of a halftone screen, expressed in lines per inch. Typical line screens are 53 to 150 lines per inch.

lines per inch

Abbreviated *lpi*, lines per inch is the yardstick used to measure halftone resolution.

lithography

Another name for offset printing, which is a reproduction process in which sheets or continuous webs of material are printed by impressing them with images from ink applied to a rubber blanket on a rotating cylinder from a metal or plastic plate attached to another cylinder.

luminance

The brightness or intensity of an image. Determined by the amount of gray in a hue, luminance reflects the lightness or darkness of a color. See also *saturation*.

LZW (Lempel-Zev-Welch) compression

A way of reducing the size of TIFF files using the Lempel-Zev-Welch compression algorithm.

M

mask

To cover part of an image so it won't be affected by other operations.

mechanical

Camera-ready copy with text and art already in position for photographing.

mezzotint

An engraving produced by scraping a roughened surface to produce the effect of gray tones. Image editing and processing software can produce this effect with a process called error diffusion.

midtones

Those portions of an image with a value between black and white, usually in the 25 percent to 75 percent range.

moiré

In scanning, an objectionable pattern caused by the interference of halftone screens — often produced when you rescan a halftone and the sampling frequency of the scanner (spi) interferes with the halftone or dither pattern of the original.

monochrome

Having a single color. Typically refers to a black and white image, but could be any single-color image.

N

negative

A representation of an image in which the tones are reversed. That is, blacks are shown as white, and vice versa.

noise

Random information that distorts an image, especially the background distortion of an analog image before it is converted to digital format.

O

OCR (optical character recognition)

The process of converting printed characters into the ASCII characters and other attributes of a bitmapped image of text.

offset printing

See *lithography*.

optical resolution

The "resolution" of a scanner that is calculated by dividing the width of the scanned area by the number of pixels on the CCD. Optical resolution is also often called "true" resolution and does not include any interpolation to increased pixels. (See *interpolation*.)

P

palette

A set of tones or colors available to produce an image. For example, a standard VGA graphics adapter has a total palette of about a quarter of a million colors but can display only 16 of them on the screen at once.

parallel

To move data several bits at a time, rather than one at a time. Parallel operation usually involves sending all 8 bits of a byte along 8 separate data paths at one time, which is faster than serial movement. Many scanners use parallel connections to move image information (SCSI or printer parallel) but fast serial interfaces (USB and FireWire) are becoming more common.

peripheral

Hardware that extends the capabilities of the computer, such as a printer, modem, or scanner.

pixel

A picture element of an image.

pixels per inch (ppi)

The number of pixels captured per inch by a scanner. This is more a more accurate term than dpi (dots per inch) when applied to scanners because scanners capture pixels. See *samples per inch (spi)*.

PNG (Portable Network Graphics)

A lossless file format created to overcome deficiencies of the Graphics Interchange Format (GIF), such as the limited number of colors.

point

Approximately 1/72 of an inch, except in the Macintosh world, in which a point is *exactly* 1/72 of an inch. Points are used by printers to measure things such as type and other vertically oriented objects.

port

A channel of the computer used for input or output with a peripheral. The serial and parallel ports of the PC are the most widely used. A scanner interface board includes a special port that the scanner can use to communicate with the computer.

portrait

The orientation of a page in which the longest dimension is vertical.

posterization

A banding effect produced by reducing the number of gray tones in an image.

PostScript

A language developed by Adobe Systems for describing resolution-independent pages that can be used by printers, typesetters, or imagesetters to generate a given page.

preview scan

A preliminary scan that can be used to define the exact area for the final scan. A low-resolution image of the full page or scanning area is shown, and a frame of some type is used to specify the area to be included in the final scan.

process colors

Cyan, magenta, yellow, and black. The basic ink colors used to produce all the other colors in four-color printing.

proof

A test copy of a printed sheet, which is used as a final check before a long duplication run begins.

proportionally spaced

Text in which the distance from the center of one character to the center of the next is varied according to the shape and size of the character. The letter *i* would take up much less space than the letter *m*, for example. In contrast, monospaced characters all occupy exactly the same amount of space. Some OCR programs require you to specify whether the text is proportional or monospaced.

Q

quantization
Another name for posterization.

R

raster image
An image defined by rows and columns of pixels. Scanners capture images as raster images, although some can convert them to vector images (see *vector images*).

raster to vector conversion
The process of examining a raster image for lines and strokes, and creating a new image that looks the same but is made up of lines rather than pixels. When a person draws, he or she is creating a vector image. Vector images can be enlarged much more accurately and often have a smaller file size.

reflection copy
Original artwork that is viewed and scanned by light reflected from its surface, rather than transmitted through it.

register
To align images — usually different versions of the same page or sheet. Color separation negatives must be precisely registered to one another to ensure that colors overlap in the proper places.

rescale
To resize an image.

resolution
The number of pixels or dots per inch in an image. Also, the capability of a scanner to resolve detail — which requires quality optics as well as high ppi or spi.

retouch
To remove flaws or to create a new effect in an image.

RGB (Red, Green, Blue) color model
A way of defining all possible colors as percentages of red, green, and blue.

S

sample rate or samples per inch (spi)

The number of pixels per inch captured by a scanner.

saturation

An attribute of a color that describes the degree to which a pure color is diluted with white or gray. A color with low color saturation appears washed out. A highly saturated color is pure and vivid.

scalable black-and-white image

Some HP scanners can create scalable black-and-white images. These images are vector drawings instead of raster drawings and can be enlarged and reduced after the scan without introducing scaling defects.

scale

To change the size of a piece of artwork.

scanner

A device that captures an image of a piece of artwork and converts it to a bitmapped image.

screen

The halftone dots used to convert a continuous tone image to a black-and-white pattern that printers and printing presses can handle. Even expanses of tone can also be reproduced by using tint screens that consist of dots that are all the same size (measured in percentages, a 100 percent screen is completely black).

screen angle

The alignment of rows of halftone dots, measured from the horizontal (which would be a 0-degree screen angle).

SCSI

Small Computer Systems Interface. An intelligent interface, used for some scanners (particularly in the Macintosh world) and for other devices, including hard disk drives.

secondary color

A color produced by mixing two primary colors.

separations

Film transparencies, each representing one of the primary colors (cyan, magenta, and yellow) plus black, used to produce individual printing plates.

serial

Transmitting information one bit at a time in sequential order. Used with modems as well as some scanners. USB and FireWire are very fast serial interfaces. The World Wide Web runs on serial connections.

shade

A color with black added.

shadows

The darkest part of an image, generally with values ranging from 75 percent to 100 percent.

sharpening

Increasing the apparent sharpness of an image by increasing the contrast between adjacent tones or colors.

smoothing

To blur the boundaries between tones of an image, usually to reduce a rough or jagged appearance.

solarization

A digital effect borrowed from photography, in which some tones are reversed.

spot color

Individual colors used on a page. Usually limited to one or two extra colors besides black to accent some part of a publication.

subtractive colors

The primary colors of pigments cyan, magenta, and yellow.

T

threshold

A predefined level used by the scanner to determine whether a pixel will be represented as black or white.

thumbnail

A miniature copy of a page or image, which gives you some idea of what the original looks like without having to open the original file or view the full-size image.

TIFF (Tagged Image File Format)

A standard graphics file format that can be used to store grayscale and color images.

tint
A color with white added to it. In graphic arts, often refers to the percentage of one color added to another.

triad
Three colors located approximately equally distant from one another on the color wheel. Red, green, and blue make up a triad; cyan, magenta, and yellow make up another. However, any three colors arranged similarly around the wheel can make up a triad.

TWAIN
A software driver that interfaces between a scanner or other image capture device and a computer and its applications.

U

undercolor removal
A technique that reduces the amount of cyan, magenta, and yellow in black and neutral shadows by replacing them with an equivalent amount of black. It can compensate for trapping problems in dark areas. See also *gray component removal*.

unsharp masking
A technique used by scanners and image editors to increase the sharpness of an image.

USB (universal serial bus)
An advanced serial interface that supports up to 127 devices. USB is much faster than traditional serial interfaces.

V

vector image
An image defined by the beginning and ending points of each line.

Z

zoom
To enlarge a portion of an image.

Index

Numbers

A

U